A16 Food+Wine

photography by Ed Anderson

A16 Food+Wine

Nate Appleman + Shelley Lindgren

with Kate Leahy

TEN SPEED PRESS
Berkeley | Toronto

Ten Speed Press
PO Box 7123
Berkeley, California 94707
www.tenspeed.com

Distributed in Australia by Simon and Schuster Australia, in Canada
by Ten Speed Press Canada, in New Zealand by Southern Publishers
Group, in South Africa by Real Books, and in the United Kingdom
and Europe by Publishers Group UK.

Cover and text design by Ed Anderson
Map on page 8 by Greg Lindgren

Library of Congress Cataloging-in-Publication Data

Appleman, Nate.
  A16 : food + wine / by Nate Appleman and Shelley Lindgren ; with
Kate Leahy ; photography by Ed Anderson. — 1st ed.
      p. cm.
  Includes index.
  Summary: "A cookbook and wine guide from the San Francisco
restaurant A16 that celebrates the traditions of southern Italy"
—Provided by publisher.
  ISBN 978-1-58008-907-4
  1. Cookery, Italian—Southern style. 2. Wine and wine making—Italy,
Southern. 3. A16 (Restaurant) I. Lindgren, Shelley. II. Leahy, Kate. III.
Title.
  TX723.2.S65A67 2008
  641.5945—dc22

                       2008011502

Printed in China

2 3 4 5 6 7 8 9 10 — 12 11 10 09 08

RECIPES

ACKNOWLEDGMENTS

This book is a collection of the great ideas we have received from A16 staff members, partners, investors, family, and friends. Your presence resonates within these pages, and we offer our deep gratitude for your inspiration and support.

To everyone at Ten Speed Press, especially Aaron Wehner, who guided our thoughts into the story we wanted to tell. To Sharon Silva, for her expert judgment and careful eye, and to Leslie Evans, Brie Mazurek, and Ken DellaPenta, for their help with the final stages. And to Amanda Berne, for helping us on the first leg of the journey.

To Ed Anderson, who captured the spirit of southern Italy in his evocative photography and inspired design.

To our partner, Victoria Libin, for her support, acumen, and deep understanding of Italian food, wine, and culture.

To Alan Freeland, for starting us out on the right foot.

To our restaurant family, past and present, without whom we wouldn't have a story to tell.

In particular, Shelley would like to thank Kellie Dunmore, Andrew Mosblech, Kevin Wardell, Ehren Jennings, Anais Radonich Galvin, Diane Desmond, Massimiliano Conti, and Tim Baumann, for their friendship and devotion to southern Italian wine and hospitality.

Nate would like to thank Chris Behr, Chris Gerwig, Justin Green, Felipe Te Hernandez, Beth Ann Simpkins, Huw Thornton, and Rae Lynn Vasquez, for understanding and respecting the food of Campania.

A special thanks to Liza Shaw, for her insight, attention to detail, and dedication, both to the book and to A16.

To Jane Tseng, for her thoughtful dessert recipes and for always ensuring that there is chocolate gelato in the freezer.

To Amanda Haas, whose careful recipe testing and kind encouragement kept us on track.

To A16's opening crew, especially former executive chef Christophe Hille, for your vision and dedication, and for inviting us to play along.

Our wine list would not be the same without the warm friendships we have made along the way. A special thanks to Amedeo Barletta, Rino Botte, Antonio Caggiano, the Cantele family, Roberto Ceraudo, Marisa Cuomo, the D'Ambra family, Bruno De Conciliis, the De Corato family, Gunther and Klaus Di Giovanna, Francesco Domini, the Favati family, the Fucci family, the Iacono family, Dino and Stefano Illuminati, Salvatore Geraci, Danila Lento, Nicodemo Librandi, Alberto Longo, Lucio Mastroberardino, Salvatore Molettieri, Penny Murray, the Paternoster family, Alessio and Francesca Planeta, Clelia Romano, Maria Schinosa, Francesca Simonini, Robin Shay, and Roberta Tanzi, for sharing your stories, your food, and your wine.

To the wine professionals and companies who have supported our efforts, especially Tony Bernardini and Vias Imports, Dino Capriotti and Vinity, Chiara Di Geronimo and Italia Wine Imports, Leonardo LoCascio Selections, Jeff Meisel, Hans Purohit, Lorenzo Scarpone and Villa Italia, Jens Schmidt and Montecastelli Selections, and Rand Yazzolino and Estate Wines. And to the Court of Master Sommeliers, for the continual encouragement.

To Peter Meehan, for his food-sourcing savvy.

To Eleanor Bertino, for always getting the word out.

Last but not least, to our families, especially Suzanne Robinson, Marie and Rick Lindgren, the Wickersham family, the Appleman family, Kathy and Tom Leahy, and Barbara and David Sutton, for providing a network of support.

A special thanks to Clarisse and Oliver Appleman and Greg and Phineas Lindgren, who make what we do possible. We can't express enough gratitude for all that you bring into our lives.

Overleaf: The view of one hundred cellars in Barile, Basilicata

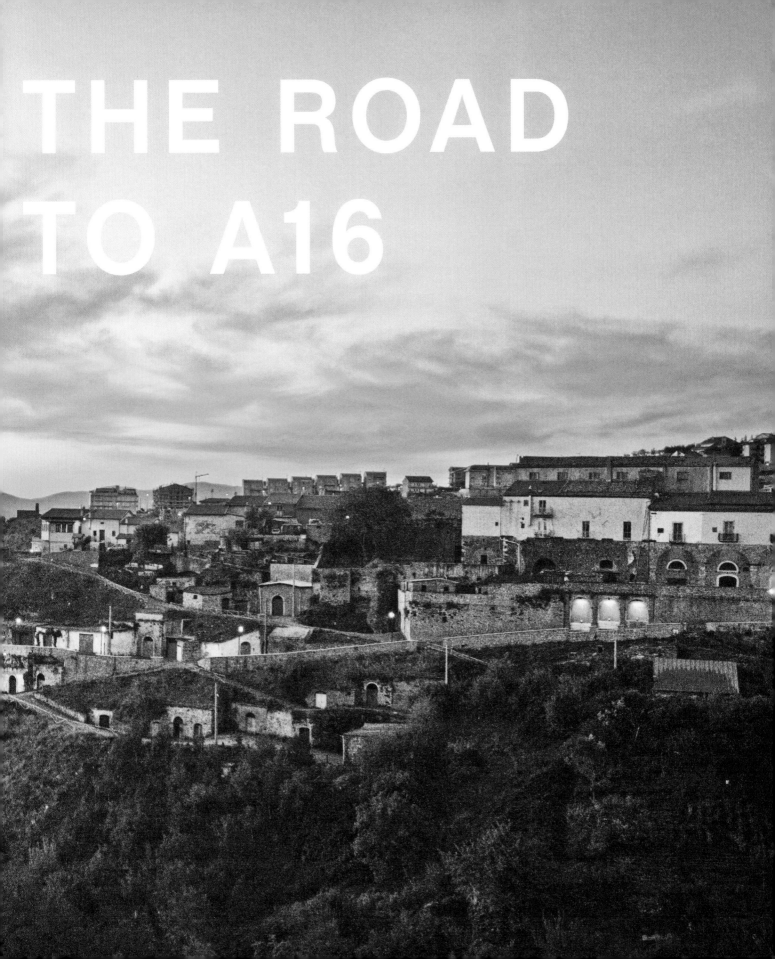

THE ROAD TO A16

Entering through the narrow storefront of A16, a bustling restaurant on Chestnut Street in San Francisco's Marina district, can be simultaneously welcoming and daunting. The place vibrates with energy as black-clad servers weave their way through the dining room, mirroring the traffic pattern of the restaurant's namesake, the Italian motorway that runs from Naples to Canosa, Puglia. A crush of eager diners waiting for a table, glasses of wine in hand, are teased by the smoky aromas emanating from the dual wood-fired ovens in the kitchen. Despite the hum of activity, the restaurant has a relaxed, welcoming glow about it—an extension of the generous, no-fuss food-and-wine ethos of southern Italy that inspired it.

The road to A16 began, appropriately, over dinner. Out to eat at the same restaurant, Shelley Lindgren struck up a conversation with Victoria Libin about Italian food and wine. At the time, Shelley and her husband, Greg, both San Francisco restaurant-industry veterans, had drafted plans for an Italian wine bar that served pizza. Meanwhile, Victoria, a lawyer with a deep appreciation for Italian food and culture, wanted to bring the incomparable thin-crust pizza she had enjoyed in Naples to San Francisco. Shelley and Greg began to meet regularly with Victoria and her husband, Paul, to enjoy home-cooked meals complemented by Italian wines and to develop a business plan. A chance encounter in an online forum discussing Neapolitan pizza brought the two couples in contact with Christophe Hille, a French-trained chef with a passion for Neapolitan-style pizza. Soon the newly formed team began developing the concept that would eventually become A16.

The initial plans for the restaurant—a wine bar that served great pizza—didn't include offerings like hearty bowls of *minestra maritata* or slowly braised *ragù alla napoletana*. But this changed once Christophe returned from a six-week stay in Campania, where he encountered unique regional pastas, such as *maccaronara*, that he felt deserved a place on the menu. Next, Nate signed on as sous chef and the menu quickly expanded to include sausages and house-made *salumi*. When Liza Shaw, a line cook with a knack for fresh pasta, joined the opening team, she went to work with Christophe on refining the pasta dishes.

While the menu concept expanded beyond just pizza, the wine list took on a life of its own. Grounded in French wines from her years working at Hubert Keller's Fleur de Lys in San Francisco, Shelley began exploring southern Italian wines with a blank slate and few expectations. As she tasted these unfamiliar wines, she found them to be delightful and intriguing, so much so that she decided to craft her wine list around the unheralded regions of southern Italy.

With the wines chosen and a menu in place, A16 opened its doors in February 2004. Four years later, the journey is far from complete. Nate, who became the executive chef in 2006, refines the menu daily, working closely with *chef de cuisine* Liza Shaw to broaden the southern Italian repertoire. Shelley continues to be an ambassador for the wines of the south, sourcing little-known producers that deserve attention, and sharing her passion and knowledge with our servers, sommeliers, cooks, and guests. The restaurant evolves as new inspiration strikes, whether from travel, an interaction with a purveyor, or just the changing seasons. But a devotion to the foodways of southern Italy—honest country cooking, wines of character and place—remains our focus as we move forward.

The wine and food of southern Italy have developed alongside each other, creating a singular bond. We honor that connection in the restaurant, with a wine list that draws heavily from southern Italy, and we have done so as well in this book. In part one, Shelley explores the exciting developments taking place in the vineyards of southern Italy. She discusses the history, key producers, and grape varieties of each region, and offers food pairings that correspond to Nate's recipes, which follow in part two. There is no better way to become familiar with the fascinating Sicilian grape Nerello Mascalese than to make a meal that complements it (in this case, the tubular pasta *paccheri* tossed with a bracing combination of sardines, capers, and olives). And for anyone already enchanted by Aglianico from Taurasi, Nate presents two beguilingly rustic dishes—lamb *crespelle* with ricotta and braised pork shoulder with chestnuts—to serve with that powerful wine. The best part of pairing Italian wine with Italian food, however, is that most Italian wines are made to be drunk with food. That means it is hard to make a mistake. Just explore, cook, and taste. And most of all, have fun.

WHAT'S IN A NAME?

When we travel through southern Italy, introducing ourselves to winemakers and chefs, they always chuckle a bit. "Ah, Autostrada Sedici," they say, recognizing the highway that passes west to east, from Naples to Canosa in Puglia. This so amused Antonio Caggiano, a winemaker in Taurasi, that he photographed the A16 Taurasi exit sign, blew it up poster size, and mailed it to us. A smaller rendition of the photograph hangs on a wall in his winery.

So, you ask, how did we name a restaurant after a road? On one of our early, hectic research trips, we often found ourselves caravanning back and forth on the A16, stopping off at restaurants, nurseries, *agriturismi*, and hotels. While the places we visited were not directly off the highway, the A16 always gave us a sense of direction in the unfamiliar surroundings. We knew that we weren't lost once we found our way back to it. As we neared the end of one of our trips, we still hadn't figured out what to call the restaurant. While the list of prospective names grew, nothing stuck. Finally, with all of us road weary and full from one too many meals, Victoria quipped, "Let's just call it A16." Almost immediately Greg began to see the possibilities, drafting a logo in his head inspired by road signs. We all looked at one another in unison. We had found our name.

PART ONE

A16 WINE

A glass of crisp Bombino Bianco paired with a piece of creamy Burrata. Ruby red Nero d'Avola served with a blistered *pizza margherita*. Juicy Casavecchia beside a plate of grilled rabbit. Serving these southern Italian wines, and many others, with our regional menu is our way of paying homage to the corner of the world that inspires us. Through the weekly exercise of tasting, exploring, and talking with producers and importers, we are constantly exposed to the breadth and depth of wines that southern Italy offers. Some of them contain nearly extinct grape varieties, while others are blends of indigenous and international grapes made by winemakers who flout tradition as if it were the speed limit on a southern Italian motorway. We don't just offer these wines to our guests for the sake of discovery, though. The wines simply belong with the gutsy country cooking of Campania.

SOUTHERN ITALY

ADRIATIC SEA

L'Aquila
Pescara
ABRUZZO

Rome
LAZIO

MOLISE
Lucera
Foggia
Campobasso
Trani
Bari

A 16

Caserta
Taurasi
Mt. Vulture
Barile
PUGLIA

Avellino
CAMPANIA
Mt Vesuvius
Brindisi

Naples
Salerno
Potenza
Matera
Lecce

Sorrento
Amalfi
Ischia
BASILICATA

Capri

TYRRHENIAN SEA

Cirò Marina
IONIAN SEA

CALABRIA
Crotone

Lamezia Terme

Sassari
Alghero
SARDINIA

Oristano

Cagliari

Reggio di Calabria

Palermo
Messina
Marsala
Mt Etna

SICILY
Syracuse

Modica

Pantelleria

When we began planning to open a restaurant that serves Neapolitan-style pizzas, I sampled a few Campanian wines out of curiosity. With little knowledge of the region's offerings, I was intrigued by my first tastings. My learning curve was steep but invigorating. Coming across wines made with honey-hued Pallagrello Bianco, a grape that less than twenty years ago grew in only one vineyard, inspired me to dig deeper into the region's viticultural history. But it was the expression of Aglianico emanating from a glass of Antonio Caggiano's Taurasi that gave me the confidence to focus the wine list on southern Italian wines.

Once A16 opened, our enthused staff began urging Sauvignon Blanc drinkers to take a chance on Greco di Tufo from Campania and professed Pinot Noir fans to try Cirò from Calabria. While at first we had to endure the inevitable requests for Chianti, our decision to promote southern Italian wines was timely. Regions such as Abruzzo, Puglia, and Sicily were just beginning to show what they are capable of producing. Meanwhile, forgotten regions such as Basilicata, Calabria, Sardinia, and Molise had been rediscovered. Southern Italian wine clearly deserved attention, and we soon found we had a dining room full of curious customers interested in expanding their wine horizons.

THE MEZZOGIORNO

Even though interest in the wines of southern Italy continues to grow, I am still amazed when guests ask for a glass of Falanghina without blinking. Recognition has come quickly, a testament to the accessibility of the wines and the many charms of southern Italy. Often called the Mezzogiorno for the way the sun hovers over the country's southern horizon at midday, Italy's south—Abruzzo and Molise east of Rome, Campania on the shin of the peninsula's boot, Calabria on its toe, Puglia at its heel, Basilicata in between, and Sardinia and Sicily past its shores—comprises rocky cliffs overlooking the azure Tyrrhenian, Ionian, and Adriatic seas; dormant and active volcanoes; arid plateaus; thick pine forests; and fertile valleys. It is not unusual in either Calabria or Sicily for an hour's drive to take you from a lush mountain forest to a dry Mediterranean coast where cacti thrive, or to see water buffalo native to India grazing in Campania's fertile valleys. It is a land of natural drama and splendor, a place where the Greeks worked and the Romans played. It's also a land full of grape biodiversity, where volcanic soil

preserved some ancient varieties from the deadly vine pest phylloxera.

For all this natural wonder and formidable history, there are plenty of reasons why modern wine drinkers have long ignored Italy's south. In fact, it wasn't too long ago that most Italian wine had the reputation for being worth less than the bottle it came in, a criticism that was especially true of southern wines. The southern Italian countryside, already poor throughout much of Europe's history, was not helped by the wars of the nineteenth and twentieth centuries, which shook apart the region's tenuous economy. A tourist visiting Campania in 1950 en route to the region's coastal resort towns Amalfi and Sorrento would have driven by peasants walking barefoot through crowded streets with baskets on their heads. In an effort to stimulate the rural economy, numerous government-backed subsidies supported prolific vineyard plantings. While all of Italy ended up swimming in indistinguishable surplus wine as a result, the effect was particularly enduring in the south, where a system of cooperatives relieved small vintners of selling modest lots of grapes by collecting them and selling them with other vintners, thus encouraging high yields for bulk wine production.

Yet modern history overshadows the region's ancient viticultural practices, varied but favorable growing climates, and abundance of indigenous grape varieties. When the Greeks arrived on the Italian peninsula four thousand years ago, they named it Oenotria, "land of wine," in reference to southern Italy's shores, which were already thick with grapevines. The Romans followed the Greeks' example and also prized southern Italy's wines, particularly Campania's sweet, amber Falernum made with Falanghina grapes harvested on the slopes of Mount Massico, believed to have been blessed by Bacchus himself.

While grapes were growing across southern Italy before the Greeks arrived, the gnarled, twisted, low-lying vines wouldn't be recognizable as vineyards to the modern eye. It wasn't until the Greeks introduced the albarello method, in which vines are trained up posts to resemble short trees, that the plants were tamed into neat rows. Ancient vintners also practiced other trellising methods to control vine vigor. One of the most memorable vineyards I have ever seen is in the northern Campanian town of Aversa, where Asprinio vines climb up tall poplar trees, and vineyard workers use ladders to harvest the grapes used in the Aversa DOC. This ancient method of trellising vines in trees is also used on a smaller scale. Eating lunch at a small

AMPELOGRAPHY AND ORAL TRADITION

For centuries, trade routes carried grapevine cuttings west, from Greece and Croatia to Italy and the rest of Europe. Over time, vines mutated to adjust to varied climates, making it difficult to pinpoint exactly where a grape originated, even with the help of DNA analysis. Nowhere, it seems, is it as hard to do as it is in southern Italy, which is a challenge for anyone interested in ampelography, the science of identifying and classifying grapevines.

In my own early research on the wines of the region, many of the stories passed on to me by winemakers, merchants, sommeliers, and importers were grounded in oral tradition. Like most folklore, these accounts were not always precise, nor were they always in agreement. I am still waiting to hear the definitive story on how Aglianico came to be planted in Campania and Basilicata: Campanian vintners argue the grape arrived on their shores first, while their counterparts in Basilicata claim the grape traveled across Puglia before settling into the soil in Mount Vulture. Even so, the stories of Aglianico's origins provide a sense of heritage to the current generation of winemakers, which they are thoughtfully building on. To those of us who have the good fortune of drinking their work, a little fiction adds to the romance in the glass.

trattoria near Avellino, I sampled a simple table wine made on the property. Outside, the trattoria's vines curled up tree branches, freeing up a patch of land for the proprietor's vegetable garden.

Even during the dark years of the modern era, a few producers in each region of the south remained focused on quality winemaking. Families such as Paternoster in Basilicata, Illuminati in Abruzzo, and Mastroberardino in Campania made wines worthy of the Mezzogiorno's noble traditions. The perseverance of these producers was finally rewarded in the 1990s, when interest in making wines of character and class began to grow.

Today, southern Italy is well on its way to reclaiming its rich winemaking heritage. Encouraged by regulations put forth by the European Union and the Italian government discouraging bulk wine production, clever Italian wine mavericks and entrepreneurs began to realize the undertapped potential for making wines of place in one of the world's oldest wine regions. Modern technologies, such as temperature-controlled fermentation tanks, paired with an allegiance to traditional grapes, have reinvigorated the area, making it one of the world's most intriguing winegrowing regions. At the restaurant, our chalkboard proudly lists some of my favorites, such as Campania's versatile Fiano, Calabria's easygoing Gaglioppo, Abruzzo's crowd-pleasing Montepulciano, Sardinia's elegant Vermentino, and the compelling Nerello Mascalese wines made near Sicily's Mount Etna. I'm also keeping an eye on Puglia, where producers whisper that the fickle Nero di Troia grape might bring forth southern Italy's next cult wine.

INTERPRETING THE GRAPES

Most wine drinkers in America think about wine in terms of the grape used to make it, rather than the place where it was made. Because of this tendency—and also because when I began learning about southern Italian wines, I found the stories of how the grape varieties persevered through time stuck with me more than the place designations did—I have adopted the grape-forward approach to organizing the wines in this book. It also happens that some of southern Italy's best wines are made with only one grape variety, *cento per cento*.

Each of the regional wine sections that follow (with the exception of Molise and Basilicata) features a catalog of the area's grapes. I have ordered the grapes from can't-miss varieties—The Classics—to intriguing grapes on the horizon, grouped under A Closer Look. While not every shop will carry southern Italian wines, chances are that if they do, they will be wines made with grapes from the former category. But with the wine regions of southern Italy evolving so quickly, some of the lesser-known grapes could well become classics in a handful of years.

THE LAWS

The grape-forward approach doesn't entirely align with Italy's unwieldy wine classification system, so it helps to have a basic understanding of the country's viticultural laws. It is also important to keep in mind that such regulations have a way of bending without breaking.

Inspired by the French Appellation d'Origine Contrôlée system founded in the 1930s, the Italian classification was instituted in 1963 as a way to control the quality, protect the distinctive regional character, and raise the stature of the country's wines. There are four levels of classified wines in Italy, and even if you aren't looking for the classifications on a bottle, the appropriate band circles the neck, a mark of quality as designated by the Italian Ministry of Agriculture and Forestry. The highest level, Denominazione di Origine Controllata e Garantita (DOCG), has the strictest production requirements, while the lowest, Vino da Tavola, has the most relaxed. Following DOCG is Denominazione di Origine Controllata (DOC), which has similar regulations without the same amount of prestige (there are many more DOCs than DOCGs). Indicazione Geografica Tipica (IGT), which refers to wines produced in specific regional areas, follows DOC. It is generally a zone much larger than a DOC, though more defined than Vino da Tavola.

While the majority of Italy's most prestigious zones are in the north, the southern island of Ischia was awarded the country's second DOC in 1966, just a few months after Vernaccia di San Gimignano in Tuscany was granted the first. The south didn't have a DOCG until Taurasi was granted the distinction in 1993. Ten more years passed before two additional Campanian regions, Fiano di Avellino and Greco di Tufo, joined the DOCG ranks. Cerasuolo di Vittoria in Sicily and Colline Teramane in Abruzzo soon followed, as southern winemakers continued their march on quality.

While some producers believe that too little regulation in the DOC system discourages quality production, others feel that too much regulation stifles creativity; and here is where Italian wines get a little more complicated. Some producers prefer to be classified as an IGT wine because they want to make wines outside of the strict guidelines of the DOC and DOCG. While an IGT classification carries restrictions, they are not as limiting as the DOC regulations, generally allowing for more experimentation. IGT wines made by bohemian winemakers can often be so distinctive that some of the most collected and sought-after wines in the market are classified IGT. Silvia Imparato makes one of Campania's cult wines, Montevetrano, using Cabernet Sauvignon, Merlot, and Aglianico grapes under the Colli di Salerno IGT designation.

So winemakers are divided. The traditionalists produce wines that are admired for expressing the character of an area, and they are likely to be designated as DOC or DOCG wines. In contrast, modernist winemakers also plant native grapes, but they aren't afraid to blend them with international varieties. They are content with IGT status as long as they are permitted to make wines in their preferred style. Finding the best producers isn't always about following quality designations set by the government's classification system. Whether DOCG or Vino da Tavola, each viticultural area is only as strong as the current generation of winemakers working within it. This leaves wine lovers the rewarding task of venturing beyond the label to learn about the grapes, the regions, and the independent philosophies of winemakers.

WINE DESIGNATIONS

DENOMINAZIONE DI ORIGINE CONTROLLATA E GARANTITA (DOCG)

This designation, which translates as "controlled and guaranteed place of named origin," asserts that only certain grapes from a designated area are used in a given wine. Of all the designations, this one is the most highly regulated and prestigious. DOCG wines are subjected to maximum-yield restrictions on the vineyards, minimum alcohol and acidity levels, and regimented aging requirements. Each DOCG also has to follow general guidelines on how the wine should taste, though there is often room for interpretation. For example, a wine from the Taurasi DOCG must be made with at least 85 percent Aglianico grapes, harvested from vines that are at least nine years old, and must be aged for at least three years, one of them in barrels. A Taurasi *riserva* is aged even longer—at least four years—and spends a year and a half in barrels. For this reason, a cellar such as Antonio Caggiano's has layers of dusty bottles waiting to be released onto the market.

DENOMINAZIONE DI ORIGINE CONTROLLATA (DOC)

This designation, which translates to "controlled place of named origin," regulates the same factors as a DOCG designation, such as permissible grapes, maximum yields, areas of production, and aging requirements. It is a lot harder to achieve DOCG status, however, so regulations are stricter in those zones than in DOCs. Unlike the Taurasi DOCG, for example, the Ischia DOC, off the coast of Campania, includes both white and red wines. The basic Ischia Bianco comprises primarily Biancolella and Forastera, with up to 15 percent of other local white grapes contributing to the blend. It must be aged in the bottle for just one month before being released. The Ischia Rosso is similarly flexible. Primarily made up of Guarnaccia and Piedirosso grapes (with other local red grapes rounding out the blend), it is bottle aged for a minimum of three months. The more relaxed requirements notwithstanding, producers often exceed the DOC standards. For example, Pietratorcia's Ischia Bianco is bottle aged for about four months before it is released.

INDICAZIONE GEOGRAFICA TIPICA (IGT)

The designation IGT, which translates as "typical to the geographical growing area," is the newest category among the four. It defines a broad regional area (generally much larger than a DOC zone) in which the wine production is loosely regulated. The Paestum IGT includes white, red, *frizzante* (semisparkling), and sweet wines made with grapes grown around the ancient city of Paestum in southern Campania. Bruno De Conciliis produces Selim, a sparkling wine made with Aglianico and Fiano grapes, under the Paestum IGT designation. The standard of quality for an IGT wine depends largely on the producer.

VINO DA TAVOLA

The broadest category, "table wine," signifies a wine produced in Italy, though generally the growing area is narrowed to a particular region. This designation can also be the escape route for winemakers whose wines clash with even the looser IGT regulations. Great wineries such as Planeta in Sicily make wonderful Syrah under the Vino da Tavola designation.

CAMPANIA A16

From the moment I first started tasting Campanian wines, they have captivated me. In fact, my excitement over these wines can be all consuming, leading me to plan overly ambitious research trips and forgo nearly every opportunity to wander around a village with the intention of getting lost in a Mezzogiorno moment. When visiting Campania, I keep the bustling pace of Naples even in sleepy, inland Taurasi or sunny Amalfi, because I can't seem to curb that feeling of adventure, the sense that the next road will lead to another wine epiphany. There are always new people to meet, old friends to visit with, and new wines to taste in too short a time to warrant a break.

The energy pulsing through the region, coupled with growing interest in its singular wines, gives Campania the feel of a winemaking frontier. Yet as the ruins of Pompeii attest, Campania is hardly a wine newcomer. To grasp Campania's rich winemaking tradition, it is important to slow down and take a look back. Way back.

Considering that Campanian wines were among the most coveted during the Greek and Roman empires, it is remarkable how far they fell out of favor. By the 1960s, most wine made here was consumed locally or shipped in bulk for blending to Argentina or to northern Italy and Germany. A few producers, notably Mastroberardino in Taurasi and Casa d'Ambra on the island of Ischia, pulled the region through its bulk winemaking days, showing others that quality production was possible. (Mastroberardino's past still stands strong; in 2007, the winery garnered a rare ninety-nine-point rating by the Italian wine journal *Gambero Rosso* for its incredible 1934 Taurasi.) As recently as the mid-1990s, Mastroberardino produced more than half of the region's DOC wines, setting the standard for new producers such as Antonio Caggiano, a local architect and photographer who took up winemaking in 1994. By 2000, wine professionals, recognizing the favorable, temperate climate and topography, were still lamenting Campania's untapped potential.

Today, however, several more producers have not only joined into quality-conscious DOC production, but they have also helped reestablish the region's reputation as a source of world-class wines. When farmer-turned-vintner Salvatore Molettieri received *Gambero Rosso*'s Red Wine of the Year award in 2006 for his noble 2001 Taurasi Vigna Cinque

Querce, the national media descended on this humble, reserved winemaker with curiosity. Today, framed articles picturing Salvatore, dressed in a suit and beaming, hang proudly in his refurbished hillside winery.

With new winemaking technology and a renewed interest in indigenous grapes, life pulses through Campania's vineyards. On my last trip to the region, with winemaker Bruno De Conciliis at the wheel negotiating our way through Naples, I could sense the excitement. Bruno has become a good friend of A16, hosting members of our restaurant family on visits and always stopping in to say hello when he comes to San Francisco. He makes wine from grapes grown in southern Campania, a region recent history recognizes more for bulk wine than for fine wine. Yet Bruno's father, a chicken farmer who had dreamed of cultivating grapes, encouraged Bruno to pursue winemaking. Bruno's Naima, a big wine made with pungent, Cilento-grown Aglianico grapes, became an immediate international hit when it was first released in 1997. Today Bruno has more than realized his late father's dream, not only by making wine but also by gradually making the transition to biodynamic viticulture.

By the time we reached the city limits, the peak of Mount Vesuvius emerging above a thick layer of clouds to our west, Bruno began to articulate the heart of his winemaking philosophy. "Wine must be the mirror of a vintage. We can play with it in soft ways, but we must be faithful to the vintage," he explained, with an earnest gesture. "If you force a wine in a particular direction, it will become angry with you. You lose its life if you control it too much. I don't want to make Coca-Cola."

The idea of allowing crushed grapes to turn into the wine they are naturally inclined to become resonates with many of Campania's best winemakers. Sure, they will remind you that technique is important, but one look at Antonio Caggiano's cellar in the village of Taurasi shows that winemaking is as much art as science. Bottles carefully inlaid into crevices along the stone walls in his subterranean cellar, gathering dust as they await their release, reflect this patient, artisanal approach to winemaking. Part of what draws me to Campania is how willingly its winemakers cede control to nature. But if you come from a culture that has survived volcanic eruptions, earthquakes, and centuries of conflict, it seems only natural to think less about controlling one's life and more about living it.

When most people think about southern Italian wines, they think of inky reds, assuming that lively, crisp whites can only be made in the north. In fact, two-thirds of Campania's native grape varieties are white. The region's whites vary in complexity, from the bright acidity of wines made from the Asprinio grape to the distinctive pleasures of mineral-laden Greco di Tufo. That's not to overshadow the red grapes grown here, most significantly Aglianico, which produces bold, spice-driven, potentially profound wines. Fortunately, at A16 we find it is easy to explain to our guests what is so great about Campania; we just pour them a glass of Fiano, and if coaxing is needed, assure them that the wine rivals a white Burgundy in complexity and intrigue. Then the adventure begins.

The Bay of Naples shares certain physical features with the San Francisco Bay Area. Tunnels bore through hillsides and ferries cross the bays. Our backyard Meyer lemon trees parallel the citrus orchards that stretch all the way down to Calabria. Like California, the terrain in Campania is dramatic, though much more compact. Its rolling hills and fertile valleys punctuated by mountain peaks, volcanoes, and cliffs that jut up against the Tyrrhenian Sea are accessible within an easy day's drive. Within this topography, more than half of which is covered in hills and mountains, lies a variety of soil types: the volcanic soil around Campi Flegrei on the coast and Mount Massico in the north; the stony, rocky soil covering the cliffs of Ischia; the loose, tufaceous soil near the town of Tufo.

This landscape has provided more than beneficial growing conditions. The existence of some of Campania's historic grape varieties is indebted to its acidic volcanic soil. During the nineteenth and early twentieth centuries, when the vine pest phylloxera devastated many of Europe's best vineyards, volcanic soil created a sanctuary for Campania's indigenous vines, saving varieties such as the widespread Falanghina and the obscure Pepella, a grape used in white wines from the Costa d'Amalfi DOC, from extinction.

Campania's most recognizable wines come from Avellino province, home of the heralded Taurasi DOCG, which produces red wines from the Aglianico grape, as well as two ageworthy white wines, Fiano di Avellino and Greco di Tufo, made, respectively, with Fiano and Greco grapes. Hilly Avellino province can be damp and bone-chilling in the winter, while the summers are clear, dry, and notably cooler than they are on the Campanian coast; it's not unusual for

vintners to harvest Aglianico grapes as late as November. The city of Avellino, a forty-five-minute drive east from the outskirts of Naples, seems to be in perpetual construction, still recovering from the 1980 earthquake. But small surrounding communities, such as Taurasi, with narrow, winding roads and old road signs, seem tucked away from modernity.

Northwest of Avellino, toward Campania's border with Lazio, the Apennines fill the horizon. Wedged in the foothills are historic vineyard areas such as Falerno del Massico, where grapes have grown on the slopes of Mount Massico since before Roman times. Here grape varieties such as fruity Piedirosso are blended with Aglianico for red wines that mirror the earthy richness of a Bordeaux. Between Mount Massico and Avellino lies the small town of Aversa in Caserta province, where the acidic white wine Asprinio di Aversa can be traced back to Bourbon rule, when it accompanied glamorous, multicourse meals before falling out of favor. Thankfully, vintners in Caserta have taken pains to preserve grapes with a long history of production in the region. While some historic grape varieties were destroyed by phylloxera or ripped out and planted with other grapes, lawyers Peppe Mancini and Alberto Barletta banded together in 1990 to form the Vestini Campagnano project to cultivate indigenous grapes and make wine under the Terre del Volturno IGT designation. Although the two have parted ways (Peppe started producing wines under the Terre del Principe label, and Alberto and his family continue to make wine under the Vestini Campagnano label), their efforts have saved the grapes Pallagrello Bianco, Pallagrello Nero, and Casavecchia from extinction.

In contrast to the quiet, introspective inland towns, Campania's coastal hills and islands feel carefree, a mood shaped in part by vacation-goers sipping chilled white wine with their fresh calamari and octopus dishes. I love Ischian Biancolella, a grape that grows on cliffs so chiseled and steep that it is a wonder how vintners tend to their vines. Capri also produces light, delightful white wines, but the island's steady tourism ensures a strong market for them, and few bottles are exported. On the coast just west of Naples, the Campi Flegrei DOC is known for its volcanic soil, which imparts a racy minerality to the white grapes Falanghina and Coda di Volpe that thrive in the area. It is here that Marisa Cuomo makes one of Italy's most revered white wines.

Marisa returned the obscure white grapes Fenile and Ginestra, of the Costa d'Amalfi DOC, to prominence through her late-harvest, barrel-aged Fiorduva, a blend of the two varieties, along with a little Ripoli. The ravine where Marisa grows the grapes for Fiorduva lies just south of the tiny Amalfi coast town of Furore. In the summer, workers place tarps over the grapes to prevent them from scorching in the unyielding sun. And in the winter, rainstorms and wind stress the vines, which cling for their life to the rocky soil. While the view overlooking the ravine is breathtaking, a true, backbreaking passion for wine is required to achieve the results Marisa gets under these adverse conditions. The fruits of these stressed vines taste as fresh as the air after the rain, with notes of mango and white peaches and a firm backbone of acidity that make the wine capable of aging for five years.

In Salerno province, south of Amalfi, lie the warm, dry hills of Cilento. Although the clay and lime soil can be difficult to till, it can bring forth powerful expressions of Aglianico, Piedirosso, and Fiano. The wines from Bruno De Conciliis and the nearby producer Luigi Maffini are discreetly modern renditions of these classic Campanian grapes. Cilento vintners also grow a number of Italian varieties not native to Campania, such as Trebbiano Toscano, Sangiovese, Barbera, and Primitivo, to be used as blending grapes.

WHITE GRAPES: THE CLASSICS

FALANGHINA

One of the most important white grapes in Campania, Falanghina has seen its fortunes rise and fall over the centuries. When the Greeks ruled Campania, the grape was held in high regard. During Roman times it was literally the toast of the empire, vinified as the wine Falernum, and the grape was worth more than gold. Falanghina has since endured wars and the demise of several empires, dodged phylloxera, and been relegated to the role of blending grape in bulk wine production, from which it is still recovering.

Falanghina wines are a deep straw color and have a ripe, honey- and almond-scented nose with a hint of nectarines. On the palate, a zesty finish brightens the initial sweet aromatics and flavor. The grape flourishes in the volcanic soils of the Campi Flegrei and Falerno del Massico DOCs, which are known for expressive, pure Falanghina wines. Northeast of Benevento province, Falanghina has been recognized as one of the most successful white grapes to grow on the slopes of Mount Taburno, thanks to the work of producers such as Cantina del Taburno and Ocone. The grape also grows along the coast, blended with local grapes in the Capri, Costa d'Amalfi, and Penisola Sorrentina DOCs, yielding wines of low acidity that are best when consumed young. Falanghina is often surprisingly inexpensive considering its many virtues.

FOOD PAIRING: Wines made from Falanghina have a fruit-forward character, balanced by notes of dried herbs, that enhances the sweet, acidic *peperonata* and creamy ricotta bruschetta (page 97). Their zesty quality makes them a palate-refreshing complement to the anchovies and olives on our *pizza romana* (page 120), and brings out the sweetness in our grilled shrimp (page 168).

RECOMMENDED PRODUCERS: Alois, Cantina del Taburno, Cantine Farro, Dedicato a Marianna, Fattoria Prattico, La Sibilla, Montesole, Ocone, Villa Matilde

FIANO

Lucio Mastroberardino presented his wines from the Terredora di Paolo winery at A16's first wine dinner. After standing up to talk, Lucio exclaimed without hesitation, "Fiano is the greatest grape in the world." I will admit I was a little startled, but his bold statement showed the deep passion that winemakers like him have for the grape and the wine made from it. With the wine's near-perfect balance of acidity, mineral complexity, and body, I certainly agree with Lucio that Fiano deserves a broader following.

Today Fiano has come into its own in the Fiano di Avellino DOCG production zone, but the grape has thrived in the area for centuries. I have been told that Fiano and Chardonnay are related—allegedly, the same boat carrying vine cuttings made stops in both France and the port of Naples—but the lineage has not been proven. The grapes do have many similarities, however. Fiano produces the most full-bodied Campanian white wine, but its fullness varies greatly depending on the maker. Its flavor profile can evoke pine nuts and herbs, or taste like pears, orange blossoms, and earth captured in a glass. Versions from the Fiano di Avellino DOCG have a smoky quality, with notes

Winemaker Bruno De Conciliis amid the Greek ruins in Paestum, Campania

of baking spices and white pepper. At the same time, even when vinified dry, Fiano wines evoke the sweetness and body of honey. Many people believe the sweet, aromatic Fiano grape attracts bees, perhaps explaining its underlying honeyed character—and the number of factories producing *torrone* (a nougat made with honey) that flank the road toward Avellino. At harvesttime, bees hover over the fruit, providing a sense that Avellino's ecosystem is, quite literally, buzzing away.

FOOD PAIRING: With their complexity and balance, Fiano-based wines pair well with a range of dishes, from seafood preparations to lighter meat courses. Fiano di Avellino wines have a pronounced saline minerality, which complements the varied preparations of tuna *conserva* (page 105). I also appreciate Fiano di Avellino paired with *minestra maritata* (page 132); the braising greens simmered in the prosciutto and cheese *brodo* bring out the honeyed side of the wine. The rich, round character of a late-harvest Fiano accents the creaminess of our liver terrine (page 206).

RECOMMENDED PRODUCERS: Benito Ferrara, Clelia Romano, Colli di Castelfranci, I Favati, Feudi di San Gregorio, Mastroberardino, Pietracupa, Terredora di Paolo

GRECO

When the Greeks arrived in Paestum, just north of Cilento, in the sixth century BC, they brought with them a white grape that became known as Greco. While planted throughout southern Italy, Greco grown in the hills surrounding the old mining town of Tufo in Avellino province acquires the acidity and complexity necessary for making distinctive wine. Recognition of Greco di Tufo spread, and the area became a DOCG in 2003. Here the loose, tufaceous soil has a greenish tint that reflects its limestone content. This soil is fragile, however. In 2004, heavy rain caused the Ferrara family's Greco vines to slide down the hill.

Both the Greco di Tufo and the Fiano di Avellino DOCGs are located in the Irpinian hills, but the differences in the wines are pronounced. While Fiano di Avellino wines can age well, Grecos are generally best when consumed young. Examples from such producers as Dedicato a Marianna and Terredora di Paolo can be as lean and racy as a Sauvignon Blanc. When made from grapes that have been given a longer hang time, however, Greco can take on more weight. Benito Ferrara's Vigna Cicogna Greco di Tufo, made by Gabriella Ferrara and her husband, Sergio, is full bodied, with notes of honeysuckle and slate. It is a benchmark wine for the region.

Asprinio grapes in Aversa

FOOD PAIRING: It is a running joke at A16: When I ask a server to suggest a wine for a certain dish, he or she says Greco. It's a cheeky response, but it carries some truth. Lean Grecos complement lighter appetizers, while fuller-bodied examples pair brilliantly with a range of foods, from delicate seafood preparations to roasted meats. Greco di Tufo classically complements the dark, bitter flavors of rapini and balances well with the sweetness of the crab in our Dungeness crab bruschetta (page 94). I also frequently recommend it with our shellfish *acqua pazza* (page 172) and our grilled shrimp (page 168).

RECOMMENDED PRODUCERS: Benito Ferrara, Colli di Castelfranci, D'Antiche Terre, Dedicato a Marianna, Feudi di San Gregorio, Mastroberardino, Pietracupa, Terredora di Paolo, Villa Raiano

WHITE GRAPES: A CLOSER LOOK

ASPRINIO DI AVERSA

Asprinio, which means "slightly sour," produces a lean, crisp white wine. I love its sour edge—as thirst quenching as lemonade, as aromatic as orange blossoms. The acidity of the wine, which can be just this side of searing, also makes it a good base for *spumante*.

Although Asprinio was once planted more widely, today it is mostly confined to the region of Aversa and is the main grape in the Aversa DOC. Yet more producers are beginning to experiment with the grape. I Borboni, a producer that has always championed the grape, makes the most well known Asprinio wine. Villa Carafa and Caputo also make quality renditions.

FOOD PAIRING: The pencil-lead minerality of lean, dry Asprinio complements earthy beets, while its citus notes pair well with the fennel and olives in our beet salad (page 99).

RECOMMENDED PRODUCERS: Caputo, I Borboni, Villa Carafa

BIANCOLELLA

One look at the island of Ischia's impossibly steep vineyards makes me marvel that anyone ever started cultivating grapes here. The first vines predate the Phoenicians, and the confluence of the maritime air, rocky soil, and indigenous grapes, particularly Biancolella, yielded a wine

Luigi Barletta of Vestini Campagnano, holding a bottle of Asprinio

that was a prized commodity throughout the Mediterranean. With such a legacy of quality wine production, it is fitting that Ischia was awarded Italy's second DOC in 1966.

With their white flower, lemon, and honey aromatics and slatelike minerality Biancolella-based wines reveal their environment in each sip. The island became a popular tourist destination in the latter half of the twentieth century, and many Ischians turned their attention away from winemaking and toward the lucrative tourist trade. Fortunately, the D'Ambra family never lost sight of producing top-quality Ischian wine. Their wines made primarily with Biancolella, such as Frassitelli, are the standard for Campanian white wine. Although newer on the scene, Pietratorcia also produces great wines, blending Biancolella with the local grapes Forastera, Uva Rilla, and San Leonardo for their Vigne Del Cuotto bottling. Both producers grapple with the challenge of working on steep hillsides, where vineyard workers must gingerly balance themselves during harvest. Even though outside interest exists in exporting this wine, Ischia's natural borders will always guarantee small production. Biancolella also grows in the coastal appellations of Campi Flegrei and Costa d'Amalfi.

FOOD PAIRING: Easygoing wines made with Biancolella are perfect fits for light, casual fare such as our arugula salad with almonds and green olives (page 101). The vibrant acidity and acacia-honey notes in the wine meld with the textures and bright, sweet-salty flavors of the dish.

RECOMMENDED PRODUCERS: Casa D'Ambra, Marisa Cuomo, Pietratorcia

CODA DI VOLPE

This grape, named by Pliny for how its curved cluster resembles a fox's tail, has been grown on the slopes of Mount Vesuvius for centuries. It is most notable for its inclusion in the Vesuvio DOC, where it has been traditionally blended with Falanghina or Greco for Lacryma Christi del Vesuvio *bianco*, of which Mastroberardino makes a popular version. Today, though, some vintners are experimenting with making 100 percent Coda di Volpe wines. Even so, the grape is largely overlooked in favor of Fiano, Falanghina, and Greco.

Wines made with Coda di Volpe are light and crisp, with delicate aromas of lemon verbena and mandarin, and

should be consumed young. Sometimes when wines are as light as this, they are seen as weak and inconsequential. But these wines typically convey a wonderful sense of place when carefully vinified. In a well-made Coda di Volpe–based wine, the grapes seem to have eaten through the volcanic soil, giving an edgy, mineral backbone to the wine's zesty fruit flavors.

FOOD PAIRING: Coda di Volpe's mineral undertones pair well with marinated olives (page 91), and its citrus notes complement braised halibut seasoned with preserved lemons and pistachios (page 175).

RECOMMENDED PRODUCERS: D'Antiche Terre, De Anglis, Grotta del Sole, Mastroberardino, Terredora di Paolo

PALLAGRELLO BIANCO

Less than two decades ago, only a few untended vineyards were left in Caserta that grew its native Pallagrello Bianco and its sibling, the red Pallagrello Nero. Peppe Mancini and Alberto Barletta's Vestini Campagnano project took up the cause of preserving these rare, native grapes as heritage varieties. The lawyers-turned-vintners took cuttings from remaining vines, some of which were more than a century old, and began to cultivate them for quality wine production. By 2000, ten years after they started their preservation project, Vestini Campagnano produced six thousand liters of wine made from Pallagrello Bianco and Nero and Casavecchia. In 2003, Peppe left Vestini Campagnano and started Terre del Principe, which also makes wines with the same three heritage grapes.

It is still rare to find Pallagrello Bianco grown outside of the Terre del Volturno IGT, but word is gradually getting out about the grape's merits. Pallagrello-based whites typically are a deep gold and have mellow acidity and a waxy, weighty presence, especially when made from late-harvest grapes, as in Vestini Campagnano's barrel-aged Le Òrtole.

FOOD PAIRINGS: The roundness of Pallagrello-based wines balances the tang of the local Friarelli peppers or the gamey richness of pork *ciccioli* (page 205). They also pair seamlessly with the rich walnut *crema* and pungent, truffle-flecked pecorino that accompany our roasted asparagus (page 102).

RECOMMENDED PRODUCERS: Alois, Terre del Principe, Vestini Campagnano

RED GRAPES: THE CLASSICS

AGLIANICO

One of Italy's greatest red grapes, Aglianico yields wines that range from humble *vino da tavola* to the rich, structured Taurasi's worthy of frequent comparison to Piedmont's Barolos and Barbarescos. As a sommelier, I like the flexibility the Aglianico grape gives me when pairing wines with different dishes. I can travel the spectrum from light to weighty and still retain the spicy, earthy flavors inherent in the grape.

Grown in Campania for more than three thousand years, this deep red, thick-skinned grape never had to fear extinction. It did, however, suffer in quality and was produced primarily for local consumption through most of the twentieth century. Today, it flourishes throughout the region in vineyards planted in both volcanic soil and in coastal vineyards. The number of notable wines made with the grape continues to expand, from the distinctive, award-winning wines of Taurasi to lesser-known bottles of exceptional quality.

A book could be devoted to the haunting, masculine wine made with Aglianico grapes grown in and around the quiet, rural village of Taurasi. In 1968, the Mastroberardino family released Radici, which means "roots." Made with Aglianico grapes grown around Taurasi, it was the first southern Italian wine to receive critical acclaim in recent history. It was also the first time a producer used the Taurasi name to indicate the origin of an Aglianico wine. Yet nearly three decades would pass before more local vintners started producing comparably great wines.

For all of the recent recognition Taurasi has received, its winemakers remain modest. I always have the sense that community and family are more important than awards and international fame. Even through Salvatore Molettieri's name carries significant weight in the Italian wine scene, he is more likely to be found chatting over espresso with members of the Favati family, who make wine in the basement of their suburban Avellino home, than flying around the world to industry events. The residents of the region have an honest style of hospitality that I seek to bring to each table at A16.

Below: Aglianico vines in Taurasi
Overleaf: Bottles of Taurasi in Antonio Caggiano's cellar

Taurasi's tight-knit community and welcoming spirit proved to be helpful during one of our early research trips to Campania. Wherever we dined, nearly every sommelier we encountered raved about Caggiano Taurasi. Curiosity piqued, we decided to visit the winery before heading back to California. Antonio Caggiano, a short, gregarious winemaker, with a close crop of gray hair and expressive eyes, quickly invited us in. He hit it off with our group as we delighted in tasting his powerful Vigna Macchia dei Goti Taurasi, a full, modern-style wine with elegant notes of baking spices. Since that visit, Caggiano Taurasi has become my good luck wine, and I reach for it whenever I need a wine to tell a story about Campania's renaissance.

According to the DOCG regulations, Taurasi must age three years, at least one of them in barrels, before it is released on the market. Yet most Taurasi producers age their wines for at least four years before releasing them, thus earning the *riserva* designation. When young, Taurasi can be tough and austere, owing to its considerable tannins. But as these wines mature, the tannins mellow and subtle fruit flavors emerge. This balance of tannic backbone and generous, nuanced fruit makes Taurasi one of Italy's most structured, ageworthy wines. Within the Taurasi zone, though, styles vary. Mastroberardino, along with Pietracupa and Di Meo, produce elegant and luscious wines that are medium-full bodied, while wines from Caggiano, Feudi di San Gregorio, Molettieri, and Villa Raiano are full bodied and intense. In both styles, the Taurasi *terroir* expresses itself in characteristic aromas of evergreen pine, clove, bittersweet chocolate, and tar.

There is more to Aglianico than Taurasi. Cool Benevento province north of Avellino produces serious red wines under the Aglianico del Taburno DOC, which, though lesser known, can be just as brooding as their counterparts from Taurasi. Like Taurasi, this zone enjoys a long growing season, concentrating the flavors of the grapes as they hang on the vine. Ocone, a biodynamic vintner, produces a stern, ageworthy Aglianico del Taburno. Meanwhile, Cantina del Taburno, a large co-op winery, makes a dark, oaky Aglianico del Taburno called Bue Apis. One of my favorite discoveries from Benevento, however, was the small family producer Lorenzo Nifo Sarrapochiello. It took me four years to secure an order of his D'Erasmo Aglianico del Taburno Riserva, a deep, plush wine with notes of dark berries.

Wines made under the Aglianico d'Irpinia IGT classification have some of the austerity found in Taurasi DOCG wines but to a lesser extent, making them more accessible when younger. I Favati's Cretarossa exemplifies the character that can be found in Irpinian Aglianico. One of the most renowned Campanian Aglianico wines also happens to be made under the Aglianico d'Irpinia IGT. Feudi di San Gregorio's powerful Serpico is made with grapes harvested from century-old, pre-phylloxera vines that grow within the Taurasi DOCG zone. But it is categorized as an Irpinia Aglianico because it isn't aged as long as the Taurasi DOCG requires. Meanwhile, in Cilento, Aglianico takes on a rich, ripe aspect due to the warmer weather, creating a wine with a modern flavor profile and softer tannins.

FOOD PAIRINGS: Since chestnuts grow throughout Taurasi, the wines of the area pair naturally with our braised pork shoulder with chestnuts and olives (page 222). When I drink Taurasi with this dish, I feel like I am watching the sunset over the Avellino hills. Our staple pasta dish, *maccaronara* with *ragù alla napoletana* (page 148), is such a Campanian classic that I feel as if Aglianico must be part of the sauce (it isn't). Drinking Aglianico with ragù-coated *maccaronara* garnished with Ricotta Salata brings forth a true sense of place. Our meatballs braised in tomato sauce (page 213) are also a natural match with Aglianico wines. Several different styles of Aglianico complement the ragù or meatballs; the choice depends on the occasion. A simple Monday meal might warrant a medium-bodied Aglianico d'Irpinia such as I Favati, while a celebration calls for Feudi di San Gregorio's Serpico.

RECOMMENDED PRODUCERS (TAURASI): Antonio Caggiano, Contrade di Taurasi, Di Meo, Feudi di San Gregorio, Mastroberardino, Pietracupa, Salvatore Molettieri, Terredora di Paolo, Villa Raiano

RECOMMENDED PRODUCERS (REGIONAL AGLIANICO): Alois, Cantina del Taburno, De Conciliis, Feudi di San Gregorio, Galardi, I Favati, Lorenzo Nifo Sarrapochiello, Luigi Maffini, Luigi Moio, Marisa Cuomo, Masseria Felicia, Michele Moio, Ocone, Salvatore Molettieri, Villa Carafa, Villa Matilde, Villa Raiano

PIEDIROSSO

The base of the native Piedirosso vine has a rusty hue and forms a distinct L shape, which resembles the foot of another native of the Campi Flegrei region: the rock pigeon. (Piedirosso literally means "red foot.") After Aglianico, Piedirosso is the second most planted red grape in Campania. It thrives on the seaside cliffs and coastal mountains of the region and plays a significant role in the legend of Lacryma Christi. As the tale goes, when Lucifer fell from heaven, he landed on Mount Vesuvius, which provoked Christ to cry, thus watering the slopes of the volcano with heavenly tears. Soon after, Piedirosso vines sprung from the earth. Some locals still say the way to tell the Piedirosso grape is ripe is when it sheds a tear in remembrance.

Piedirosso-based wines (which frequently include Aglianico in the blend) tend be light- to medium-bodied with a spicy, strawberry character. The grape is most notably grown in the provinces of Naples, Salerno, and Caserta, and aside from the Vesuvio DOC, it is also the main red grape in the Costa d'Amalfi, Campi Flegrei, Falerno del Massico, and Ischia DOCs. Mastroberardino has taken on Piedirosso as a pet project to help with the restoration of Pompeii. The resulting wine, Villa dei Misteri, made with Piedirosso grapes grown near Pompeii, is spice driven, with a medium-full body; it is also very pricey, but all proceeds go to preserving Pompeii. On the Amalfi coast, Piedirosso is made into a *frizzante* wine that is served chilled—the perfect accompaniment to a lazy afternoon spent gazing at the sea.

FOOD PAIRING: The soft, delicate red fruits of Piedirosso work seamlessly with a *pizza marinara* (page 119), while its notable spiciness adds another peppery kick to our *bucatini* with fava beans (page 159).

RECOMMENDED PRODUCERS: Grotta del Sole, Luigi Maffini, Marisa Cuomo, Masseria Felicia, Mastroberardino, Montevetrano, Terredora di Paolo

RED GRAPES: A CLOSER LOOK

....

CASAVECCHIA

Named for the old house that supported one of the last remaining rows of its vines, Casavecchia is another of winemakers Peppe Mancini and Alberto Barletta's preservation projects in the vineyards of Caserta. Alberto's son Amedeo recalls that when his father started cultivating Casavecchia seriously, no one believed that the juicy grape could produce great wine. It was Amedeo's mother, Maria, who urged her husband not to give up on the grape.

Casavecchia grapes are large and sweet, not unlike Concord grapes. They make such great table grapes that Caserta locals preferred to eat them rather than press them. The grape itself has inky juice with a vibrant flavor, and the wines made from it can burst forth with plummy fruits. Judicious barrel aging can tame the grape and give it tannins. Trebulanum, from Alois, is an example of a larger-than-life, juicy Casavecchia. Villa Carafa's rendition, which we often pour by the glass at A16, is also full bodied and well rounded. Vestini Campagnano makes a more elegant, linear Casavecchia with spicy accents. The annual production of Casavecchia is still small, so it can be difficult to find these wines outside of the region.

FOOD PAIRING: The herbaceous bite of spring onions and fennel-infused sausage in the *salsiccia* pizza (page 125) balance well with the concentrated dark-fruit flavor of Casavecchia. This wine goes equally well with grilled sausages and cured meats. I also like serving it alongside our grilled rabbit (page 186).

RECOMMENDED PRODUCERS: Alois, Terre del Principe, Vestini Campagnano, Villa Carafa

PALLAGRELLO NERO

Sibling to Pallagrello Bianco, the once nearly extinct Pallagrello Nero vine is now spreading in popularity thanks to the initiatives started by Vestini Campagnano. The grape's recent obscurity belies its storied past, which includes the distinction of producing a favorite wine of Ferdinand IV. It is also a grape with a bright future for making wines of consequence. Compared with juicy Casavecchia, Pallagrello Nero has a decidedly serious tone, its austere tannins and acidity more closely aligned with Aglianico. When vinified, Pallagrello Nero similarly benefits from being aged in oak. The wine is still being produced in limited quantities, mostly within the Terre del Volturno DOC. But its history and potential make it worth a search.

FOOD PAIRING: Pallagrello Nero's austere tannins and acidity make it a good match for rich rabbit or pork dishes, such as pork shoulder with olives and chestnuts (page 222) and *ciccioli* (page 205). It also counterbalances the richness of our lamb and ricotta *crespelle* (page 190).

RECOMMENDED PRODUCERS: Terre del Principe, Vestini Campagnano

ABRUZZO A24

The first time I drove to L'Aquila, Abruzzo's capital, I wasn't expecting to encounter a road so steep and winding. But the twists and turns of the highway made L'Aquila, perched 2,150 feet above sea level, seem like a true getaway spot. Although it lies only seventy miles east of Rome, it is removed from the urban bustle, tucked away in the thick forests surrounding the Gran Sasso national park. Despite its remoteness, L'Aquila is a sophisticated university town steeped in history—a vibrant pocket in a region that is full of geographic and cultural contrasts.

From the Gran Sasso massif and its Corno Grande, the highest point in the Apennines, mountains cascade across the landscape of Abruzzo, and it is rare to find a stretch of flat land. But where the dramatic terrain relaxes into rolling foothills dotted with sheep and wide, sandy beaches along the Adriatic Sea, grapes enjoy ideal growing conditions: porous clay and gravel soils, dry summers, and cool sea breezes.

Some readers might question whether Abruzzo belongs in a discussion of southern Italian wine, given its proximity to the central regions of Lazio and Marche. But its formidable mountains have shielded it from northern influences, aligning its culture more closely with that of the south. Abruzzo's southern exposure is evident in its cuisine, specifically in its choice of cooking fat and its prevailing style of pasta. Lazio, Marche, and the regions north use both butter and olive oil, while Abruzzo, Molise, and the regions south, including Sardinia and Sicily, use olive oil almost exclusively. Every region in Italy consumes dried pastas, yet Abruzzo, Campania, and Puglia are renowned for their dried-pasta production.

The enological history of Abruzzo also follows the classic story of the south. While the local wines received praise from the ancient Greeks and Romans (who also loved the region's beaches), modern history has not been as kind. Poverty inhibited the production of quality wines, which in turn drove up bulk-wine production through the proliferation of cooperatives. Today, bulk wine still comprises most of the wines produced here, but fortunately, just as Campania has restored dignity to its wine industry, so, too, has Abruzzo. The late winemaker Edoardo Valentini, who spent more than fifty years making some of Italy's most beguiling white wines, always claimed that the climate and soil of Abruzzo could produce expressive wines evocative of the region. A

new generation of winemakers, including Edoardo's son Francesco, is striving to make Abruzzesi wines that fulfill Edoardo's vision.

The Trebbiano d'Abruzzo and the Montepulciano d'Abruzzo DOCs cover more than half of the region. A crisp, racy Abruzzo white made with Trebbiano or Pecorino grapes is the perfect way to start a meal, while the reds of Montepulciano d'Abruzzo (made from the grape of the same name) range from velvety smooth to full bodied and tannic, with enough range in between to keep a wine taster engaged. The northeastern area of Abruzzo, close to the border with Marche, is home to the region's most noble Montepulciano d'Abruzzo wines in the DOCG Colline Teramane. While most of the wines made here are immediately enjoyable, some are capable of extended aging, and many producers have wine libraries that go back decades. The century-old Emidio Pepe winery, which makes Montepulciano d'Abruzzo and Trebbiano d'Abruzzo wines in northeast Abruzzo, is just now releasing bottles that are twenty to thirty years old.

To taste an example of why Abruzzo is on my radar, seek out the deep red Colline Teramane *riserva* Pieluni from Dino Illuminati. The Illuminati family has grown grapes in the region since the late nineteenth century and played an instrumental role in pushing for the DOCG designation in Colline Teramane. An engaging yet humble winemaker, Stefano Illuminati makes rich wines with Montepulciano that have brought him acclaim from outside of the region. Not content to dwell on one style, he also crafts an astounding variety of wines, including one of the region's rare sparkling wines made in the traditional French *méthode champenoise*. Stefano is quick to point out all of the new projects, including vineyard land acquisition and growth in such varieties as Chardonnay, Riesling, and Cabernet Sauvignon. But the most significant projects are focused on bringing forth the best qualities of the Trebbiano and Montepulciano grapes.

Farther inland, near the foot of the southern side of the Gran Sasso, is the town of Ofena, known as *il forno dell'Abruzzo*—"the oven of Abruzzo"—for its sizzling-hot summer days despite its mountain setting. It is also an important center of saffron production and sits at the heart of an area with the potential to be Abruzzo's next great wine region. The Luigi Cataldi Madonna estate has been making wine here since the 1920s, and in the late 1960s, the family began to shift their focus to quality production, planting new vineyards and modernizing their cellar. In time, they built a reputation for making singular wines. The Cataldi Madonna Montepulciano d'Abruzzo Tonì is one of the purest expressions of the Montepulciano grape I have tasted.

These are only two of the growing number of producers worth seeking out in greater Abruzzo. New producers such as Binomio, Fattoria La Valentina, and Villa Medoro are bringing forth modern, high-quality Montepulciano d'Abruzzo and Trebbiano d'Abruzzo. The diversity among producers in the region—from the size of their production to the methods they employ—has resulted in an exciting range of wine styles. The upsurge in quality is rapidly raising the profile of the region, and I eagerly anticipate tasting what these producers do next.

WHITE GRAPES: THE CLASSICS

TREBBIANO

Since it grows easily in Abruzzo, Trebbiano is by far the most cultivated white grape in the region. Pliny referred to a wine made here called Trebulanum, which may well have been made with Trebbiano. The grape yields a deep gold wine with intriguing essences of honey, yellow wax bean, and green almond–qualities that have been largely overshadowed by its role in Modena's balsamic vinegar production.

Stimulated in part by the allure of the late Edoardo Valentini's Trebbiano d' Abruzzo, the grape is beginning to make a comeback in quality. Producers such as Dino Illuminati, Emidio Pepe, Pasetti, and Villa Medoro are working to revive Trebbiano as a grape that can shine on its own. The Illuminati Brut, a rare, sparkling Abruzzesi wine, is produced with 100 percent Trebbiano; the firm acidity of the wine elegantly frames notes of brioche and star fruit. In contrast, Emidio Pepe, who practices biodynamic farming methods and prefers to crush his harvest by foot, makes an ageworthy, golden Trebbiano d'Abruzzo with a waxy, rich texture imparted by the thick skin of the grapes.

There is a bit of mystery surrounding the identity of Trebbiano. While Edoardo and fellow winemakers referred to the grape as Trebbiano, others believed it was actually the Puglian grape Bombino Bianco. Meanwhile, the large Puglian producer Rivera believes the grapes are two distinct varieties. Perhaps in an effort to hedge bets, the Trebbiano d'Abruzzo DOC permits the use of both Trebbiano and Bombino Bianco grapes.

FOOD PAIRING: While Trebbiano can produce ageworthy wines, most Trebbiano d'Abruzzo wines are light, with subtle fruit notes and a refreshing mineral undertone that complement our seafood *acqua pazza* (page 172). Their firm acidity cuts through the richness of *coppa di testa* (page 208).

RECOMMENDED PRODUCERS: Bruno Nicodemi, Cantina Frentana, Cantina Tollo, Dino Illuminati, Emidio Pepe, Franco Pasetti, Fratelli Barba, Masciarelli, Torre Zambra, Valentini, Villa Medoro

WHITE GRAPES: A CLOSER LOOK

PASSERINA

Believed to have originated in Greece, Passerina grapes grow well in Abruzzo, especially in the north around Controguerra. A wine made from 100 percent Passerina tends to be medium bodied and floral, with notes of peach and Golden Delicious apple. The grape is often blended with Pecorino and Trebbiano, and it is also one of the main components of the regional sweet wine Controguerra Passito Bianco.

FOOD PAIRING: A tart glass of Passerina complements a bowl of marinated olives (page 91) at the start of a meal. If it is a Controguerra Passito Bianco, however, reach for a plate of cookies (page 258).

RECOMMENDED PRODUCERS: Dino Illuminati, Lepore

PECORINO

With the region's textile industry to support, Abruzzo has always been full of sheep. The story of the indigenous Pecorino grape is tied to these woolly inhabitants. According to local folklore, sheepherders used to guide their flocks through the mountains when a particular white grape was ready for picking. After nibbling on the fruit, the sheep sprung to life with energy, giving the grape its name, Pecorino, derived from the word *pecora*, or "sheep." Another, less evocative theory holds that the grape was cultivated by sheepherders because it could thrive in the high altitudes where they kept their flocks.

Characterized by citrus aromatics and a lean, flinty minerality, Pecorino is often used as a blending grape with Passerina and Trebbiano to make an everyday white wine. Recently, however, it has become popular for producing a refreshing, crisp white wine on its own. The Giuseppe Ciavolich winery makes a particularly excellent Pecorino-based wine called Aries. Cantina Frentana also makes a racy, elegant Pecorino that we recommend for customers who like crisp, thirst-quenching whites such as Sauvignon Blanc.

FOOD PAIRING: The citrus notes of Pecorino are a wonderful accompaniment to roasted sardines with garlic and mint (page 171).

RECOMMENDED PRODUCERS: Caldora, Cantina Frentana, Cantina Tollo, Contesa, Dora Sarchese, Faraone, Giuseppe Ciavolich, Gran Sasso

RED GRAPES: THE CLASSICS

MONTEPULCIANO D'ABRUZZO

When we opened A16, the Montepulciano d'Abruzzo from Il Feuduccio di Santa Maria d'Orni quickly became a staple and guest favorite. With an earthy richness and heady dose of blackberries and cherries, this wine appeals to those who favor the bold, fruit-forward qualities of New World wines.

Montepulciano is one of Italy's most important red grapes, and it is the defining grape variety for Abruzzo, much as Sangiovese is for Tuscany and Aglianico is for Campania. Although the dark, inky quality of Abruzzese wines made from Montepulciano might make them seem daunting, the best examples have a warm, inner glow that appeals to a range of wine drinkers. They also vary in style. The more common fruit-forward type seduces with its velvety mouthfeel, mimicking a lush Merlot balanced by a rugged edge that keeps it intriguing. These wines typically have low to medium tannins and are meant to be enjoyed young. Meanwhile, a more tannic, ageworthy style is emerging, particularly in the Colline Teramane zone. When the Montepulciano d'Abruzzo DOC was created in 1992, this area in the northeast corner of Abruzzo near the Adriatic Sea was singled out as optimal for growing Montepulciano grapes. Thanks in part to producers such as Illuminati, who campaigned to have the growing area recognized, Colline Teramane was awarded DOCG status in 2003. After a few years of aging, these wines unfold with an elegant structure layered with bold, dark plum fruits.

One quirky thing to remember about this grape: Despite its proliferation in Abruzzo, it is often confused with the town of Montepulciano in Tuscany, home to the DOCG wine Vino Nobile di Montepulciano. But the main grape in Vino Nobile is Prugnolo Gentile (a Sangiovese clone), not Montepulciano.

FOOD PAIRING: Montepulciano d'Abruzzo has a velvet finish that pairs well with rib roast with *mosto* (page 193). But my favorite match is with the rich cheeses and briny green olive that top the *pizza bianca* (page 123).

RECOMMENDED PRODUCERS: Binomio, Cantina Tollo, Centorame, Dino Illuminati, Emidio Pepe, Farnese, Fattoria La Valentina, Il Feuduccio di Santa Maria d'Orni, Luigi Cataldi Madonna, Marramiero, Masciarelli, Orlandi Contucci Ponno, Valentini, Villa Medoro

MOLISE A14

When my friend Massimiliano introduced me to the producer Di Majo Norante, I was delighted to find such intricate wines from one of Italy's most remote corners. As the region with the second fewest residents in Italy (Valle d'Aosta has the fewest), Molise feels insulated from outside influence, particularly in its inland villages, where time seems to have stood still. When my husband, Greg, and I drove through Molise's rocky Apennines, our car soaring across the bridges that connect each peak, we marveled at how difficult it must have been to travel here before the *autostrada* was built. The physical isolation has not helped the economy. From the turn of the twentieth century through World War II, the population of Molise shrunk as its inhabitants, including my mother-in-law's family, emigrated to the north and abroad. Isolation has its benefits, though, as the lack of industry has helped preserve local traditions. The northern city Agnone produces some of Europe's finest church bells. When I heard its bells chime though the mountains, I felt as if I had found a hidden treasure. Some of Molise's wines resonate with the same sense of discovery.

During my first visit to the region, I was surprised to see acres of vineyards lining the road from Campania to Molise's capital, Campobasso. For a small wine region, there seemed to be a good deal of activity. Enrico and Pasquale Di Giulio, who founded the Borgo di Colloredo winery in 1994, have noticed a heightened interest in the region's winemaking in recent years, and the general feeling among producers here is that Molise will become appreciated as more people try its wines. The rebirth of the wine industry has coincided with the emergence of the region as a distinct entity. As recently as 1963, Molise was part of Abruzzo, and centuries ago it was part of Puglia. It has a long tradition of viticulture dating back to the Etruscans, but it suffered a severe setback when phylloxera wiped out most of its vines in the nineteenth century. It has only been within the last thirty years that vineyards have been replanted, and only in the past twenty years have some vintners begun to devote their production to quality wines.

Unlike Campania, Molise is not known for its wealth of indigenous grapes. Its strength as a wine region comes from its mountainous terrain and its enterprising producers. White wine is produced here, but red wines, made primarily from Montepulciano and Aglianico, are the main draw. When fashioned from well-managed vines, Montepulciano from Molise has a dusty, earthy quality balanced by concentrated fruits and firm tannins, paired with an addictive, velvety

finish—the perfect complement to *trippa alla napoletana* (page 137) or a rib roast with rosemary and *mosto* (page 193). One indigenous red variety, Tintilia, a tannic grape that can be hard to grow, is gaining interest among some winemakers. Although currently unproven, it may be the best candidate for crafting a uniquely Molisan wine.

The climate in Molise can be harsh and prone to drought, with freezing temperatures in the winter and hot summers. Even so, the region has a lot to offer winemakers. Di Majo Norante was one of the first estates to recognize the region's potential, campaigning for the Pentro di Isernia and Biferno DOCs, which were granted in 1980. (A third DOC, Molise, which encompasses the entire region, was created in 1998.) The most prominent, the Biferno DOC, stretches from Campobasso all the way to the Adriatic, where coastal hillsides slope east toward the sea and vines benefit from long summers and sea breezes. The mountainous, inland Pentro di Isernia DOC, which is split into a northern and a southern section, is more obscure. Yet there is a growing consensus that the area's stressful growing conditions— poor soil and dramatic variations in climate and altitude— have the potential to yield concentrated red grapes ideal for making ageworthy wines.

Situated in the northeastern coastal city of Campomarino, Di Majo Norante is Molise's benchmark estate. Reflecting his aristocratic, Neapolitan heritage, owner Alessio Di Majo makes wine with the noble Campanian grapes Aglianico, Fiano, and Falanghina. But the producer's flagship wine, Don Luigi, is pure Molise. A blend of Montepulciano and Tintilia, it is infused with concentrated, dark-berry fruits and an earthy, tarmac quality. Di Majo Norante also produces one of my favorite dessert wines, Apianae, named for the bees (*api* in Latin) that hover over the sweet Moscato Reale grapes from which it is made. After three years of aging in oak, the wine delivers beautiful aromatics and a well-balanced palate of mandarin and honey, making it a perfect end to a special meal.

Apart from Di Majo Norante, there are a growing number of sophisticated estates producing unique wines of understated elegance. Also located close to the coast, Borgo di Colloredo's vineyards grow on steeply pitched hillsides facing the Adriatic. Here the Di Giulio family makes ambitious whites and reds worth seeking out. Its Biferno Rosso Gironia, made with Montepulciano and Aglianico, offers a combination of plum and cherry notes coupled with baking spices derived from barrel aging. Other producers worth a look include Azienda Agricola Colle Sereno, Cantina Valbiferno, Cantino Cliternia, and Di Tullio.

PUGLIA A14

Prior to my first visit to Puglia, what little I knew about its topography and economy had led me to expect a dull and dry landscape, with tractors, irrigation systems, and other indications of the region's agricultural focus scattered across the countryside. I couldn't have been more wrong. Driving up the Salento peninsula for the first time, the Adriatic and Ionian seas beckoning from either side and rows of vines competing with olive trees for attention, the picture in my head switched from black and white to full color.

Puglia came into sharper focus as I toured the striking southern city of Lecce. Surrounded by sand-hued Baroque architecture and Roman ruins, I felt an unmistakable youthful energy from the throngs of university students walking briskly by. My tour guide, Paolo Cantele, who works in marketing and sales for his family's winery, blended into the crowd with his curly, cropped hair, carefully styled goatee, and designer jeans. The Cantele family, which has made wines on the Salento peninsula for three generations, is proudly forward looking. They recently moved their operations into a new, state-of-the-art building outside of town. With the winery's rows of towering fermentation tanks, it is clear the family makes a lot of wine (more than two million bottles in 2007), but they remain focused on quality in their pursuit of innovation. The fundamentals of modern winemaking—limiting yields in the vineyards, controlling temperatures during fermentation, aging wines prior to release—were late to arrive in Puglia, a region formerly awash in bulk wine. But as local producers like Cantele, coupled with outside investors who have taken an interest in the rich soil and such native grapes as inky Nero di Troia, Puglia is penning an exciting comeback story.

When I began tasting Puglian wines for the A16 list, it was hard to know where to start. Puglia is one of the most challenging southern Italian wine regions to comprehend because of the sheer quantity of wine produced and the varying levels of quality. According to the Associazione Enologi Enotecnici Italiani, Puglia's total wine production in 2006 was 185 million gallons, the most of any region in Italy. (Piedmont, the region known for its noble Barolo and Barbaresco production, produced about 75 million gallons.) Yet even though Puglia has twenty-five DOCs, only about 5 percent of its production is categorized as DOC wine.

My early tastings were uneven. Some wines were pleasantly surprising and terrific values; others lost me in cooked-fruit tedium. Even when I was presented with a fine example, it wasn't always easy to find a local importer. After visiting Puglia, my business partner Victoria Libin introduced me to Rivera's Il Falcone, an excellent Nero di Troia wine. Then a year and a half passed before we found a local importer and began to offer it by the glass. Rivera, located in Andria in central Puglia, is a significant producer. That it took so long to source its wine for our list speaks to how this region's quality production has remained under the radar. But that is part of the excitement of discovery. Il Falcone is just one of the wines that has kept me tuned into what Puglia will do next.

Located across the Adriatic from Greece, Puglia is atypically flat compared to its neighbors, stretching in a narrow band from Italy's spur down the length of its heel. Throughout history Puglia has been an important point of entry for Mediterranean goods, including grapes from Greece. The region's long tradition of winemaking was given a boost when phylloxera devastated vineyard land in northern Italy and France in the nineteenth century. It was during this period that local producers began to regularly export grapes and bulk wine to other regions in Italy and abroad for blending, a trend that continues today.

Red grapes have always grown exceptionally well in the region. Puglia's *terra rossa* clay imparts a mineral richness to the vines, while limestone ensures good drainage. Warm weather allows the grapes to achieve a dark color once envied by northern producers, and sirocco winds keep vines free from mold, at times drying the grapes and concentrating their juices. These factors contribute to the region's bold red wines, which often carry notes of Bing cherries, black currant, and sagebrush. Of Puglia's main red grape varieties, Primitivo is the best known in the United States, largely due to research conducted by scientists at the University of California, Davis, who discovered that the grape is genetically identical to Zinfandel. In the American market, Puglia suddenly became thought of as a source for "Italian Zinfandel," and some producers even added the Zinfandel name to their labels in an effort to boost sales abroad. (In some cases, this is justified: the Accademia dei Racemi winery in Manduria, southwest of Brindisi, makes a Primitivo-Zinfandel blend, Primitivo di Manduria Zinfandel Sinfarosa, with Zinfandel grown from cuttings imported

from Paul Draper's iconic Ridge winery in California.) While Primitivo produces delightful, fruity table wines perfect for everyday consumption, it is only part of the story here.

Despite the region's robust output, making wine in Puglia is not without its challenges. The intense sun can scorch vines before the grapes have fully matured, and the heat makes it difficult to achieve the acidity level needed for quality white wine production. Today, some producers are experimenting with blending Chardonnay with local varieties Bombino Bianco and Verdeca, with encouraging results. Puglian *rosato* (rosé) offers another refreshing alternative to the region's ubiquitous reds. Rosa del Golfo makes one of Italy's best, a sparkling *rosato* made with Negroamaro.

The flat, windswept Salento peninsula has the highest concentration of DOCs in Puglia. The proximity of the peninsula's vineyards to the sea is said to advantageously season the *terra rossa* clay and limestone soil with salt. This is red wine country, and despite the host of different DOC names—the most famous of which is Salice Salentino—the wines have much in common, due to the relatively uniform climate across the peninsula. Negroamaro is the dominant grape, usually accented by Malvasia Nera or Primitivo.

At the Tormaresca estate in the upper Salento peninsula, the Tuscan house Antinori operates outside of DOC restrictions to produce its Masseria Maime bottling, a Salento IGT made from 100 percent Negroamaro. Rich and structured, the wine is one of my favorite expressions of Negroamaro. The vineyards on the estate jut up against the Adriatic Sea, and groves of tall, sturdy olive trees divide rows of Primitivo, Chardonnay, and Cabernet. Antinori originally invested in the property—and the Bocca di Lupo estate in the Castel del Monte DOC farther north—to create mass-market wines with international varietals for export. But after noticing the potential for fine red wines in both areas, the company shifted its focus toward building up the Tormaresca name for quality Puglian wine.

A growing number of producers have joined Antinori in investing in the Castel del Monte DOC. Located in central Puglia west of Bari, this DOC is the leading candidate to create Puglia's first great ageworthy red wine. Named for an octagonal castle built by Frederick II in the thirteenth century, Castel del Monte is hilly by Puglian standards, and the soil here is the same mineral-rich *terra rossa* clay and limestone composition found on the Salento peninsula. Nero di Troia is the main grape, with most of the wines in the zone containing small percentages of Aglianico and Montepulciano. In addition to Rivera's Il Falcone, the producer makes a top wine, Puer Apuliae, that is a benchmark in the region. The growing local interest in Nero di Troia has spurred producers such as Tenuta Cocevola to make a Castel del Monte wine exclusively with this grape.

Newcomers to areas other than Castel del Monte and the Salento peninsula also see Puglia's potential as a wine region. Outside of the nondescript northern city Foggia, Alberto Longo is revitalizing the once-fading DOC Cacc'e Mmitte di Lucera. A Puglian native, Alberto worked in northern Italy as a consultant before deciding to start a wine venture in a former granary close to home. His powerful Le Cruste, a full-bodied Nero di Troia–based wine with a violet scent and restrained blackberry and cherry notes, is another indication this grape is one to watch.

WHITE GRAPES: THE CLASSICS

BOMBINO BIANCO

One of the most widely planted white grapes in Puglia, this bright, fleshy variety is a workhorse cultivated for blending. Yet it can come into its own when thoughtfully combined with Trebbiano or Chardonnay, which balance out Bombino Bianco's greener notes, resulting in bright wines with grapefruit, lemon verbena, and honeydew melon characteristics. Some believe Bombino Bianco is the same grape as Trebbiano d'Abruzzo, the principle grape in Abruzzo's best white wine.

FOOD PAIRING: The weighty, round character and herbaceous edge of Bombino Bianco wines seem designed for a creamy plate of Burrata (a Puglian specialty) drizzled with extra virgin olive oil (page 92).

RECOMMENDED PRODUCERS: Rivera, Tenuta Coppadoro

MOSCATO BIANCO

One of the most popular strains of the Moscato family of grapes, sweetly aromatic Moscato Bianco (known locally as Moscato Reale) is used to make Moscato di Trani, one of Puglia's few dessert wines. It is a classic: golden, medium bodied, with a touch of acidity to balance the sweetness, and possessing a light fragrance of orange blossom on the nose. It is also one of the best values I have found in dessert wines. One of only a few producers of the wine,

family-run Villa Schinosa makes an ambrosial Moscato di Trani from grapes grown on their estate, just inland from the scenic, slightly weathered seaside city of Trani. Even though the Schinosa family practices labor-intensive methods to produce the wines, concentrating the Moscato flavor by drying the grapes on straw mats *appassimento* style, the wine is a bargain compared with similarly made dessert wines in northern Italy or France.

FOOD PAIRING: Perfect with creamy desserts or citrus, Moscato di Trani also pairs well with a plate of cookies (page 258).

RECOMMENDED PRODUCERS: Rivera, Torrevento, Villa Schinosa

WHITE GRAPES: A CLOSER LOOK

FRANCAVILLA

Compared to how long grapes such as Aglianico and Greco have been cultivated in southern Italy, Francavilla is a relative newcomer. It arrived in Puglia in the early twentieth century and was planted around the town of Martina Franca. Today it is primarily cultivated around Ostuni, a town in the northern Salento peninsula, where it is blended into a delicate, light white wine with notes of mango and guava that is best when consumed young. Some producers make single-variety wines from Francavilla in order to preserve part of Puglia's viticultural heritage, though it is going to take time before these wines are available in the United States.

VERDECA

One of the primary grapes in vermouth, green-tinged Verdeca is widely planted in Puglia, especially south of Bari, where it is blended into the Martina Franca and Locorotondo DOCs. But vermouth production has declined significantly in the last twenty years, making Verdeca's future tenuous. However, some Puglese winemakers see potential in the flinty, acidic grape, which complements the ripe roundness of locally grown Chardonnay.

FOOD PAIRING: The clean, straightforward flavors of Verdeca complement the refreshing raw zucchini salad with green olives and mint (page 101).

RECOMMENDED PRODUCERS: Cantina Due Palme, Rubino

RED GRAPES: THE CLASSICS

....

NEGROAMARO

For years I have told customers and staff that the grape Negroamaro translates in Italian to "black-bitter." The translation is commonly used, and I never questioned it. Francesco Domini, general manager of Tormaresca, set me straight when I visited the Masseria Maime estate, explaining that *amaro* comes from *maros*, the Greek word for "black." So this grape is really "black and black," referring to its nearly black skin and deep-purple flesh. Still, it makes perfect sense that the grape is often described as black and bitter, for the wines made from Negroamaro not only have a deep hue but also aggressive acidity and an earthy bitterness.

Negroamaro is the most widely planted grape in Puglia, and it is the principal grape in most of the DOCs on the Salento peninsula, including Alezio, Brindisi, Copertino, Leverano, and Salice Salentino. The best examples bring forth assertive notes of dried cherry with hints of star anise and clove. Valle dell'Asso's Piromafo, a Salento IGT wine, shows the elegant and aromatic side of the grape, while Conti Zecca's appropriately named Nero (which has some Cabernet blended in for structure) is deep purple and full bodied. Cantele's plush, aromatic Amativo falls somewhere in between, thanks to the generous proportion of Primitivo.

FOOD PAIRING: Orecchiette with rapini (page 158) is a classic Puglian dish, its bold chile, garlic, and bitter-green flavors typically accompanied by a rustic red wine such as a Salice Salentino. More refined renditions of the Negroamaro grape, such as the Conti Zecca's Nero, perform well alongside our Genova-style short ribs (page 194), with the richness of the sauce complementing the earthy, dark-berry character of the wines.

RECOMMENDED PRODUCERS: Agricole Vallone, Al Bano Carrisi, Cantele, Conti Zecca, Cosimo Taurino, Masseria Li Veli, Messapicus, Michele Calò & Figli, Rosa del Golfo, Tormaresca, Valle dell'Asso

NERO DI TROIA

This dark, thick-skinned grape, thought to have originated in Troy, is one of the most distinguished in Puglia, particularly when grown in the Castel del Monte DOC. While for centuries the grape was used to make a coarse peasant wine, the De Corato family, who owns the Rivera winery, believed in its potential and has built a compelling case with their Il Falcone and Puer Apuliae bottlings. A well-made Nero di Troia is supple and full, with a nose evocative of violets. Some producers, including Rivera, age the wines in oak barrels, while others such as Santa Lucia forgo oak in order to preserve the freshness of the palate. Taming the grape is not easy. Nero di Troia demands careful attention in the vineyards, or it can become unforgivably tannic. Yet these tannins, when handled properly, give the wines the structure needed to evolve over years in the cellar. Fortunately, newer high-density plantings of Nero di Troia vines are beginning to mature, giving winemakers higher-quality fruit and more reason to experiment with this variety.

FOOD PAIRING: Nero di Troia–based wines shine alongside ricotta gnocchi in cheese *brodo* with peas and meatballs (page 155). The ricotta gnocchi and rich *brodo* counter the tannins of the wines, while the peas complement their floral notes.

RECOMMENDED PRODUCERS: Alberto Longo, Rivera, Santa Lucia, Terre Federiciane, Torre Quarto, Torrevento

PRIMITIVO

When we first opened A16, we took great pride in selling bottles of Primitivo to guests who liked bold, jammy Zinfandels. Yet some diners were wary, having tried unbalanced renditions of this grape in the past. Fortunately, the quality of imported Primitivo wines has improved greatly as awareness of the variety (driven by the trendy Zin connection) has spurred quality-minded production among producers in Puglia. Cultivating the early-ripening Primitivo grape takes some care. It is prone to oxidation, uneven ripening, and an imbalance of high alcohol, low acidity, and soft tannins. But in the hands of the right winemakers, a Primitivo wine can be deliciously fruit-forward with notes of raspberry, well balanced, and a good value. When aged in small oak barrels, as is the practice at Accademia dei Racemi, the wine gains more structure and substance, helping it age gracefully for a few years. Antica Masseria del Sigillo's Terre del Guiscardo bottling (a blend of Primitivo, Cabernet, and Merlot) is surprisingly complex, with assertive red-fruit and spice notes. The local climate also influences the style of the wine. Primitivo grapes from the central DOC Gioia delle Colle benefit from a longer growing season, giving them time to build up acidity that adds balance to the finished wines.

FOOD PAIRING: A fruit-forward Puglian Primitivo wine, such as one from Antica Masseria del Sigillo, is a perfect match for hearty vegetable pastas such as penne tossed with eggplant, tomatoes, and olives (page 163).

RECOMMENDED PRODUCERS: Antica Masseria del Sigillo, Cantele, Cantine Coppi, Le Fabriche, Masseria Monaci, Mille Una, Rosa del Golfo, Tenuta Viglione, Tormaresca, Valle dell'Asso, Vetrere

RED GRAPES: A CLOSER LOOK

ALEATICO

This sugar-packed grape, which may be a mutation of Moscato Rosso, makes Puglia's most unique (and hardest to find) wine, the exceptionally sweet *liquoroso* Aleatico di Puglia. For a rare wine, it has an extensive DOC, incorporating all of Puglia into its boundaries. However, the best Aleatico di Puglia is produced around Salice Salentino and Gioia del Colle. This is grappa meets a spicy flourless chocolate cake: initially dry from the alcohol, yet becoming dense and chewy with a long, sweet finish.

RECOMMENDED PRODUCERS: Al Bano Carrisi, Duranti

MALVASIA NERA

This sweet grape was once considered one of Puglia's most important varieties. Malvasia Nera has retained a significant amount of vineyard territory and is grown in most southern Puglian DOCs. Yet it has been relegated to a blending grape in the wines of the Salentino peninsula, providing a delicate, perfumed counterpoint to earthy, tannic Negroamaro. While quite rare, dry 100 percent Malvasia Nera wines have a juicy, fresh taste with rose-petal aromatics. My nostalgic side would love to see Malvasia Nera make a comeback as a single-variety wine, but it is too soon to tell whether the grape will attract the attention needed to spur production.

SUSSUMANIELLO

Known both as "little gypsy," for the belief it came from the Near East, and "little donkey," because donkeys were used to transport the grapes through the countryside, this intense grape has formidable acidity and is mostly used for blending. Yet with the heightened interest in Puglia's indigenous grapes, some producers are trying their hand at single-variety bottlings of Sussumaniello. Accademia dei Racemi is at the forefront of the Sussumaniello experiments, and their Torre Guaceto Sum is a young, fresh Vino da Tavola that is immediately enjoyable. Such a wine reminds me of the Piedmont grape Barbera; if we can call Aglianico from Taurasi the Barolo of the South, can't we have a Barbera of the South too? With minimal tannins and a lovely punch of juiciness, Sussumaniello-based wines refresh the palate with hints of raspberry.

RECOMMENDED PRODUCERS: Accademia dei Racemi, Rubino, Torre Guaceto

BASILICATA SS658

The last decade has been a boon for winemakers in Basilicata. The region has garnered international praise for its intriguing Aglianico del Vulture DOC, and it was awarded a second DOC, the Terra dell'Alta Val d'Agri, in 2003. Such acknowledgment represents significant progress for a region once better known for Italian author and activist Carlo Levi's 1945 novel *Christ Stopped at Eboli*, a tale portraying the destitution of Basilicata's population. The book brought to light the "problem of the south"—the region's notorious poverty—and shocked many in northern Italy. Much has changed in Basilicata since Levi wrote his account, and fortunately for its residents and visitors, there is a sense of newfound excitement and discovery afoot. Still, the region has managed to stay off the regular tourist route.

Basilicata is a sparsely populated, cool, mountainous region known for chile-spiked vegetable dishes and the deep red-green, hot Senise pepper, which enjoys DOP (Denomination of Protected Origin) status. While the region has experienced extensive deforestation, it has retained pockets of wooded beauty around Mount Vulture, a dormant volcano north of Potenza. To the east, the drama of the sand-hued caves in Matera—I Sassi di Matera, literally "the stones of Matera"—also draws visitors (including film crews, who often use the location for movies set in biblical times). Formed out of tufa soil, the prehistoric caves had been inhabited for centuries until the 1950s, when the government moved the local population into modern homes. The caves, once a symbol of the south's problems, are now enjoying distinction as a UNESCO World Heritage site.

The Aglianico del Vulture DOC produces one of Italy's most memorable wines. The volcanic soil of Mount Vulture imbues the local Aglianico grapes with a wild, intriguing character that shows through in the distinctive wines of the area. Yet the DOC territory is large, and variations in soil composition can result in wines of inconsistent quality, from the deep, complex wines for which the region is known to lighter, thinner styles. For this reason, not everyone in Basilicata has welcomed its recent acclaim. While talk circulates of a DOCG designation in the near future, the change is on hold until new boundaries are drawn that restrict the size of the growing area, ensuring more consistent quality in Vulture wines.

I was first made aware of this concern while dining at Il Cantinone, a great *enoteca* in Barile owned by sommelier Vito Giuseppe D'Angelo. Joining me were some of Basilicata's best producers, including Sergio and Vito Paternoster; Salvatore Fucci and his daughter Elena; and restaurateur and hotelier Rino Botte, who started the Macarico label in conjunction with Vito Paternoster. When I congratulated the group on the growing recognition for Aglianico del Vulture, they began to discuss their frustration with the loose boundaries set for the zone. Vines for true Aglianico del Vulture, they asserted, need to grow in the volcanic soil along the sides of the Vulture. These producers take their soil seriously: Paternoster's central vineyard, Rotondo, and the Fuccis' vineyard, Titolo, are named after the Vulture lava flows on which they rest. Yet the DOC boundaries stretch well beyond the limits of the volcanic soil, creeping into Basilicata's clay soil, which yields less concentrated grapes. Many at the table feared that inferior winemakers would dilute the area's reputation for quality that they had worked so long to build.

For all of the controversy, I am hopeful that the historic names of the area will only benefit from the recognition Vulture is receiving. Anselmo Paternoster, one of the original wine pioneers in Basilicata, settled in the town of Barile in 1925 and began crafting fine wines out of the local Aglianico crop growing in the volcanic soil around Mount Vulture. Today, Anselmo's grandsons—Vito Paternoster, who manages the estate, and his brothers, Sergio and Anselmo, both trained enologists—continue to build on the tradition their grandfather started. The family still uses their original facility but has also constructed a modern rammed-earth cellar in the center of its prized Rotondo vineyard. The building's low, sloping roof echoes the silhouette of Mount Vulture's foothills, elegantly complementing the landscape that surrounds the winery.

Paternoster makes two distinctively different Aglianico del Vulture wines. The first, Don Anselmo, named after the winery's founder, is made according to a traditional method using large chestnut casks. The wine rests in cask for eighteen months before being transferred to smaller oak barrels for an additional year of aging. It is then bottled and aged for another year before it is released. The combination of acidic, tannic Aglianico fruit and prolonged aging in wood results in a wine with the structure to last for several decades. While tightly wound and tannic on release, Don Anselmo comes into its own after a decade, its tannins resolving into an elegant, earthy wine with notes of baking spices. Paternoster's second Aglianico,

Cellar door in Barile, Basilicata

Rotondo, is a modern interpretation that is made to be enjoyed at a younger age. It is aged in small oak barrels for fourteen months, and the result is a bigger, richer wine with distinctive notes of black cherry. Both wines are excellent, and together they exemplify how different stylistic approaches to the same grape can yield two very different but equally compelling expressions of it.

In addition to making their own wines, the Paternoster family shares advice with other Aglianico del Vulture producers, particularly in the small town of Barile. Sergio Paternoster has provided guidance and technical analysis to nearby producer Elena Fucci, a true boutique winery whose single vineyard, Titolo, lies close to Paternoster's Rotondo. Salvatore and Carmela Fucci, both teachers, make wines with their daughter Elena (the winery's namesake), who has a degree in enology. The Fuccis produce only one wine, the noble, concentrated Titolo, with dark fruits balanced by hints of spice and oak. In 2002, when Elena was twenty-two and studying at the University of Pisa, Titolo received the prestigious Tre Bicchieri award from *Gambero Rosso*.

Spurred by the successes in the Vulture zone, new vineyards are springing up throughout Basilicata. The Terra dell'Alta Val d'Agri DOC has seen growth with international varieties such as Cabernet Sauvignon and Merlot, some of which are being blended with Aglianico. There are also a few new noteworthy developments with the red

Vito Paternoster

grape Tamurro Nero. The variety was near extinction when producer Tenuta Le Querce started cultivating it, making a concentrated wine with tannins more gripping than Aglianico. White wines are also produced here, including Fiano, Malvasia, and Moscato, but most of Basilicata's best wines, and the ones you are most likely to find imported, are from Aglianico del Vulture.

In addition to Paternoster and Elena Fucci, look for Vito Paternoster's joint venture with Rino Botte, Macarico, which produces a pair of elegant, juicy Aglianico del Vultures. Another reliable source, Cantine del Notaio, barrel ages its aromatic Aglianico in ancient caves dug out of the tufa soil. Outside recognition of the region is also evident in the interest taken by Gruppo Italiano Vini. Its Terre degli Svevi label produces a modern, refined Aglianico. Other producers to try include Basilium, which makes light-bodied Aglianico, and Basilisco, a boutique winery specializing in concentrated renditions of the grape. Some producers of Aglianico del Vulture are also trying their hand with the international varieties Syrah and Chardonnay.

While Aglianico del Vulture is interchangeable with Taurasi for wine and food pairings, I am partial to pairing it with braised goat (page 189). The compelling spice and herb flavors in the wine bring out the rosemary and cinnamon that perfume the braise. Or, honor a classic pairing in Basilicata by serving Aglianico del Vulture with roasted sausages (page 211) and *peperonata* (page 77).

TAURASI AND AGLIANICO DEL VULTURE: BAROLOS OF THE SOUTH

The great heights that Aglianico reaches in Taurasi and Vulture have brought both areas into the international wine spotlight, intensifying the long-running debate as to whether the grape's first home in Italy was Campania or Basilicata. I have heard both sides, and each sounds plausible. It is generally accepted that the grape came from Greece, but it is less certain whether it arrived in Campania first via Naples's busy port or landed in Puglia, where the grapes traveled over the mountains to Basilicata before reaching Campania. Over time, the grapes have evolved to suit their surroundings, and some winemakers say the differences are visible, insisting the grapes from Vulture grow in pointier, longer clusters than the grapes in Taurasi. But I am less concerned with the origin and evolution of the Aglianico grape than I am with the varied styles of wine it inspires.

The cool climate and loose, volcanic soil of both the Aglianico del Vulture and Taurasi zones allow the Aglianico vines to enjoy the extremely long growing seasons, which concentrate the flavor of the grapes. As of this writing, the wines of Taurasi are more consistent in quality than those of Vulture, mainly because of the more uniform growing conditions in Taurasi. The wines from both areas are best when aged at least a few years in the bottle, but the requirements differ. Taurasi must age for three years before it is released on the market, while Aglianico del Vulture can be released after one year (though many producers hold back their inventory voluntarily for three years).

Young Vulture Aglianico expresses spices such as clove, star anise, cardamom, and juniper berry complemented by dusty undertones, whereas young Taurasi tends to have hints of mint, black pepper, and baking spices, with background notes of gravel. As both wines mature, the spice, tannins, and fruit in each meld into a complex aroma and suave texture. The propensity for aging that Taurasi and Aglianico del Vulture share, and the alluring qualities of the best examples, justify the title Barolo of the South often given to both wines.

CALABRIA A3

The dark corner of the duomo in Strongoli, in eastern Calabria, might seem to hold little interest for someone studying the region's viticultural history. Looking as if it were carved out of the steep hillside, Strongoli is a compact town, with narrow streets that snake around ashen buildings. Nearly every vantage point has expansive views of rolling hills, vineyards, and the Ionian Sea, yet the town itself feels weary and impenetrable, a legacy of the hard times that have led to a steady population decline over the years. But within its cavernous duomo stand two ancient Greek stone tablets praising the region's wines, a testament to a noble viticultural tradition that a new generation of producers is committed to restoring.

Winemaker Roberto Ceraudo, who took me to see the tablets, embodies the revivalist spirit at work in the region's vineyards. Roberto's *agriturismo*, Dattilo, just down the road from Strongoli, is a pastoral oasis, where mature grapevines grow among olive and fruit trees almost as if they were pulled from central casting. Their charm matches that of Roberto, whose tweed blazer and distinguished graying hair give him the look of a country gentleman. He divides his time between making wine, pressing olives for oil, and running a fine-dining restaurant, yet of all his duties, winemaking is his passion. To Roberto, the key to Calabrian wines gaining recognition in the international market is preserving their sense of place while exploring the possibilities with international varieties. His offerings, including the Val di Neto IGTs Dattilo and Imyr (made from 100 percent Gaglioppo and Chardonnay, respectively), reflect this balanced, open-minded approach.

Calabria is a picturesque peninsula, with the rugged, snow-capped Apennines running down its center and 460 miles of coastline flanking its borders. Citrus varieties flourish in the warm coastal area, and the region is prized for bergamot, the orange used in Earl Grey tea and pricey perfumes. Meanwhile, in the thick inland forests of Pollino National Park, porcini thrive. Calabria is also one of the oldest wine regions in Italy, with vines already rooted in the soil when the Greeks arrived to colonize the area. It was the Greeks who first introduced serious vine cultivation and winemaking techniques, and today, the Greek *albarello* trellising method, in which vines are trained up posts, is still common.

Despite the region's natural resources—or perhaps, to some extent, because of them—self-sufficient Calabria remains an enigma not only to foreigners but also to many Italians. And many of those who have passed through have done so at a brisk pace, traveling on the A3 *autostrada* en route to Reggio di Calabria to catch the ferry to Sicily. The region retains its rough character, the legacy of wars, earthquakes, and poverty. Coastal highways are lined with unfinished construction, from modest two-story skeletons in the newer cities that spill out along the low-lying Ionian coast, to new hillside castles that were clearly started with enthusiasm until ambition, money, or both ran out. As many locals acknowledge, Calabria has not enjoyed the most secure governmental infrastructure, which has contributed to it lagging behind its neighbors in the southern Italian wine renaissance.

The region's leading DOC is Cirò, located along the eastern coastline where the Gulf of Taranto meets the Ionian Sea. Composed primarily of Gaglioppo, Calabria's most important indigenous variety, Cirò Rosso is a light- to medium-bodied red that is aromatic, spicy, and immediately enjoyable, with a rustic edge suggestive of the region's surroundings. The nearby coastal DOCs of Melissa and Sant'Anna di Isola Capo Rizzuto make similarly styled, albeit lesser-known, red wines with Gaglioppo. On the western side of the peninsula, the Lamezia and Savuto DOCs combine Gaglioppo with Greco Nero, Nerello Cappuccio, Magliocco, and Nerello Mascalese. Here the cooler climate gives the grapes more acidity and concentration. Longtime producer Odoardi's supple Scavigna Vigna Garrone, a red wine made primarily of Gaglioppo with Cabernet Sauvignon, Cabernet Franc, Nerello Cappuccio, and Merlot, is showing the potential of the cool Savuto area for serious red wine production, and other producers, such as Statti, are building on Odoardi's success. Only a fraction of the wine produced in Calabria is white, but some of the region's reliable names offer zesty examples made from the predominant white grape, Greco Bianco, and the up-and-coming variety Mantonico. Other native varieties, such as white grapes Guardavalle and Pecorello and red grapes Marcigliana and Prunesta, are just beginning to show potential for making notable wines.

Located immediately off the highway in Cirò Marina, the family-owned Librandi estate has been a bastion of quality in the area for decades. Tall and indefatigable, with a thick crop of white hair, Nicodemo Librandi has blue eyes that brighten when talk turns to Calabria's potential. Librandi, which produces two million bottles of wine annually, is an anomaly in a region known for small, local production. The winery gleams, its towering, temperature-controlled stainless-steel tanks evidence that the family has embraced modern enology. The technological advances introduced to the winery in the 1970s allowed it to improve quality quickly and expand rapidly. Twenty years ago, Nicodemo and his brother, Antonio, believed that in order to sell wine abroad, they needed to make wines with international varieties such as Chardonnay and Cabernet Sauvignon. Today, although the winery still uses some international grapes for blending, the brothers have changed their focus to indigenous vines, which they believe will distinguish Calabria in the global marketplace.

As Nicodemo gave us a tour of his expansive Val di Neto vineyards, south of Cirò Marina, where Gaglioppo and Cabernet Sauvignon grapes are grown for the winery's lauded Gravello wine, he explained the importance of rejuvenating indigenous grape species. Wild-looking vines of Gaglioppo, Magliocco, and Arvino grapes curl around posts in one of Librandi's *campo sperimentale* (experimental fields), where he studies different strains of local varieties. Indeed, Nicodemo seems to be enthusiastic about biodiversity, not just in grapes but also in any edible plant. One of his orchards, where we stopped to pick up fragrant clementines for the road, had sixty different varieties of citrus flourishing in the late-January sun.

Southwest of Cirò, perched on a sunny hillside of Italy's narrowest stretch of land, Cantine Lento presents another face of new Calabria. The winery is in transition from its old compound in the middle of the bustling city Lamezia Terme, where the Lento family has lived and made wine since the nineteenth century, and Amato, its new, grand 173-acre estate. During one of my visits to the area, the cheerful, elegant Danila Lento (daughter of Salvatore and Giovanna Lento) explained the family's plans for Amato and for the *agriturismo* they plan to install in a newly restored nineteenth-century villa. On a clear day, of which there are many in Calabria, you can see both the Tyrrhenian and Ionian seas from the site. At the winery, modern and traditional viticulture meld. Extensive soil sampling lead the family to cultivate the international varieties Cabernet Sauvignon, Merlot, and Chardonnay, which proved well suited to Amato's gravelly soil. At the same time, they continue to plant local varieties Greco, Magliocco, and Gaglioppo, trellising some vines in the traditional *albarello* method.

For all the energy being poured into Calabrian wines, the region's future remains uncertain. "In Calabria, we're not as focused on producing wine," reflects Danila. "Calabria needs to communicate to show what the wines can be and what the wines can do. We are very far away from the market. A lot of people still don't know where Calabria is." But from my experiences with the people, places, and wines of the area, Calabria is busy shaking off its welcome mat, ready to invite the world in.

WHITE GRAPES: THE CLASSICS

GRECO BIANCO

While Campania's Greco di Tufo and Calabria's Greco Bianco grapes share a Greek heritage, Bianco-based wines have tropical aromas of passion fruit, guava, and pineapple that set them apart from their mineral-driven Campanian counterparts. Cirò Bianco, from the most prominent DOC in Calabria for whites, is made with at least 90 percent Greco. Librandi makes a crisp, steel-fermented Cirò Bianco entirely from Greco. Meanwhile, Cantine Lento produces a Greco wine redolent with tropical fruits while maintaining a racy edge of acidity.

Near the southeastern tip of Calabria, Greco Bianco is made into one of Italy's rarest dessert wines in the Greco di Bianco DOC. Or at least I am told it is; I have yet to try it, as bottles of this fabled wine are scarce, even in Italy.

FOOD PAIRINGS: A glass of Cirò Bianco is the perfect *aperitivo* to complement marinated olives (page 91) or a handful of toasted almonds. And like Campania's Greco di Tufo, it also works well with seafood dishes such as *acqua pazza* (page 172).

RECOMMENDED PRODUCERS: Cantine Lento, Ceraudo, Librandi, Statti

MANTONICO

Indigenous to Calabria, Mantonico is quickly gaining recognition for its potential to make a range of stylish wines. Depending on the producer, Mantonico can yield a lean wine with fresh aromatics of jasmine, Key lime, honeysuckle, and mandarin, or a rounder, richer wine akin to Chardonnay. Both Statti and Librandi barrel age their 100-percent Mantonico wines, and both also make a *passito* with the grape.

FOOD PAIRINGS: A fuller, dry Mantonico-based wine pairs well with our bruschette, from Dungeness crab with rapini and anchovy (page 94) to ricotta and *peperonata* (page 97). The roundness of the wine complements the richness of the crab and ricotta, while its bright fruit accents the rapini and *peperonata*.

RECOMMENDED PRODUCERS: Librandi, Odoardi, Statti

RED GRAPES: THE CLASSICS

GAGLIOPPO

The first time I tasted Fattoria San Francesco's Quattroventi, from the Cirò DOC, I was hooked. It had an aromatic nose of ripe tomato, cranberry, oregano, and tart red cherry—a wine at once refined, elegant, and gripping. Cirò, made almost exclusively with Gaglioppo, has become a favorite at A16, and our servers often recommend it to diners who like Pinot Noir.

Gaglioppo is the noblest grape of Calabria, cultivated in the region for more than four thousand years. It is also the most planted variety. Yet only in recent years, with the help of modern practices, have we started to see its charming side. The light- to medium-bodied wines made from Gaglioppo exhibit fresher fruit than they have in the past, while still retaining their characteristic earthy undertones. Because the grape has such low tannins, it benefits from being blended with Cabernet Sauvignon for structure, as Librandi does for its Gravello bottling. Gaglioppo also produces lovely *rosato* wines.

FOOD PAIRINGS: Gaglioppo-based wines are versatile at the table, complementing both fish and lamb. Unusual for red wines, they pair well with chiles because their mild tannins don't exasperate the palate. I frequently suggest a Cirò Rosso with the octopus *zuppa* (page 135) and the squid ink *tonnarelli* with calamari (page 152). If the *tonnarelli* did not have squid ink, a white wine would be my first choice, but the squid ink gives the dish a weightier presence that works well with Gaglioppo. And for people who like the Pinot Noir–salmon pairing, I will pour a glass of Gaglioppo beside our braised salmon with basil and almonds (page 177).

RECOMMENDED PRODUCERS: Ceraudo, Fattoria San Francesco, Ippolito 1845, Librandi, Luigi Vivacqua, Malena, Odoardi, Statti, Terre di Balbia, Vinicola Zito

MAGLIOCCO

Thick skinned and muscular, Magliocco is one of Calabria's most promising indigenous varieties. Wines made from it show characteristics of dark plum and blackberry, with notes of clove, juniper berry, and white pepper. With their deep color and dark-berry depths, the wines are reminiscent of Nero d'Avola from Sicily. Magliocco is most commonly used as a blending grape in the Lamezia and Savuto DOCs, but some of Calabria's best new wines are Magliocco based. Odoardi and Cantine Lento blend Magliocco with Gaglioppo, and Librandi makes a 100-percent Magliocco wine, Magno Megonio, that is barrel aged and best consumed after five years. Some say this red grape will be the star of Calabria. Based on the incredible quality of the Magliocco wines I have tasted, I am excited to watch how the grape evolves in the hands of capable vintners.

FOOD PAIRINGS: The dark fruits and earthy tannins of Magliocco-based wines make them an admirable match for our roasted pork loin and its sweetly pungent pine nut, currant, and garlic *soffritto* (page 216).

RECOMMENDED PRODUCERS: Cantine Lento, Librandi, Odoardi, Statti, Terre di Balbia

RED GRAPES: A CLOSER LOOK

ARVINO

Often described as having a mineral, smoky quality, wines made with the Arvino grape are medium bodied with a deep ruby color and strong aromatics of licorice, prune, and boysenberry. They typically have a higher concentration of tannins and alcohol than most of the medium-bodied reds found in Calabria. Arvino is grown in small amounts and is not a required grape for any DOC, though Librandi is cultivating it in their experimental field.

GRECO NERO

As its name implies, this variety is another import from Greece. It is most commonly cultivated in the provinces of Catanzaro and Crotone, but it is planted all over Calabria and used primarily as a blending grape in DOCs such as Bivongi, Lamezia, and Melissa.

RECOMMENDED PRODUCERS: Cantine Lento, Odoardi

SICILY A20

The trip from Reggio di Calabria on Italy's mainland to the Sicilian city of Messina isn't very long, about forty minutes by ferry, but the contrast between the two regions' wine industries is profound. While the southern Italian wine boom got off to a slow beginning in Calabria, it may well have started in Sicily, where the winemakers are some of the most forward looking in all of Italy.

An imposing island—the largest in the Mediterranean Sea—Sicily has plenty to offer the casual visitor, from atmospheric coastal cities such as the ancient port of Cefalù to majestic Mount Etna. It is also a promising land for wine producers, with its dry, predictable climate and more acres dedicated to vine cultivation than any other region in Italy. Quantity has not meant quality, however. Of the more than 180 million gallons of wine produced in 2006 (second only to Puglia, according to statistics from the Associazione Enologi Enotecnici Italiani), only about 3 percent was classified higher than table wine. But in the past decade, adventurous winemakers have worked to turn the island into a significant source of compelling wines.

One of the pioneers of modern Sicilian wine came from within the co-op system. In the early 1980s, Diego Planeta, the president of Sicily's largest co-op, Cantine Settesoli, began to see the potential of the rocky Sicilian soil and warm, dry climate to produce wines of character. But he knew that changing the minds of the more than two thousand co-op associates would be a difficult task. Instead, he remained Settesoli's president while starting a side project with his family. In 1985, the family began cultivating international grapes such as Chardonnay and aging the wine in oak, which was then a rarity. Planeta's attention to detail set his new-style wines apart, and the acclaim they received encouraged other winemakers to follow suit. In the 1990s, the family began experimenting with indigenous grape varieties, building two wineries on the western side of the island near Menfi and two others on the southeastern side near Ragusa, all making wine under the Planeta umbrella. Today Planeta cultivates vines on 865 acres and produces more than two million bottles a year. Across the zones, Diego's nephew, winemaker Alessio Planeta, makes balanced, sophisticated wines with both international and indigenous grape varieties. Recently, the family's hunt for the next breakthrough growing area in Sicily led them to the island's literal hotspot: Mount Etna.

At 11,056 feet, Mount Etna is the largest volcano in Europe, and it remains quite active. As recently as ten years ago, the Etna region looked as if it would never recover from the phylloxera blight that hit Sicily hard a century earlier. But today, grapes thrive in the volcanic soil of the mountain's cool slopes (oblivious to what might be a tenuous existence), producing some of Sicily's most praiseworthy red and white wines. One producer, Giuseppe Benanti, makes both a triumphant Etna Bianco with the white Carricante grape, and an Etna Rosso with Nerello Mascalese and Nerello Cappuccio, earning Benanti the Winery of the Year award from *Gambero Rosso* in 2007.

The cool climate of Etna is a stark contrast to the hot coastal vineyards where most of Sicily's grapes are still grown. The western province of Trapani alone grows more than half of the island's wine grapes, particularly Catarratto Bianco, some of which is used in Marsala production. Yet like Planeta, many western Sicilian producers have shifted their focus to quality production. One such producer, the Di Giovanna family, has grown grapes outside of Sambuca di Sicilia, in Agrigento province, for five generations. In 1985, they began studying their land composition and determined that a mix of native and international grapes was well suited to the gravely soil, dry climate, and high altitude, where temperatures can reach 90°F during the day and drop to 30°F at night. Today, Di Giovanna, which produces more than 200,000 bottles annually, is an exemplary modern Sicilian winery, dedicated to both indigenous and international grapes vinified in a fresh, modern style. The estate is now run by Gunther and Klaus, sons of Aurelio and Barbara di Giovanna, and the family continues to refine their product, including making the switch to organic farming. A visitor who has heard the fun-loving brothers sing Frank Sinatra songs at the top of their lungs, as I have, might question their seriousness of purpose. But their work ethic, passion, and focus are evident in their remarkable range of wines, including bold, single-variety Nerello Mascalese, Nero d'Avola, Grillo, and Grecanico.

Interest in quality wines also continues to grow in other parts of the island. In 2005, Cerasuolo di Vittoria became Sicily's first zone to attain DOCG status. Tucked in the island's southeast corner, Cerasuolo (which means "cherry red") wines are made with Frappato and Nero d'Avola grapes. Delicate, with a vibrant garnet color and a pronounced nose of strawberry, cranberry, and juniper, these wines are food friendly. Other zones are quietly rising into prominence. Just outside of Messina, the small Faro DOC includes only a handful of wineries, but one of them produces a sophisticated red wine worth seeking out. Salvatore Geraci's Palari Faro, made primarily with Nerello Mascalese, is the kind of wonderfully aromatic, earthy wine I pour when trying to impress French wine aficionados. Markedly different from the jammy reds typically associated with southern Italy, it is another example of the breadth of styles the island is capable of producing. Meanwhile, Sicily remains a prominent producer of heady dessert wines. My favorite, from the southern island of Pantelleria, is a natural *passito* made with Zibibbo, a local name for the Moscato di Alessandria grape. These grapes take their time drying on the vines, completely in sync with the relaxed pace of the island, where citrus flourishes and the food is filled with locally harvested capers and sardines.

WHITE GRAPES: THE CLASSICS

CARRICANTE

Even though there is more white wine produced in Sicily than red, it can be a challenge to make a balanced, nuanced white in such a warm climate. So I get excited when I come across a well-made white with firm acidity and an understated elegance—a profile that the Carricante grape often delivers. When grown in the volcanic soil around Mount Etna, where it is the main grape in Etna Bianco wines, Carricante yields wines that are crisp on the palate with a quenching minerality. These qualities are evident in Benanti's 100-percent Carricante wine Etna Bianco Superiore Pietramarina. Barone di Villagrande's Fiore, also a single-variety Carricante from Etna, has a honey and almond character, with slate overtones and a structure that can hold up to ten years in a good vintage.

FOOD PAIRING: When I see pistachios, I think of the meaty, sweet variety for which Sicily is famous. The subtle nutty nose of a Carricante-based wine complements the pistachio, lemon, and caper paste that tops our braised halibut (page 175).

RECOMMENDED PRODUCERS: Ajello, Barone di Villagrande, Benanti

MARSALA

The town of Marsala on the west coast of Sicily has been famous for wine since the sixth century BC, when the Greeks used the port as a trading center. The fortified wines made here became popular in eighteenth-century England, thanks to English importer John Woodhouse. To satisfy the demands of the new market, industrial-scale viticulture took hold in surrounding Trapani province, supplying Marsala producers with grapes. After more than a century of popularity, Marsala began a long decline in quality, during which it became better known as a cooking wine. New laws were enacted in 1984 to improve production standards, but high-quality Marsala remains the exception.

Marsalas are made in a myriad of styles. They can be slightly off-dry, semisweet, or very sweet, and vary in color from golden (*oro*) to amber (*ambra*) to red (*rubino*). Like sherry, Marsala is made using the *solera* method (in which a wine is transferred though a progression of barrels as it ages), and much of its character comes from oxidation. This method also adds to its complexity and price, depending on how long it is aged. The least-expensive Marsala, known as *fine*, is aged one year; this is the type to reach for when you are cooking. *Superiore riserva* is aged for four years, *vergine* for five years, and the oldest and most valuable, *vergine stravecchio*, for ten years. The best *oro* and *ambra* Marsalas tend to be made with predominantly Grillo grapes, though many producers blend Grillo with Catarratto Bianco and Inzolia or Damaschino, with varied levels of success. Rare *rubino* is made with Perricone and Nerello Mascalese or Nero d'Avola. In the hands of top producers such as Marco De Bartoli and Carlo Pellegrino, Marsala is a sophisticated drink, sipped as an *aperitivo* or paired with dessert to prolong a relaxed dinner.

CATARRATTO

Grown intensively in Trapani province, Catarratto is the most planted grape in Sicily. In fact, it does so well in the hot, dry climate of western Sicily that *catarratto* is a local term for "abundance." Catarratto is often used for blending in bulk wine and Marsala, and it is the main grape in the Alcamo DOC west of Palermo. There are two varieties of the grape, Catarratto Bianco Comune and Catarratto Bianco Lucido, but it is rare to see a distinction made between them. It is also rare to see a 100-percent Catarratto bottling, beyond a locally consumed table wine. But the producer Donnafugata fashions pleasing wines by using a significant proportion of Catarratto in blends with Inzolia, Viognier, and Zibibbo.

FOOD PAIRING: A glass of round, simple Catarratto-based wine complements Sicily's myriad seafood preparations. I like it with our grilled shrimp topped with pickled pepper sauce and toasted almonds (page 168).

RECOMMENDED PRODUCER: Donnafugata

GRILLO

This hearty white grape with an odd name (it means "cricket" in the local dialect) was brought to Sicily from Puglia. During the phylloxera epidemic, it proved to be one of the most resistant vines, which encouraged over-planting, particularly in Trapani province. The grape is used in Marsala, and excellent Marsala producers, such as Marco De Bartoli, prefer to make their wines with 100 percent Grillo for a richer flavor profile. When left untended in the vineyard, Grillo can produce wines that range from flabby to astringent; the better examples are round and mild. Di Giovanna is starting to tease out the grape's potential in its single-variety Grillo, which shows floral and citrus notes. Meanwhile, Marco De Bartoli's steel-fermented Grappoli del Grillo is mineral rich and lean.

FOOD PAIRING: Swordfish is eaten often in Sicily, and its rich meat, complemented by a savory tomato-fennel *agrodolce* (page 173), matches well with the bright, rich characteristics of a Grillo wine.

RECOMMENDED PRODUCERS: Ajello, Di Giovanna, Marco De Bartoli

WHITE GRAPES: A CLOSER LOOK

DAMASCHINO

Legend has it that Arabs brought this grape from Damascus, though recent history has relegated it to the status of anonymous grape grown in Trapani province and used in Marsala production. Many have dismissed its potential for making single-variety wines of character, but in a step toward its rediscovery, Donnafugata has started making a pleasant, light white table wine that blends Damaschino with Catarratto.

RECOMMENDED PRODUCER: Donnafugata

GRECANICO

Di Giovanna's racy Grecanico was one of the first wines that tipped me off to the potential of Sicily's whites. With their effusive mineral and citrus character (not unlike Sauvignon Blanc), Grecanico-based wines are enjoying more recognition among quality producers. Like many of the white grapes in southern Italy, Grecanico is a relative of Greco, and it has also been linked to Garganega, the main grape in the Soave wines of the Veneto. While used in western DOCs Delia Nivolelli and Menfi, Grecanico achieves greater depth of flavor when grown in the hills around Sambuca di Sicilia.

FOOD PAIRING: Artichokes are a notorious hard-to-pair food, but when they are served with chicken livers, as Nate does for one of our bruschette (page 96), the lean, precise nature of a Grecanico wine balances with the richness of the liver and mellows the metallic edge of the artichokes.

RECOMMENDED PRODUCER: Di Giovanna

INZOLIA

Often blended with Catarratto, Inzolia is planted throughout Sicily, especially in Trapani province and in the Contessa Entellina DOC, where it is the principle white grape. Sometimes called Ansonica, it ripens early and can verge on being too lean, but at its best, it produces a fresh-tasting wine that should be consumed young. It is also commonly blended in Marsala, along with Grillo and Catarratto.

RECOMMENDED PRODUCERS: Ajello, Cusumano, Donnafugata, G. Milazzo, La Parrina

MALVASIA

Grown in Sicily for more than three millennia, Malvasia comes into its own on the northeast island of Lipari when harvested late and made into Malvasia delle Lipari Passito, a highly aromatic dessert wine that evokes scents of almonds, walnut skins, orange marmalade, and jasmine.

FOOD PAIRING: Malvasia della Lipari Passito is highly versatile, making it my go-to wine when a questionable pairing comes up for dessert. It complements a simple slice of pecorino and a decadent chocolate *budino* tart (page 249) equally well.

RECOMMENDED PRODUCERS: Barone di Villagrande, Cantine Colosi, Hauner

ZIBIBBO/MOSCATO

While Moscato is widely planted throughout Italy, the particular Moscato di Alessandria strain cultivated on the southern Sicilian island of Pantelleria is known as Zibibbo. Here, thick-skinned clusters of Zibibbo dry on the vine for *passito* production, yielding an exotic dessert wine with a sweet tang of apricot that captivates the senses and soothes the soul.

The Moscato di Noto DOC, on the southeastern tip of Sicily, offers another distinctive expression of the Moscato grape. Planeta's offering brings a new elegance (and availability) to Moscato di Noto Passito, with notes of petrol, candied orange peel, and lemon curd.

FOOD PAIRING: Sicilian Moscato wines—particularly those from Pantelleria, with their stone-fruit essences—are elegant complements to roasted peaches and amaretti (page 254).

RECOMMENDED PRODUCERS: Abraxas, Donnafugata, Marco De Bartoli, Planeta, Salvatore Murana

RED GRAPES: THE CLASSICS

FRAPPATO

Thought to be a relative of Calabria's Gaglioppo grape, Frappato yields wines that are light to medium bodied, with lively aromatics of cranberry, rose petals, and oregano. While Frappato is grown throughout Sicily, its most significant role is in the island's only DOCG, Cerasuolo di Vittoria, where it is blended with Nero d'Avola.

FOOD PAIRING: Cerasuolo di Vittoria wines are delightful with vegetable *cianfotta* (page 130). Their characteristic bright fruit lifts out the flavor of the stewed vegetables with a lively acidic touch.

RECOMMENDED PRODUCERS: COS, Gulfi, Planeta, Valle dell'Acate

NERELLO MASCALESE

In a matter of a few years, Nerello Mascalese has become one of the most prized grapes of Sicily. The volcanic soil of Mount Etna is particularly suited to the grape, giving it admirable structure lifted by an aromatic bouquet. The grape is also the main variety in the small Faro DOC, home to one of my favorite Sicilian reds, Salvatore Geraci's Faro Palari. Nerello Mascalese–based wines, which are often blended with Nerello Cappuccio or Nero d'Avola, have a richness grounded in the earth that reminds me of Pinot Noir. And just as Pinot Noir is used for making Champagne, Nerello Mascalese is also made into sparkling wine. Producer Emmanuel Scammacca del Murgo makes notable *brut* and extra *brut* sparkling wines from 100-percent Nerello Mascalese grapes.

FOOD PAIRING: One of my favorite pasta dishes is the flavorful combination of sardines, olives, capers, garlic, and breadcrumbs tossed with wide, tubular *paccheri* (page 156). The briny acidity of this dish is a perfect match for the vibrant red fruits of Nerello Mascalese. As my friend Carl says, this match gets "two yums and a wow!"

RECOMMENDED PRODUCERS: Barone di Villagrande, Cottanera, Murgo, Palari, Passopisciaro, Tenuta delle Terre Nere

NERO D'AVOLA

At A16, customers always seem to gravitate toward Sicilian reds, particularly the deeply colored, robustly flavored wines made with Nero d'Avola. Although it is the best-known and most-planted red grape on Sicily, its origin remains unclear. Its strapping flavor led some to identify it as the precursor of modern-day Syrah, a theory proven wrong by DNA fingerprinting. In the 1980s, as international varieties came into vogue, Nero d'Avola vineyards were replanted with Cabernet Sauvignon and Syrah, among other varieties. But with the recent revival of indigenous varieties throughout the south, this grape has been reinstated as one of Sicily's finest, thanks in part to the foresight of producers such as Planeta.

Used in the Cerasuolo di Vittoria DOCG, as well as in the Alcamo and Delia Nivolelli DOCs in the west and the Eloro DOC in the southeast, Nero d'Avola wines tend to be thick, with dark-berry flavors. But this grape also has the knack for stumping professionals in blind tastings because it can produce wines in a surprising variety of styles, from soft and plush to sturdy, particularly when it is blended with Cabernet Sauvignon.

FOOD PAIRING: The sweetness of *peperonata* with roasted chicken meatballs (page 185) is given added dimension by the dark fruits of a Nero d'Avola. It is also a great pizza wine, pairing particularly well with our *pizza margherita* (page 120).

RECOMMENDED PRODUCERS: Abbazia Santa Anastasia, Ceuso, Donnafugata, Firriato, G. Milazzo, Gulfi, Mirabile, Morgante, Planeta, Tasca d'Almerita, Tenuta Barone La Lumia

RED GRAPES: A CLOSER LOOK

NERELLO CAPPUCCIO

A natural hood of leaves grows over the clusters of Nerello Cappuccio, and for this reason, some believe the grape was named after the traditionally hooded Capuchin monks. Although not as widely planted as Nerello Mascalese, Nerello Cappuccio is a significant blending grape, particularly for red wines in the Etna DOC, where it is used to round out the body of Nerello Mascalese.

RECOMMENDED PRODUCERS: Barone di Villagrande, Benanti, Palari, Tenuta della Terre Nere

PERRICONE

Grown in Sicily for centuries, this late-ripening variety is often relegated to the roll of a blending grape in *rubino* Marsala and in DOCs such as Alcamo, Contea di Sclafani, Delia Nivolelli, and Eloro. But when handled with care, Perricone can lend a balanced profile of medium tannins and bright, juicy fruit to the wines made with it. With examples like Firriato's rich, award-winning Ribeca, a blend of Perricone and Nero d'Avola, drawing attention to the grape, it is poised for a revival.

RECOMMENDED PRODUCERS: Barone di Villagrande, Cottanera, Duca di Salaparuta, Firriato

SARDINIA SS 131

For more than two thousand years, Sardinians steeled themselves from coastal invasions, guarding their unique perspective on life and culture while enduring the island's fate as a spoil of war between mightier powers. This insular disposition, combined with the island's physical distance from the Italian mainland (111 miles across the Tyrrhenian Sea), can make Sardinia feel more foreign than any other region in Italy. Its rugged, mountainous landscape and intense heat and winds can add to its formidable impression. But just as the mysterious *nuraghi,* the Bronze-Age towers of stacked stone scattered around the island, have captivated scholars for centuries, the people and terrain of Sardinia stir something inside the casual visitor.

Sardinia was the first Italian region I explored, well before the days of A16. My husband, Greg, and I drove from France to the Italian port city of Livorno and caught the overnight ferry to Sardinia. When the ferry docked in the early morning, we were welcomed by a rare, quiet moment at Porto Cervo on the Costa Smeralda, a resort area that fills with vacationers during the summer holiday season. From Costa Smeralda, we drove west through the northern region of Gallura, passing forests of cork oak along the way. The roots of these trees, stressed by the island's poor, dry soil, encourage dense bark growth, resulting in high-quality corks. Observing the trees stripped bare of their bark, I wondered how many of the countless number of corks I have extracted from wine bottles might have come from these woods.

The windswept region of Gallura is home to Sardinia's sole DOCG wine, Vermentino di Gallura, made from the Vermentino grape. After tasting several examples during our visit, I was taken by its crisp minerality drawn from the local granite-flecked soil; its nose of brush, stone fruits, and almonds; and its clean finish. I decided it was the perfect seafood wine and started ordering Vermentino di Gallura whenever we were eating fish or shellfish. But when dining in a restaurant in Rome later in the trip, the sommelier, a native of Gallura, urged me to try a *vendemmia tardiva* (late-harvest) version. I worried that what I assumed to be a sweet wine would clash with my seafood dish, but it proved to be a perfect match. The wine was surprisingly dry, not unlike a dry German *spätlese,* and its rich, round, stone fruit–inflected profile had just enough acidity to brighten the meal. Today this unexpected find, from the producer Capichera, is still one of my favorite white wines.

Many of the grapes grown on Sardinia are thought to have originated in Spain, a legacy of the nearly four hundred years of Spanish rule that began in the fourteenth century. But the particular climate and soils of Sardinia have given the transplanted grapes their own identity. Vineyards are spread evenly across much of the island, though the grapes they produce differ in style depending on the local conditions. Northern Gallura and the northwestern DOC of Alghero are slightly cooler, benefiting from temperate breezes off the Atlantic Ocean, while the central and southern regions, such as the Sulcis district, endure blasts of heat from the *scirocco* winds. The total wine production in Sardinia is modest compared to Sicily—about one-tenth of Sicily's output in 2006, from roughly the same landmass—and only recently have the wines become more readily available on the international market (though distribution is still limited). Acreage is slowly growing, but Sardinia has considerably less land planted to vine than Sicily, and due to a low water supply and prevalence of poor, rocky soil, its vineyards tend to have lower yields than Italy's average.

The predisposition of some of Sardinia's growing areas to low quantities—and its corresponding beneficial effect on quality—is one of the reasons Sardinia has attracted outside interest, most significantly from winemaker Giacomo Tachis, who is best known for creating Italy's first Super Tuscan wine, Sassicaia, and who later worked with Antinori on its famed Tignanello. Tachis recognized the potential in Sardinia's soil, climate, and native grapes, and then convinced Sebastiano Rosa, the managing director for Tenuta San Guido (the Tuscan estate that makes Sassicaia) to invest in the island. The result is Agricola Punica, a joint venture between Tenuta San Guido and the Sardinian cooperative Cantina di Santadi. Punica makes one wine, the full-bodied Barrua, first released in 2002. This dense, refined wine packed with dark-berry fruits consists primarily of Carignano, blended with Merlot and Cabernet Sauvignon. Aged in one-third new French oak, it exemplifies the modern face of Sardinia's wine industry.

Giacomo also consults with Argiolas, Sardinia's most consistent quality producer and a champion of local grapes. Based in the town of Serdiana, which lies eleven miles north of the port city of Cagliari on the southern coast, the Argiolas family has grown grapes on the island since 1918. In addition to Carignano and Cannonau, the winery cultivates the local variety Bovale Sardo, which they use as the primary grape in Korem, an Isola dei Nuraghi IGT wine redolent of black currants and earth. The Turriga Isola dei Nuraghi is Korem's more polished cousin, an elegant wine with subtle oak nuances made primarily with Cannonau and Carignano, accented by small percentages of Bovale Sardo and Malvasia Nera.

There are still some traditions on Sardinia that remain closely aligned with the island's mysterious past. Distilled from either red myrtle berries or myrtle leaves, *mirto* is the *digestivo* of choice, and it is as coarse and strong as grappa. Sardinian brandy, I've been told, is equally potent. Yet in the midst of the island's folkways and prehistoric ruins, a fascinating, modern wine region is emerging.

WHITE GRAPES: THE CLASSICS

NURAGUS

This grape, sometimes called *burda* ("wild" in a local dialect), is the most planted white grape in Sardinia, comprising almost one-third of the island's total wine production. Grown mostly in the southern province of Cagliari, Nuragus is popular less for the quality of the wine it produces than for its ability to thrive in poor soil. The whites made from it can be bracingly acidic, though better examples show aromatics of stone fruits and almonds. Argiolas's single-variety Selegas is a classic expression of Nuragus, and it also happens to be a great value.

FOOD PAIRING: The almond and peach flavors in this light- to medium-bodied wine give lift to the richness of the cannellini bean bruschetta (page 94), pairing well with the tang of the pecorino.

RECOMMENDED PRODUCERS: Argiolas, F.lli Pala

VERMENTINO

Although this vigorous grape variety is grown throughout southern France and along the Tuscan and Ligurian coasts of Italy, it develops a distinguished character in Sardinia, particularly in the barren granite soils and windy slopes of Sardinia's Vermentino di Gallura DOCG zone. Sardinians liken the nose of a well-made Vermentino wine to *macchia*, the stubby brush that covers the island's hillsides. Vermentinos from Gallura have firm acidity and a clean finish, and they can carry some weight when harvested late for *vendemmia tardiva* bottlings. When made from

grapes grown in warmer areas of the island, the wines, which fall under the island-wide Vermentino di Sardegna DOC, demonstrate a more tropical, ripe expression of the grape. There is also a Vermentino-based *frizzante* from the northwest Alghero district, a perfect refresher for the blistering-hot summer months on the island (though it is rarely exported).

FOOD PAIRING: Vermentino di Gallura is particularly suited to seafood, cutting through the richness of roasted sardines with bread crumbs and garlic (page 171) and pairing well with most shellfish dishes.

RECOMMENDED PRODUCERS: Argiolas, Cantina del Vermentino, Cantina Gallura, Capichera, Giovanni Cherchi, Pedra Majore, Piero Mancini, Sardus Pater, Tenute Dettori

VERNACCIA

Vernaccia is a name used for several white and red grapes grown throughout Italy, though they have little in common with one another. The Vernaccia grown in the western province of Oristano is fashioned into a rich, nutty, sherrylike wine capable of long aging. While the origins of Vernaccia di Oristano are contested, some believe that the style of wine was introduced during the period of Spanish rule in an effort to replicate sherry.

FOOD PAIRING: With its nutty aroma, Vernaccia di Oristano is a beautiful complement to our cucumber salad with almonds, ricotta, and *bottarga* (page 98).

RECOMMENDED PRODUCERS: Attilio Contini, Josto Puddu

WHITE GRAPES: A CLOSER LOOK

NASCO

Grown in the southwest region of Cagliari, where it is the main grape in the Nasco di Cagliari DOC, Nasco is thought to be the only variety truly native to the island. Its very limited cultivation is concentrated in the production of *passito* wines. Yet with interest shown by producers such as Argiolas (whose Angialis bottling is a refined *passito* made primarily from Nasco), the grape has a promising future.

RECOMMENDED PRODUCERS: Argiolas, F.lli Pala, Meloni Vini

TORBATO

This grape, which demands particular care and attention in the vineyard, almost disappeared from production until Sella & Mosca, one of Sardinia's largest producers, began making a single-variety wine with it. Today, Sella & Mosca is still the primary producer. Its Terre Bianche, made under the Alghero DOC, is a fresh, clean wine that is low in alcohol and best when consumed young.

RECOMMENDED PRODUCER: Sella & Mosca

RED GRAPES: THE CLASSICS

CANNONAU

A clone of Spanish Garnacha (and French Grenache), Cannonau is the main red variety of Sardinia. When grown in fertile conditions and left unchecked, the variety can produce fruit devoid of character, but the dry, rocky soil of Sardinia provides the necessary austerity, producing concentrated fruit capable of making quality wines. The style of Cannonau-based wines varies from medium bodied to very full bodied, depending on the area and the producer. Tenute Soletta makes a lively Cannonau di Sardegna Riserva, with bright cherry notes, while Alessandro Dettori's Tenores is an intense, high-alcohol wine that evokes dark cherries balanced by well-integrated acidity.

FOOD PAIRING: A *zuppa* of mussels and *borlotti* beans (page 133) matches well with an earthy rendition of Cannonau, while the zesty, smoky flavors in our grilled spareribs with yogurt and lemon (page 218) call for a bolder, full-bodied version.

RECOMMENDED PRODUCERS: Alberto Loi, Argiolas, Attilio Contini, Cantina Santa Maria La Palma, Feudi della Medusa, Mesa, Tenute Dettori, Tenute Soletta

CARIGNANO

Although Carignan has a reputation in France for producing bulk wine high in tannin, acidity, and alcohol, the grape finds its muse in the harsh conditions of Sardinia's southwestern Sulcis district. The wines of the Carignano del Sulcis DOC are some of Sardinia's best: full bodied with rich, dark-berry fruits, earthy undertones, and a bouquet of wildflowers. Interest is growing around Carignano's potential, led by the pioneering work of enologist Giacomo Tachis.

FOOD PAIRING: The plush berry fruit and acidity in a refined glass of Carignano complement the rich flavors of lamb and ricotta *crespelle* (page 190).

RECOMMENDED PRODUCERS: Agricola Punica, Cantina di Santadi, Mesa, Sardus Pater, Tenute Dettori

MONICA

Another Spanish import, Monica is one of the most widely cultivated red grapes in Sardinia. Production is concentrated in the southern provinces of Campidano and Cagliari, home to the Monica di Cagliari DOC. The grape tends to make a tangy wine, with high-toned raspberry fruit and subtle vegetal notes. Arigolas gives the grape more structure with its Perdera bottling, an Isola dei Nuraghi IGT wine made primarily with Monica blended with a little Bovale Sardo and Carignano, and aged in French oak for about six months.

FOOD PAIRING: The vibrant red fruits in a glass of Monica wine mirror the acidity and sweetness of in-season tomatoes. For this reason, it seamlessly complements both our eggplant *parmigiana* (page 104) and our *pomodoro* pizza with ricotta (page 123).

RECOMMENDED PRODUCERS: Alberto Loi, Argiolas, Cantina Santa Maria La Palma, Tenute Dettori

RED GRAPES: A CLOSER LOOK

BOVALE SARDO

This juicy grape is grown all over Sardinia, most often for use as a blending variety. Yet wines such as Argiolas Korem show a dark, earthy, full-bodied expression of what the grape is capable of producing, with date, black-currant, red-plum, and herbal qualities. Santa Maria La Palma also makes an excellent wine with Bovale Sardo, although it is more subtle and medium bodied, with spicy juniper and cardamom aromatics combined with a hint of cranberry.

FOOD PAIRING: *Zampone*, a stuffed pig's trotter (page 219), demands a bold wine with a hint of sweetness. The ripe-plum flavors of a Bovale Sardo–based wine work in tandem with the sweetness from the *mosto* and the trotter meat.

RECOMMENDED PRODUCERS: Argiolas, Cantina Santa Maria La Palma, Feudi della Medusa

CAGNULARI

Like the white grape Torbato, Cagnulari was close to extinction, but it is now being touted as a variety of considerable promise. Primarily grown in the northern Alghero area, it has been compared with Bovale Sardo, and some speculate that the two grapes are clones. Cagnulari is still a work in progress, and the wines made from it can be rustic with pronounced vegetal notes. But the better examples are bright hued and elegant, with a medium body and tannic grip. The producer Santa Maria La Palma makes Cabiròl, a jammy Alghero DOC wine made with 60 percent Cagnulari and 40 percent Cabernet Sauvignon.

FOOD PAIRING: *Bottarga* is a delicate ingredient that requires a wine that accents, rather than overwhelms, its salty essence. A polished Cagnulari-based wine from Alghero has the necessary restraint to complement *bucatini* with oven-dried tomatoes and grated *bottarga* (page 160).

RECOMMENDED PRODUCERS: Cantina Santa Maria La Palma, Carpante, Feudi della Medusa

PART TWO

A16 FOOD

When I was seventeen, I headed off to culinary school determined to become a chef. I thought this meant preparing fancy French twelve-course tasting menus. If you had told me a decade later I would be thriving in a kitchen filled with olive oils, peppers, pecorino cheeses, eggplants, anchovies, and capers—a kitchen where meatballs would be a signature dish—I would have called you crazy. And I would have been wrong. While I respect French technique, it is the country cooking of Campania, with its bold vegetable dishes, lively pastas, and deeply flavorful braises, that inspires me.

Southern Italy has historically been poorer than the north, and its culinary heritage, known as *la cucina povera*, essentially "peasant cooking," was born of necessity. Yet the resourcefulness of home cooks, such as serving braised meat as a ragù with pasta one day and alone as a main course the next, has ensured that everyone eats and lives well, regardless of the local economy or the politicians who control it. Just as southern Italian winemakers cherish their indigenous grapes, southern Italian cooks are rooted in the past, nearly to the point of obsession with preserving the old ways. There are famous attractions in Campania—Pompeii, Sorrento, the islands of Capri and Ischia, the Amalfi coast—yet southern Italy remains largely removed from the usual tourist route, a lapse that has helped preserve its food traditions. Today nearly every restaurant in the center of Florence has menus printed in English, French, and Japanese, while you are lucky to be handed a menu at all in Campania. The international popularity of Naples-style pizza notwithstanding, it is still rare to find regional foods, such as the *maccaronara* pasta native to the Irpinian hills, served outside of the region.

At A16, we translate rustic Campanian cooking to a San Francisco setting. Just as Italian cooks work with the best ingredients they can acquire, we source the finest local and seasonal produce we can find and treat it in an Italian manner. Our summertime corn on the cob is all-American, but roasting the delicious local yellow corn with olive oil, sea salt, and freshly ground black pepper in our wood-burning oven is completely Italian in spirit. When the season passes, we move on to butternut squash, which we roast with Calabrian chiles and pancetta, and when spring arrives, we turn to snap peas and carrots roasted with green garlic.

All of these seasonal vegetable dishes reflect an essential element of Campanian cooking: simplicity. Whenever I tinker with a recipe, I find myself removing ingredients, rather than adding them. And I try to abide by another Campanian custom: I rarely use onions and garlic or black pepper and chiles in the same dish. Campanian cooks never combine these ingredients, feeling they cancel each other out. I even resist automatically adding black pepper to every dish, whether it includes chiles or not. These simple rules make me a more conscientious cook.

The traditional thriftiness of Campanian cooks also guides the A16 kitchen. The reason our popular Monday meatballs have a lighter texture than typical American meatballs is because we use a higher percentage of bread in the mixture. In the past, Campanian cooks used bread to stretch the rare bit of meat they acquired, which results in meatballs capable of sopping up a rich braising liquid. We also use what we have on hand. When a bumper crop of *borlotti* shelling beans comes our way, our challenge is to find new ways to prepare them. We are flexible, too, just as southern Italian cooks have been for centuries. If Gypsy peppers are unavailable, bell peppers are good substitutes for our *peperonata*. Or, green garlic has a wonderful fresh, clean flavor, but scallions impart a similar bright taste to a dish. These habits of thrift and of using what is on hand teach us to approach cooking with an open mind.

What we cook reflects where we live, and one of the most important lessons I have learned from proud southern Italians is to celebrate your surroundings through the food you prepare. When you seek out the best local ingredients, combine them with good-quality pantry staples, and take some chances, the results are guaranteed to be memorable.

WOOD-FIRED COOKING

The two dueling ovens are the most recognizable features in the A16 kitchen. On cold, foggy San Francisco evenings, diners craving dry heat warm themselves by sitting at the pizza counter, the scent of burning almond wood flavoring the oven-cooked food as much as any spice.

The oven in the middle of the kitchen is for pizzas only. The pizza cook wields a long peel, pivoting from the floured marble slab, where the dough is shaped, toward the oven. On an average night, that cook will prepare between seventy-five and one hundred pizzas, making the work look effortless as the inferno blazes on, the temperature at the back of the oven reaching more than 800°F. To the left stands the oven we use for giving vegetables, fish, and braised meat dishes a final smoky sendoff. The cook covering this station sears fresh sardines on the well-seasoned oven floor to crisp their skin. When an order comes in for braised chicken, she tosses the thighs in olive oil, puts them on a pan, and roasts them in the oven for a minute or two until their skin begins to sizzle, becoming remarkably crispy while the meat stays tender. Working this oven is like cooking through a window: it isn't easy but it is what gives our food much of its character.

To ensure the ovens retain a blistering, steady heat, cooks throw almond-wood chips on the embers to stoke the flames. When ash accumulates on the oven floors, they use a long metal brush to sweep the decks clean. Once the last order is cooked for the night, the embers are spread over the ovens to burn out slowly. The next morning, the ashes are shoveled into a metal bucket, and the heat and a few glowing embers left over help start the fire for the new day.

THE
PANTRY

The more I cook, the more comfortable I am finishing a dish with just a spoonful of broth, a squeeze of lemon juice, or a few shavings of cheese. Keeping the food simple allows each ingredient to shine. The challenge, of course, is that when you use fewer elements, you cannot hide behind a bland olive oil or a stale spice. The pleasant bite delivered by a carefully chosen oil drizzled over pasta or the texture San Marzano tomatoes give to a sauce cannot be achieved with a lesser product.

This chapter is the backbone for the dishes that follow. In it, I discuss the core ingredients of the A16 kitchen, from herbs to oils to anchovies, and provide recipes for *brodo*, pickled peppers, oven-dried tomatoes, and other flavor-building components. For information on where to find specialty ingredients, such as *bottarga* and "00" flour, see Resources.

Oven-dried tomatoes

BOTTARGA

While *bottarga* is not cheap or easy to find, it gives a plain pasta or vegetable dish an unexpected, addictive complexity. Made from the pressed, dried, and salt-cured roe sac of grey mullet or tuna, *bottarga* imparts a savory flavor that, rather than fishy, is the saline essence of the ocean. At A16, we prefer *bottarga* made from grey mullet roe, which should be purchased in block form and grated directly over a dish just before serving. Pregrated *bottarga* sold in jars is much cheaper, but it lacks the flavor and intensity of freshly grated.

BREAD CRUMBS

Forget buying stale bread crumbs off the grocery-store shelf. Fresh bread crumbs made from slightly stale bread are tastier. They are also easy to make.

Cube day-old bread, crusts and all, into large croutons. If the bread is still soft and moist, place the croutons on a baking sheet and leave them on your counter for a day or so to dry out. Then pulse the bread in a food processor until finely ground. Store in the freezer in an airtight container until needed.

To toast bread crumbs, preheat the oven to 275°F. Distribute the bread crumbs on a rimmed baking sheet in a single layer (it is fine if they were just pulled out of the freezer) and toast slowly, rotating the pan front to back often, for 20 to 30 minutes, until uniformly golden. Store in a tightly sealed container at room temperature for up to 1 week.

BRODO

Lighter and easier to make than stock, its fancy relative, *brodo*, or "broth," is made from what's on hand in the kitchen. We regularly use two types, cheese and prosciutto, in our soups and pastas.

CHEESE BRODO

We make this *brodo* with the hard rinds from Grana Padano because we accumulate so many of them. Rinds from Parmigiano-Reggiano are another good choice. You can ask for the rinds from both cheeses or from another grana at counters or shops that sell them grated. Also, whenever you grate any hard sheep's or cow's milk cheese with an unwaxed, natural rind, save the rinds and freeze them. When you have accumulated enough to make a pot of *brodo*, pull them out, make this broth, and freeze it for future use in such recipes as Ricotta Gnocchi in Brodo with Peas and Spicy Pork Meatballs (page 155).

Bottarga

Makes 1½ quarts

2 quarts water
6 ounces grana rinds
1 bay leaf

Combine the water, rinds, and bay leaf in a pot and bring slowly to a boil over medium-low heat, stirring frequently to ensure that the rinds don't stick to the bottom of the pot and burn. Lower the heat to a simmer and cook, uncovered, stirring infrequently, for 1½ hours, or until the broth has taken on a nutty, creamy flavor.

Strain through a fine-mesh strainer into a clean container and let cool. Cover and store in the refrigerator for up to 1 week or in the freezer for up to 3 months.

PROSCIUTTO BRODO

This light-bodied *brodo* imparts the distinctive, unmistakable flavor of prosciutto to pastas and soups, such as Minestra Maritata (page 132). Ask the clerk at an Italian delicatessen or other specialty store to save prosciutto trimmings (including the skin, which gives the *brodo* body) and end pieces for you. These are the leftovers that can't be sliced into long strips, and the shop will likely be glad to make a few bucks by selling them. If you cannot find a shopkeeper willing to sell you trimmings and ends, use an 8-ounce hunk of prosciutto to make the broth. You can also add any scraps and ends you might have from cutting *salumi* at home.

Makes 8 to 9 cups

8 ounces prosciutto trimmings and ends
3 quarts water

Coarsely chop the prosciutto ends into chunks, removing any plastic hooks or string that came with them. Place the scraps and water in a pot and bring to a boil over medium heat. Lower the heat to a simmer and, using a ladle, skim off the foam that rises to the surface. Simmer slowly, uncovered, for about 2 hours, or until the fat from the prosciutto has melted into the *brodo*.

Strain through a fine-mesh strainer into a clean container and taste for salt. The broth will be salty, which you must take into consideration when using it in recipes. Let cool completely, cover, and store in the refrigerator for up to 1 week or in the freezer for up to 3 months. Before using, bring the broth to a simmer and stir to reincorporate the fat.

CHEESES

We rely daily on two types of cheese: aged (for grating) and fresh. *Grana* is the generic term for Italy's hard, grainy grating cheeses. I once asked the clerk at a cheese counter for a chunk of Grana Padano, a cow's milk grana produced throughout the vast Po River valley in northern Italy. She sighed and then told me that it was not as good as the more famous (and expensive) hard cow's milk Parmigiano-Reggiano. This is a common view, though I do not share it. Both cheeses have garnered DOP status, and I prefer Grana Padano for its nuttiness, salinity, and texture. However, the cheeses can be used interchangeably in the recipes calling for grana in this book.

Grana Padano, Parmigiano-Reggiano, and other grana cheeses are relative newcomers to the southern Italian table, where growing affluence has encouraged culinary experimentation. Pale gold pecorino, or sheep's milk, cheeses are more typical of southern Italy, where they are eaten young as table cheeses or aged for grating. We use mature pecorino, sometimes called *stravecchio* (extra old), for shaving on top of salads and grating over pastas. Since there are countless pecorino cheeses produced in Italy, ask a cheesemonger for a mature pecorino to be used for grating, then sample a few varieties. Pungency varies. You want a pecorino that has a full, rounded flavor. Buy it in small quantities to ensure you use it up before it dries out in your refrigerator.

When it comes to fresh cheeses, I always seek out the best mozzarella and ricotta available. This invariably means procuring ultrafresh handmade cheeses produced from good-quality milk.

In the past, Italian mozzarella was made only from buffalo milk, but demand soon exceeded supply and most of the mozzarella consumed today is Fiore di Latte, made from cow's milk. Although you can find Mozzarella di Bufala, imported from Campania, in specialty stores, I usually shy away from it since it is rarely as fresh as it should be. At A16, we use Fiore di Latte from Gioia Cheese Company based in southern California.

Fresh ricotta, with its pleasant, creamy taste, is worlds away from the commercial ricotta found in most grocery stores. The big difference is texture. The more ricotta is processed, the fewer curds remain, and that's why most commercial ricotta sold in grocery stores is as smooth as paste. For an eye-opening experiment, buy several different ricottas, including both handmade fresh and commercially manufactured, to see which ones appeal to you. You should like the taste of any ricotta you plan to use. For the recipes in this book, I recommend seeking out handmade ricotta for the best results. It may benefit from a pinch or two of salt, but always try the cheese before you season it to sample the true taste. Also, if a recipe calls for draining fresh ricotta, check to see how moist the cheese is. If it is sitting in whey, wrap it in cheesecloth, set it in a strainer over a bowl, and drain it for at least a couple of hours or overnight in the refrigerator before using.

RICOTTA SALATA
....

It is not difficult to find Ricotta Salata in grocery stores, but making your own gives you a better product with a creamier taste. It is also a great way to preserve ricotta if you have too much on your hands. We grate Ricotta Salata over pastas and salads.

Makes 1 pound

1½ pounds fresh ricotta
1 tablespoon kosher salt

Gently mix the ricotta with the salt. Suspend a fine-mesh strainer over a bowl and line it with a single layer of cheesecloth, allowing some overhang. Place the ricotta in the strainer, grab the ends of the cheesecloth, and twist them until the cheesecloth is pulled tightly over the ricotta. With your hands, squeeze out as much water from the ricotta as possible, and then return the wrapped ricotta to the strainer. Top with a weight, such as a large can, and

refrigerate for 3 days, or until the ricotta is firm. If the ricotta gives off a lot of liquid, you may need to drain the bowl to ensure the ricotta is never sitting in liquid.

Preheat the oven to 200°F. Line a rimmed baking sheet with parchment paper.

Remove the weight. At this point, the ricotta will have taken on the shape of the strainer. Invert the ricotta onto the prepared baking sheet and pull off the cheesecloth. If the ricotta does not feel firm, use your hands to pack it into a disk and then pat it dry. It is very important that the ricotta holds its shape before it is baked. Bake for about 6 hours, or until firm and dry. (If you have a convection oven, turn the fan on; the cheese should be dry in about 3 hours.)

Let the ricotta cool completely, then wrap well in plastic wrap. It will keep in the refrigerator for up to 3 weeks.

CHILES, CHILE OILS, AND PEPPERS

Whether called chiles or peppers, these members of the nightshade family are a quintessential element of southern Italian cooking. While no true distinction exists between peppers and chiles, we call the smaller spicy types chiles and the larger sweet varieties peppers.

CALABRIAN CHILES
If we could only use one chile in the A16 kitchen, it would be the bright red, fiery variety popular in Calabria. About 2 inches long, with thin walls and big seeds, Calabrian chiles, sometimes called Italian hot long chile peppers, are sold lightly brined and packed in olive oil. One brand we use, Tutto Calabria, says it all with its claim "To make hot any recipe!" Calabrian chiles are often difficult to find even in specialty stores, but they are easily ordered online (see Resources). While their sweet-hot flavor is worth seeking out, you can substitute ¼ to ½ teaspoon dried chile flakes for 2 to 3 Calabrian chiles in our recipes.

Calabrian chiles

CHILE OIL

This is such a simple staple to have on hand that you might find yourself using it on eggs, potatoes, braised greens, pizza, or nearly anything that might benefit from a little kick (for most cooks I know, that's about everything). The great thing about this chile oil is that you can change it to suit your taste. If you like it hot, use less olive oil; if you like it mild, use more.

Makes 2 generous cups

½ cup dried chile flakes
2 cups extra virgin olive oil, or as needed

Place the chile flakes in a blender with 1 cup of the oil and pulse until the mixture forms a coarse paste. Drizzle in the remaining 1 cup oil, pulsing to combine.

Transfer to a clean container. Cover tightly and store at room temperature for about 1 week. For longer storage, refrigerate for up to 3 months. The longer the oil is stored, the stronger the flavor will become. If it becomes too strong, add more olive oil until the heat level is tempered to your taste.

CALABRIAN CHILE OIL

The bright, addictive taste of this oil makes it great for finishing pastas and vegetables. It is also an essential topping on our Pizza Romana (page 120).

Makes 1 generous cup

1 cup extra virgin olive oil, or as needed
¼ cup stemmed and coarsely chopped Calabrian chiles

In a pot, warm the olive oil over low heat. Stir in the chiles and cook them slowly for about 10 minutes, or until they begin to crisp. Remove from the heat, pour through a strainer into a clean container, and let the chiles and oil cool separately (to prevent the chiles from burning).

Once both the chiles and oil are cool, combine them and then taste the oil. If it is too spicy, add more olive oil until the "heat" is how you want it. Cover tightly and store in the refrigerator for up to 3 months.

PEPERONATA

Although they are not as sweet as red and yellow bell peppers, Gypsy peppers are perfect for making this bright, versatile condiment, particularly in the late summer when this medium-sized, tapered variety has turned from green to shades of yellow or red.

This recipe yields plenty of peppers to serve with bruschetta (page 97) or chicken meatballs (page 185). If you cannot find Gypsy peppers, use a combination of red, orange, and yellow bell peppers. But stay away from green bell peppers. Their grassy flavor will overwhelm the more nuanced character of the others.

continued

Makes about 6 cups

8 Gypsy peppers (about 2½ pounds total)
½ cup extra virgin olive oil, plus more for roasting
  the peppers
Kosher salt
2 tablespoons salt-packed capers, soaked (page 84)
1 tablespoon tomato paste
½ red onion, diced (about 1 cup)
½ fennel bulb, cored and diced
½ teaspoon dried chile flakes
2 tablespoons red wine vinegar

Preheat the oven to 400°F.

In a bowl, toss the peppers with a dash of olive oil and a pinch of salt, coating them evenly, and then arrange in a single layer on a baking sheet. Roast the peppers, turning them once about halfway through cooking, for 20 to 30 minutes, or until the skins have started to blister and pull away from the flesh. Remove from the oven, place in a bowl, and cover tightly with plastic wrap—this creates steam, which will loosen the skins—until cooled enough to handle.

Remove the plastic wrap from the bowl, and peel the peppers. The skins should slide right off. Tear the peppers into roughly equal pieces about ½ inch wide, discarding the stem, seeds, and membranes.

In a large pot, heat the ½ cup olive oil over medium heat. Dab the capers dry with a paper towel, and add them to the hot oil. Fry the capers for about 1 minute, or until they bloom and become crispy. Stir in the tomato paste and cook for 2 minutes, or until the paste turns from bright red to brick red. Stir in the onion, fennel, chile flakes, and ½ teaspoon salt and cook, stirring occasionally, for about 5 minutes, or until the onion and fennel are tender.

Deglaze the pan with the vinegar, dislodging any browned bits from the pan bottom, and stir in the peppers. Cook for a few minutes, taste for the seasoning, and adjust with more salt or vinegar if needed. At this point, the peppers can be served warm or at room temperature. Or, let cool completely and store in a tightly covered container in the refrigerator for up to 2 weeks.

PICKLED PEPPERS

We pickle peppers by the gallon in the summer, when peppers and chiles are spilling from their bins at farmers' markets and produce stores. Having these pickled peppers on hand gives you the beginnings of a terrific sauce or condiment, particularly for our grilled shrimp (page 168). They are also a great addition to our roasted potatoes and cauliflower side dish (page 238), especially if you want to serve the dish at room temperature as a salad. When you remove some of the peppers for a dish, make sure the remaining peppers are still fully covered with pickling liquid, or they can spoil. For longer storage, pack the peppers into a sterilized jar, process in a water bath, and keep in a cool, dry cupboard for up to 1 year, refrigerating the jar once it is opened. If Gypsy peppers are not in season or are unavailable, banana peppers are a good substitute.

Makes 1 quart

1 pound Gypsy peppers
2 red jalapeño chiles
2 cloves garlic, smashed with the side of a knife
2 teaspoons kosher salt
2 cups distilled white vinegar
1½ cups water

Halve the peppers and chiles and remove the stems, seeds, and membranes. Cut the peppers lengthwise into ½- to 1-inch-wide strips. Coarsely chop the chiles. In a heatproof bowl, combine the peppers, chiles, garlic, and salt.

In a pot, combine the vinegar and water and bring to a boil. Remove from the heat and pour over the pepper mixture. Let stand for about 1 hour, or until cool. Using a slotted spoon, transfer the peppers to a jar or other container in which they fit snugly. Pour in the pickling liquid, making sure the peppers are fully submerged. Cover tightly and store in the refrigerator for up to 3 weeks.

DRIED BEANS

We use a variety of dried beans at the restaurant, but cannellini, *ceci* (chickpeas), and dried favas are the ones we cook with most frequently. Preparing them is easy, though you must pay attention while they are cooking, as the timing will vary depending on the type and age of the bean. Cook dried beans until they are cooked through and no longer starchy. Old dried beans take longer to cook and cook unevenly. To help ensure you are buying fresh dried beans, shop at markets where there is good turnover and store them for no longer than 6 months.

While opinions vary among cooks on soaking and seasoning beans, I have consistent results when I soak dried beans overnight and then season them after they are cooked and are cooling in their cooking liquid. The exception is when I am cooking beans that are purchased skinned, such as some dried fava beans (the tuna *conserva* recipe on page 108 uses skinned favas), in which case I skip the soaking step. Regardless of the type of bean I am cooking, I always save the cooking liquid. It provides body and a pleasant, mild bean flavor to pastas and soups, such as the octopus *zuppa* on page 135.

FLOUR

We have found that using Italian flours helps us to better replicate the classic pizzas and pastas of southern Italy.

"00" FLOUR

When we make pizzas and pastas at A16, we want to capture the taste and feel of the dough as it is made in Italy, so we buy imported "00" (*doppio zero*) flour from Antimo Caputo, a family-run mill that has been open for business on the same street in Naples since 1925 (see Resources). The "00" refers to the grade of the flour, in this case, the finest milled flour Caputo makes.

In order to replicate the texture of "00" flour, some cooks mix pastry flour with all-purpose flour, but I do not recommend the practice. While "00" flour feels nearly as fine as pastry flour, it is higher in protein than most all-purpose flours. Protein is an integral element in good-quality "00" flour, and it is essential for springy pizza

dough and strong pasta dough. The Caputo mill sells "00" flour with a protein content consistently between 12 and 13 percent, which is in line with the protein percentage in bread flour. Not all brands of "00" flour have the same protein percentage, however. For example, some U.S. flour mills market "00" flours that are much lower in protein, and although they are suitable for our cookie and cake recipes, these domestic "00" flours are not recommended for our pizzas or pastas. All-purpose flour is a better choice, and it can be used for any recipe in this book calling for "00" flour.

CHESTNUT FLOUR

The province of Avellino, east of Naples, is famous for chestnuts, and chestnut flour, or *farina di castagne*, is used frequently in Campanian cooking. We use the finely ground, smoky, white-brown flour in cookies and bread and on occasion add it to polenta. Look for it in Italian grocery stores and online (see Resources).

SEMOLINA FLOUR

This pale yellow durum-wheat flour adds strength to dried pastas and some fresh pastas. It is also convenient to have on hand for making certain breads and some types of gnocchi. Although we do not add semolina flour to the dough for our gnocchi, we do coat the shaped gnocchi with semolina to keep them from sticking together.

CROCCANTINI
....

These crackers are tasty served alongside tuna *conserva* with dried fava bean puree and dandelion greens (page 108), Burrata (page 92), or pork liver terrine (page 206). What's more, you can pulse leftover crackers in a food processor to make terrific bread crumbs. Note the use of two different salts. Kosher salt seas   ons the dough, and sea salt garnishes the cracker. The trickiest part of this recipe is rolling out the dough thin enough so that it crisps quickly and evenly in the oven. If you have access to a pasta machine, set the rollers on the third narrowest setting and send the dough through them, rather than use the rolling pin suggested here. It will guarantee that you get even sheets of dough.

continued

Makes about 30 crackers

2 cups "00" flour (page 79) or all-purpose flour
¾ cup water
½ teaspoon kosher salt
¼ teaspoon sugar
Extra virgin olive oil
Coarse sea salt
Freshly ground black pepper

Preheat the oven to 500°F. Oil two 13-by-18-inch rimmed baking sheets with olive oil.

In a stand mixer fitted with the dough hook, combine the flour, water, kosher salt, and sugar and knead on medium speed for 10 minutes. The dough will have a sticky, elastic consistency. Detach the dough hook, cover the bowl with a kitchen towel, and allow the dough to rest for 10 minutes.

Cover your hands with plenty of flour and transfer the dough to a well-floured work surface. Divide the dough in half. With a rolling pin, roll out the dough as thinly as possible into a rectangle the size of the baking sheet, using additional flour to keep the dough from sticking to the surface or to the pin. It is crucial to roll the dough very thin or it will bake up chewy and soft in the center, rather than crisp all the way through. Roll the dough around the rolling pin and transfer it to the baking sheet, laying it perfectly flat. Do not worry if it tears in some places. Once the dough is baked, you will be breaking the sheet into pieces. But do make sure there are no overlapping wrinkles in the dough, which will prevent it from crisping up evenly.

Brush the dough with olive oil, and then sprinkle with sea salt and pepper. Bake the sheets, one at a time, for 8 to 10 minutes, until the surface is golden brown and crisp. Do not be tempted to bake both sheets at the same time or the dough will not brown evenly. Remove from the oven, place the pan on a cooling rack, and let the crackers cool completely on the pan.

Break the cool cracker sheets into pieces, and store in an airtight container at room temperature for up to 1 week.

HERBS AND SPICES

Fresh and dried herbs and spices are important in our recipes, but I avoid herbal potpourris. With a few exceptions, one or two herbs are all it takes to complete the dishes in this book. With spices, I am even more sparing. The most frequently used spices in our kitchen are dried chile flakes, fennel seeds, and black pepper. Some chefs advocate toasting spices before using them, but I find that it makes the spices—particularly fennel—taste as if they would be more at home in an Indian dish than an Italian one. I prefer to buy small quantities of the most aromatic whole spices I can find, and then if they need to be ground, I grind them in a mortar or a spice grinder just before I use them.

BASIL
At the farmers' markets in San Francisco, baskets of fresh basil with the roots still attached are one of the signs of summer. If you can find basil with its roots intact, buy it. The roots prolong the life and flavor of the aromatic leaves. Basil wilts and blackens in the refrigerator, so treat a bunch like you would a flower arrangement: put it in a vase, store it in a cool corner of the kitchen, and pluck off the leaves as you need them. The basil should keep this way for about a week. Even better, grow a pot of your own in a sunny window.

BAY LEAVES
These leaves are used more often out of habit than for their flavor. That's because the specimens you have probably had for a decade in your pantry have lost their pungency. While California bay laurel is often dismissed as inferior to Mediterranean bay, I like to use the fresh leaves of our native tree for their herbaceous punch; but dried Mediterranean bay leaves with a vibrant, green color and a strong scent work just as well. You will find that a single small, aromatic leaf adds just the right amount of herbal flavor to a soup or a braise. You can elect to pull bay leaves out of a dish before serving, but I don't mind finding a leaf or two in my bowl.

BLACK PEPPER
While I like the piquant, juniper aroma of black pepper, it should not automatically be added to *every* recipe, particularly if you are already using dried chile flakes. Southern Italians rarely use chiles with black pepper, feeling that one cancels out the other. Pepper also can make food less wine friendly.

DRIED OREGANO

We tried using fresh oregano for our pizzas. It did not work. Somehow, dried oregano just tastes right. Stick with Italian or Turkish oregano, avoiding the smokier Mexican variety.

MARJORAM

Just as dried oregano is essential for a marinara pizza, our braised cannellini beans (page 234) would not be the same without fresh marjoram. A strong—and highly underrated—herb similar to oregano, marjoram has small, green leaves that impart a distinct, floral aroma to anything to which they are added.

MINT

Mint refreshes vinaigrettes and boosts the flavor of salads. But, like basil, the leaves are delicate. Wash them the day you are going to use them, and then tear them with your hands at the very last minute to prevent them from turning black.

PARSLEY

We use flat-leaf parsley (also known as Italian parsley), but the curly variety, now widely out of favor, has a similar clean, grassy flavor. The two types can be used interchangeably in this book. Parsley leaves keep for a few days after they are picked and washed, so it is helpful to have a bagful of cleaned leaves that you can chop quickly and add to a dish at the last minute.

ROSEMARY

One of the stronger fresh herbs, rosemary works best with braised meats and hearty starches. I add whole sprigs to braises, fishing them out before serving. I also like to fry the leaves in olive oil, and then drizzle the oil on steaks and roasted meats.

NUTS

Most of the nuts used in this book, save for those called for in a few dessert recipes, are toasted. The best way to ensure nuts toast evenly is to put them in a relatively low oven for a long time. If you try to speed the process by toasting them at a high temperature, the inside will stay raw while the outside burns.

To toast nuts, preheat the oven to 300°F. Spread the nuts in a single layer on a rimmed baking sheet and toast, rotating the pan front to back often, for 15 to 20 minutes, depending on the nut and whether or not it has a skin. Skinned nuts take less time. Look for the nuts to become aromatic and golden. It can be harder to gauge when skin-on nuts, particularly almonds, are ready. To test for doneness, break a nut in half. It should have a consistently light caramel color at the center.

OLIVE OIL

No ingredient permeates the A16 menu more than olive oil does. We use a range of mild and robust oils for different applications, which is a challenge for our pantry cook, who has as many as four squeeze bottles filled with different oils, for dressing salads, garnishing Burrata, giving slices of *ciccioli* a final flourish, and more.

Finding a good olive oil requires scrutiny. Like wine, extra virgin olive oil is made once a year in its place of origin. The best extra virgin oil is also a raw food product: during its manufacture, the olives, their juices, and the oil are never heated. Howard Case, a former marketing executive turned Italian olive oil importer and good friend, likes to make the point that the extra virgin olive oil purchased in August is from the same batch that went on the shelves in February. As the year goes on, that oil mellows in flavor.

Yet not all olive oils, extra virgin or otherwise, are made equal. Much of the olive oil sold as Italian is made with imported olives, with only the fine print on the label revealing their origin as Tunisia, Greece, or Spain. While each of these countries produces laudable olive oil, chances are the fruits they are shipping to Italy for blending are bruised and overripe. The differences among oils labeled *extra virgin*, *virgin*, *pure*, and the thoroughly misleading *lite* add another layer of confusion.

The first criterion for judging the quality of an olive oil is its acidity level. According to guidelines established by The International Olive Oil Council, extra virgin olive oil must have an acidity level of .8 percent or lower. Many estate oils (pressed from olives cultivated on a single estate or farm) are much lower. Virgin olive oil has an acidity level of up to 2 percent, and like extra virgin oil, it has not been heated. The next grade, pure olive oil, is a highly refined oil

that is chemically treated and heated to remove off flavors and reduce the acidity level. At that point, it has virtually no color, aroma, or taste, so it gets its flavor and color from the addition of extra virgin or virgin oil. Lite oil is a sneaky product. Despite its name, it has no fewer calories than extra virgin oil and is essentially pure olive oil with less extra virgin or virgin oil added to it.

Flavor and application are important elements to consider when selecting and cooking with olive oil. When I taste extra virgin oils with Howard, we pour the oils into wineglasses, then swirl, sniff, and slurp much like you would at a wine tasting. While it is tempting to look at color to assess quality, color only tells you the age of the oil. The same oil that is green in the winter (the *olio nuovo*, or recently pressed extra virgin olive oil) will be yellow by summer. So I focus on taste, thinking about whether the oil tastes hearty enough to stand up to a creamy slice of Burrata, or light enough not to overpower lettuce. Extra virgin oils from warm coastal regions tend to have a rounder taste, which is more suitable for salads and pizza. Oils from hilly inland regions have a robust, grassy character, making them ideal for finishing pastas, soups, and braises.

Pure and virgin oils also play critical roles in the kitchen. Just as I would never finish a pasta dish with a pure or virgin oil, I would hesitate to use a premium extra virgin olive oil for sautéing garlic because the heat and garlic will diminish the nuances of the oil. Pure olive oil has a higher smoke point than either extra virgin or virgin oil, which makes it better suited for sautéing. Yet it all comes down to flavor. If I find a well-balanced extra virgin or virgin oil in a style lighter than an estate oil, I might use it instead of a pure olive oil. If, on the other hand, the extra virgin oil is cheap and imparts an off flavor, the pure oil is preferable.

The recipes in this book call for extra virgin olive oil, a catch-all meant to encourage the use of a good-quality olive oil. But within that designation, I suggest that you experiment with both full-bodied and light-bodied oils for our recipes. Remember, too, it is better to splurge on an estate olive oil you really like and use a pure olive oil for sautéing, than it is to cook everything with a mediocre extra virgin oil. You should consider having three types of olive oil on hand:

Everyday cooking oil. This can be a lightly flavored extra virgin or virgin oil or a good-quality pure oil that includes a significant amount of extra virgin oil. We use a pure olive oil

from Puglia that has up to 15 percent extra virgin oil. I find it tastes better than many of the cheap extra virgin oils on the market.

Well-rounded extra virgin oil for salads and pizzas. Forget the peppery, grassy oils for salads and pizza. Instead, look for a good-quality extra virgin oil that feels round in the mouth and will complement, not compete with, the accompanying ingredients.

Robust extra virgin oil for finishing soups, pastas, braises, and cheeses. Drizzling olive oil over a dish at the last minute is the time to use that pricey estate-produced extra virgin oil. Since the oil is added at the end of cooking, its distinctive flavor and aroma are not lost.

SALT

One day while watching a travel show on Morocco, I saw a man setting up a stand of fresh sardines. Instead of laying the fish on a bed of ice, as is done in the United States, he coated them with salt. The image reminded me of the role of salt as a wholly natural and traditional food preservative.

Salting early is the easiest way to improve the taste of your food without meddling too much with its integrity. Thanks to such books as Judy Rogers's *The Zuni Cafe Cookbook*, it is becoming more common for cooks to use salt early and often as they prepare food. The great thing about salting such proteins as pork, beef, and poultry early is that it is easy to do. It just requires some forethought. After we butcher a pig, we season each cut, from shoulder to hock, with kosher salt, using about 1 teaspoon per pound. Then we store the meat for up to 3 days before cooking it. We rarely serve poultry or meat that has not been seasoned with salt for at least a day before we cook it.

Our practice of salting early extends to seafood and vegetables. Grilled shrimp (page 168) are tossed in salt and set aside for at least an hour before we cook them. All of the fish we will be serving in the evening are seasoned with salt earlier in the day. But it is easier to overseason seafood than pork or beef. To avoid salty seafood, season fish and shellfish for no more than a few hours before you cook it. We blanch any vegetable in heavily salted water to add flavor from the very beginning. And, of course, we salt our pasta water. As with vegetables, the salted water should be nearly as salty as seawater. Our cooks taste the water used for boiling pasta throughout the dinner rush to ensure that the balance of salt to water is maintained.

Kosher salt is the all-purpose salt at the restaurant. We use sea salt judiciously in some recipes when we want the salt to impart a distinctive salty note. In dessert recipes such as our chocolate shortbread cookies (page 259), we use a flaky grey sea salt so that it dissolves on your tongue as you taste the dark chocolate.

You can also add salt to a dish by using foods cured in it, such as preserved Meyer lemons (below) and salt-packed anchovies and capers.

ANCHOVIES

The stigma attached to American anchovy pizza has not helped the image of this distinctive fish. It is too bad because anchovies are incredible flavor enhancers. The key to rehabilitating the anchovy's reputation is to track down salt-packed anchovies, which are larger and cleaner tasting than the oil-packed fillets sold in jars or tins.

Salt-packed anchovies are also whole fish, rather than fillets, and are typically sold in large cans (1 to 2 pounds) at Italian specialty groceries and online (see Resources). It might take a while to use a whole can of salt-packed anchovies at home, but if once you open it, you keep the fish covered in salt, they will last for 6 months in the refrigerator, provided that you check on them periodically and cover them with a fresh layer of salt. Or, find some friends with whom you can share the can. Some shops sell salt-packed anchovies by weight, so you can buy only what you need in the short term, a better option if you use anchovies infrequently.

It is a good idea to prepare more salt-packed anchovies than you need for a single recipe. That way you will already have some ready when you need them. First, rinse the anchovies under cool running water to wash off the excess salt, and then let them stand in cool water for a minute or two until pliable. Working with 1 anchovy at a time, pluck off the fins and lay the fish flat on a work surface. Check for scales by running the blunt side of a paring knife against the skin, working from the tail to the head. Rinse the fish again, and use your finger to pry it open gently from the belly. Flatten the fish on the work surface, skin side down. Starting at the head, peel away the backbone in a

single motion. The tail should come off with the backbone. Halve the fish so you have 2 fillets, and then soak the fillets in multiple changes of cool water for about 30 minutes, drain, and pat dry. The fillets can be used right away. Or, to store them, arrange them in a single layer in a rectangular storage container and cover them with a layer of olive oil. As you prepare additional anchovies, add the fillets to the container and cover them with more oil. When you have finished, cover the container tightly and store in the refrigerator. The fillets will keep for at least 2 weeks as long as they are fully covered with oil.

CAPERS

While all capers are pickled to make them edible, salt-packed capers are superior to their vinegar-packed cousins, which regularly get shoved to the back of the refrigerator where they usually languish for years. Salt-packed capers should be soaked before they are used to leach out excess salt, and they do not keep as long as brined capers.

When buying salt-packed capers, make sure the salt is white, not yellow, and the capers are not sitting in their own water, which can indicate they are rancid. Some specialty stores sell salt-packed capers by weight. If you can find one that does, buy small quantities and store in a tightly covered container in the refrigerator. Small capers are pungent, but I prefer stockier capers from Sicily for their meatier texture.

To soak salt-packed capers, place them in several changes of cool water for at least 30 minutes and then drain well. If you will be adding the soaked capers to hot olive oil, be sure to pat them dry to prevent them from sputtering in the oil and burning you.

PRESERVED MEYER LEMONS

While priced at a premium in most grocery stores, Meyer lemons are common in California kitchens, often thanks to a neighbor's prolific backyard tree. At A16, we prolong their season by preserving them in salt, a trick borrowed from Moroccan cooks. If Meyers are hard to come by, you can also use a conventional lemon variety (Eureka or Lisbon). In every case, look for organic lemons. If you cannot find them, be sure to remove the waxy coat on the rind with a natural fruit and vegetable rinse. Preserving lemons is a slow process. Allow the rinds to cure for a few weeks before you use them.

Meyer lemons

Makes 8 preserved lemons

8 Meyer lemons
Generous amount of kosher salt
Freshly squeezed Meyer lemon juice as needed

Wash the lemons well and dry the skins. Working from the bottom, or blossom, end of each lemon, quarter the lemon with a paring knife, stopping just before you cut through the stem end. Each lemon will look like 4 separate wedges held together by the intact stem end.

Working from the blossom end, pack the inside of each lemon with about 2 heaping tablespoons of salt. Place the lemons in a large canning jar in which they fit snugly, and cover with a generous layer of salt. Cover the jar tightly and leave it out at room temperature for a couple of days, or until the lemons become submerged in their own juice. If the lemons do not release enough juice, add freshly squeezed lemon juice to cover. Refrigerate the container for at least 3 weeks before using, monitoring the lemons to make sure they stay submerged in juice. The lemons will keep indefinitely if they are completely covered with juice.

To use a preserved lemon, slice off the still-attached stem end to separate the wedges. Using a sharp paring knife, remove the flesh and the pith from the rind and discard them. Soak the rind in cold water for 30 minutes to leach out the excess salt, and then mince the amount of rind called for in the recipe you are making. Any leftover cleaned rind can be kept, submerged in water, in the refrigerator for up to 1 week.

SAN MARZANO TOMATOES

When I use canned tomatoes, I use only the San Marzano variety from Campania. Grown in volcanic soil from nearby Mount Vesuvius and harvested by hand when ripe, San Marzanos are nearly as integral as pizza to the identity of Naples. Fleshy, with few seeds and low acidity, and typically lower in salt than regular canned tomatoes, they are consistently the best canned tomato product I have found. In 1996, the European Union granted these superior tomatoes Denominazione d'Origine Protetta (DOP) status, which guarantees they are also regulated for quality.

It has become much easier to find canned San Marzano tomatoes in grocery stores. But if you cannot find them, look for canned domestic plum tomatoes that are low in sodium. Always buy whole tomatoes. Diced tomatoes are typically prepared from produce that was not good enough to can whole.

OVER-DRIED TOMATOES

During the late summer, Mariquita Farm's San Marzano vines in Hollister, California, supply us with a windfall of meaty, hearty tomatoes. We dry them in the oven on a bed of salt to concentrate their flavor. If you cannot find San Marzanos, use ripe Roma tomatoes in their place.

Makes 2 cups

1½ pounds kosher salt
15 San Marzano tomatoes
About ½ cup extra virgin olive oil

Preheat the oven to 200°F.

Spread the salt on a 13-by-18-inch rimmed baking sheet, creating a layer ½ inch thick. Core the tomatoes and halve them lengthwise. Arrange the halves, skin side down, in rows on the salt layer. Bake for 6 hours, or until

San Marzano tomatoes, Mariquita Farm

the tomatoes are completely dried and look like sun-dried tomatoes. (If you have a convection oven, turn the fan on; the tomatoes should be dry in about 3 hours.)

Remove the tomatoes from the salt (the salt can be reused for another batch), and pack them into a container with a tight-fitting lid. Pour in olive oil, cover, and store in the refrigerator for up to 1 week.

VINEGAR, WINE, AND MOSTO

Vinegar, wine, and *mosto* add balance and depth of flavor to many of our dishes. Wine cuts through the sweetness of slowly cooked onions in braised short ribs (page 194), vinegar brings acidity to Giardiniera (page 240), and the concentrated flavor of thick, sweet *mosto* brings out the richness in roasted meats and terrines.

VINEGAR

In Campania, white wine vinegar is more popular than red, but we often use them interchangeably at the restaurant. I prefer the less-expensive types sold in plastic gallon jugs at the grocery store over the fancy bottles infused with herbs. These modest vinegars are not as concentrated, so they are less apt to dominate the dish to which they are added. If the vinegar you have tastes very strong, cut it with a little water before using it.

WINE

Shelley has all the fun in this department. When it comes to cooking with wine, we keep it simple. Palatable dry white and red table wines work just fine. I use white wine more frequently than red wine because of its acidity. Rather than purchasing wine just for cooking, Shelley recommends holding onto bottles that have been open for too long and the wine has started to oxidize. Store them—red or white—in the refrigerator until you are ready to use them for cooking.

MOSTO

Also known as *vincotto* or *saba*, *mosto* is concentrated, aged grape must. To make it, red grapes are picked, dried, and pressed. The juice is reduced gently, and then aged in oak barrels. The result is a sweet syrup with notes of prune and spice—the perfect wintry flavors for *zampone* (page 219).

I was getting tired of buying small, precious bottles of *mosto* when it occurred to me that it could not be that hard to make. And in northern California, there is no shortage of wine grapes. So I decided to try my hand at making *mosto* with dark red Syrah grapes (omitting the barrel-aging step) and was quite happy with the results. There is one difference: barrel aging changes the color of the *mosto* from dark purple to nearly black. This recipe yields a much brighter result.

Makes about 1 cup

3 pounds dark red grape clusters with seeds and stems such as Concord or any red wine grape such as Syrah or Zinfandel
Up to 1 cup good-quality sweet vinegar such as a moscato or semisweet vinegar with low acidity

Place the grape clusters in a 3-quart stockpot, and add cool water to come halfway up the sides of the grapes. Cover, place over medium heat, and cook for 10 minutes, or until the grapes soften and plump. Remove the lid, crush the grapes with a potato masher, reduce the heat to low, and simmer, uncovered, for about 1 hour.

Strain the liquid through a fine-mesh strainer into a smaller pot, discarding the stems and seeds in the strainer. Place over medium-low heat and cook for about 20 minutes, or until the liquid is reduced to a syrup that coats the back of a spoon. Remove from the heat.

Measure the syrup. Then stir in enough vinegar to form a 3:1 ratio of syrup to vinegar (the amount of syrup will vary with each batch, depending on how much juice the grapes released). Let cool completely and store in a tightly sealed container at room temperature. It will keep indefinitely.

ANTIPASTI

Nowhere else on our menu can we react so quickly to the changing seasons, a special ingredient, or a new idea than with the antipasti. Their flexibility inspires creativity, and their variety heightens anticipation for the meal that follows. The practice of serving a few items before the *primo piatto*, or first course, which is usually a soup, pasta, or risotto, is traditional in the Italian meal. While kept purposefully simple in an Italian home—a few slices of prosciutto with a bit of fresh ricotta—the antipasto course is a theatrical event in some Italian restaurants, with countless savory plates emerging from the kitchen—bruschette, grilled shrimp, marinated vegetables—each one more impressive than the last.

When composing an antipasto course at home, depending on your mood and the occasion, you can keep it simple or stretch your skills and show off. The only rule is to consider the courses that will follow. A bowl of marinated olives served alongside slices of *salumi* will take the edge off your guests' hunger as you shuffle rustic pizzas in and out of the oven. Yet the same selection may seem skimpy preceding a larger meal. When I prepare a feast at the peak of summer, for example, I add a couple more components that highlight the season, such as a raw zucchini salad and a platter of eggplant *parmigiana.*

With their versatility and bright flavors, salads make great antipasti. Here again creativity comes into play. Our cucumber salad with fresh ricotta, toasted almonds, and shaved *bottarga* is an unlikely combo that came together in a rare "aha!" moment before one of our wine dinners. Salads can be adapted to highlight seasonal ingredients. Our arugula salad transitions to an escarole salad with shaved persimmon in the late fall and early winter, and the four takes on bruschetta and tuna *conserva* complement the changing seasons. And while radicchio, potatoes, and green olives are excellent accompaniments to the tuna, they also pair well with beets for a hearty winter salad.

Sometimes the best antipasti are composed from yesterday's meal. Most of the braised vegetables in the Vegetables chapter make a good bruschetta topping, finished with a few curls of pecorino. They can also be built from leftover pizza dough. At the restaurant, we bake any remaining dough, tear it into pieces, and toss it with tomatoes and cucumbers to make a classic Neapolitan caponata.

All of the recipes in this chapter are deliberately flexible to encourage the cook's creativity. Be imaginative in how you serve them, too, plating them in individual portions as we do at the restaurant, or passing them around the table in bowls or platters, family style.

MARINATED OLIVES

PAIR WITH CODA DI VOLPE (CAMPANIA)
MAKES ABOUT 2½ CUPS

A glass of wine and a bowl of marinated olives are the easiest way to whet your guests' appetites while you finish cooking in the kitchen. We use two kinds of olives for this preparation, small, black San Remo olives from Liguria and large, green Nocellara del Belice olives from Castelvetrano, Sicily. But any mix of good-quality black and green olives will work.

¾ cup extra virgin olive oil
4 cloves garlic, smashed with the side of a knife
1 sprig rosemary
¼ teaspoon dried chile flakes
1 cup green olives
1 cup black olives

In a pot, heat the olive oil over medium heat until warm. Stir in the garlic, rosemary, and chile flakes and simmer for 3 minutes, or until the oil is aromatic and the garlic turns golden. Add the olives, adjust the heat to low, and cook gently, stirring occasionally, for 30 minutes.

Remove from the heat and let the olives cool in the oil. Remove and discard the rosemary before serving. Serve immediately, or store in a tightly covered container in the refrigerator for about 1 month.

BURRATA WITH OLIVE OIL, SEA SALT, AND CROSTINI

PAIR WITH BOMBINO BIANCO (PUGLIA)
SERVES 6

This is the simplest item on our menu, and it is also one of the most indulgent. Before we opened, I looked into the possibility of finding a domestic producer of cream-filled fresh Burrata, a specialty of Puglia. Eventually I found the Gioia Cheese Company, headquartered in South El Monte, in Los Angeles County. We struck up a relationship, and I rely on Gioia to provide us with this delicate cheese, as well as ricotta and mozzarella.

Founded and operated by Italian-born Vito Girardi, Gioia produces hand-shaped balls of soft, fresh Burrata. Each cheese is made by flattening a ball of still-warm mozzarella, filling it with cream and *stracciatella* (the curds remaining from making fresh mozzarella), and then knotting it at the top. The filling process not only makes Burrata more challenging to master than mozzarella, but also more perishable.

Gioia Burrata is carried by several specialty-cheese shops in California and is spreading east to Chicago, Washington, D.C., and other cities (see Resources). As demand grows, more domestic producers are beginning to emerge, which should make Burrata easier to find. Some East Coast cheesemongers are also importing Burrata from Puglia. Whether you are purchasing domestic or imported Burrata, check for the date it was made, and never buy it if it is a week old. If Burrata is unavailable, substitute handmade domestic mozzarella.

To preserve the flavor and texture of this handcrafted cheese, we serve it as simply as possible: with sea salt, a drizzle of assertive extra virgin olive oil, and a few crostini on the side.

2 balls Burrata (about 1 pound each)
½ loaf country bread or a handful of Croccantini (page 79)
Extra virgin olive oil
Sea salt

Preheat the oven to 400°F. Bring the Burrata to room temperature.

Slice the bread loaf in half lengthwise, then slice each half crosswise into ¼-inch-thick pieces. Brush each side generously with olive oil, arrange on a baking sheet, and bake, flipping the pieces over halfway through, for about 10 minutes, or until evenly golden brown on both sides and crispy.

Cut each Burrata in thirds and place the pieces on individual plates or arrange on a platter. Sprinkle a pinch of sea salt over each piece, and then drizzle with olive oil. Serve with the crostini.

BRUSCHETTA
FOUR WAYS

MAKES 6 BRUSCHETTE

Franco Iacono often greets visitors to Pietratorcia, his winery on the island of Ischia, with an invitation to watch him make bruschetta. While it is a simple procedure, Franco does it with the enthusiasm of a made-for-television chef. He rubs the toasted bread slices with half of a garlic clove and then mashes cherry tomatoes into the bread. A stream of olive oil and theatrical dashes of dried oregano and sea salt finish it off.

With similar gusto, we serve up a changing list of bruschette because it is a great way to highlight a seasonal item or make use of an abundant ingredient. At home, if you have pasta sauce or braised vegetables left over from the night before, use it on bruschetta with an added element or two, such as arugula, shaved pecorino, or olives. That's the best part about bruschetta: it's hard to go wrong if you have great ingredients on hand.

Carefully choose the bread for bruschetta. Avoid loaves with a holey crumb, such as ciabatta, so the topping does not end up on your lap. Instead, select a round country loaf with a dense crumb, and slice it into ½-inch-thick slices to ensure it is sturdy enough to hold any toppings.

The word bruschetta, which is derived from bruciare, "to burn," implies that some charring on the bread is desirable. At A16, we are fortunate that our wood-fired ovens toast bread to charred perfection in less than a minute. At home, an outdoor grill is the best way to impart a nice, smoky flavor and light char. Just make sure your grill fire is not too fierce or you will incinerate the slices. If a grill is out of the question, you can toast the bread in a hot oven.

Extra virgin olive oil
6 slices country bread, ½ inch thick
1 clove garlic, halved
Toppings of choice (recipes follow)

Prepare a medium-low fire in a charcoal grill, spreading the coals evenly for direct-heat cooking, or preheat the oven to 450°F.

Brush the olive oil evenly over both sides of each bread slice. If using a grill, place the slices on the grill rack and grill for about 3 minutes, or until golden brown. Flip them over and grill for 2 minutes. If using an oven, arrange the slices on a baking sheet and toast for 3 to 5 minutes, until golden brown. Flip them over and toast for 3 minutes.

Rub each toasted slice on one side with the cut side of the garlic, and top immediately with one of the following toppings. Or, if it is fall or winter and you have acquired an olio nuovo (page 83), Franco would insist that a drizzle of the oil on each slice is all you need.

continued

BRUSCHETTA WITH BRAISED CANNELLINI BEANS, ARUGULA, AND PECORINO

PAIR WITH NURAGUS (SARDINIA)
SERVES 6

Arugula counters the richness of the braised cannellini beans in this straightforward, yet warm and satisfying bruschetta, ideal for serving in the fall and winter months.

2 cups (½ recipe) Braised Cannellini Beans with Garlic, Marjoram, and Oregano (page 234)
6 bruschette (page 93)
2 cups arugula
Block of aged pecorino for shaving
Extra virgin olive oil

In a small pot, combine the cannellini beans with a splash of water and place over medium heat. Bring to a simmer just to heat through, and then remove from the heat.

Spoon about ⅓ cup of the beans onto each bruschetta, and top with a small handful of arugula. Using a vegetable peeler, shave a few curls of pecorino on top, and finish with a drizzle of olive oil. Serve immediately.

BRUSCHETTA WITH DUNGENESS CRAB, RAPINI, AND ANCHOVY

PAIR WITH GRECO DI TUFO (CAMPANIA)
SERVES 6

During the holiday season and lasting through January, San Francisco Bay Area chefs and home cooks celebrate the local Dungeness crab season. This simple way for serving the popular crab brings out its sweet, salty flavor. Fresh sardines, roasted with olive oil and lemon, are a good choice in warmer months.

Kosher salt
2 bunches rapini (about 12 ounces total)
¼ cup plus 2 tablespoons extra virgin olive oil
1 clove garlic, thinly sliced
1 salt-packed anchovy, rinsed, filleted, and soaked (page 84) and then chopped
¼ teaspoon dried chile flakes
1 pound fresh-cooked Dungeness crabmeat
6 bruschette (page 93)

Bring a large pot of salted water to a boil. Add the rapini and cook for about 5 minutes, or until soft. Drain well, and when cool enough to handle, squeeze out the excess water and chop coarsely.

In a sauté pan, heat the ¼ cup olive oil over medium heat. Stir in the garlic and cook, stirring occasionally, for about 3 minutes, or until golden. Stir in the anchovy, chile flakes, and rapini and cook for about 5 minutes to blend the flavors. Taste for seasoning and add a pinch or two of salt if needed. Keep hot.

Pick through the crabmeat for bits of shell and place in a bowl. Taste the crab and mix in a pinch of salt if it tastes underseasoned. This may not be necessary, depending on the crab. Mix in the remaining 2 tablespoons olive oil.

Divide the rapini evenly among the 6 bruschette, and then top with the crab. Wait for the rapini to warm the crab before serving.

BRUSCHETTA WITH BRAISED ARTICHOKES, GUANCIALE, AND CHICKEN LIVERS

....

PAIR WITH GRECANICO (SICILY)
SERVES 6

Rich chicken livers and *guanciale* (cured pig's jowl) complement the sweet, herbal flavor of artichokes, which are at their peak in the spring. Pairing artichokes with these contrasting ingredients makes the bruschetta more wine-friendly. *Guanciale* (*guancia* means "cheek"), which is cured primarily with salt, pepper, and chile, is sometimes difficult to find outside of Italy, but cured pancetta or our Fresh Pancetta (page 209) can be used in its place.

ARTICHOKES
1 lemon, halved
6 medium to large artichokes
Kosher salt
¼ cup plus 1 tablespoon extra virgin olive oil
2 ounces guanciale, diced (about ½ cup)
1 red onion, diced
1 bay leaf
1 sprig marjoram

CHICKEN LIVERS
1 pound chicken livers
Kosher salt
2 tablespoons olive oil
1 ounce guanciale, diced (about ¼ cup)
¼ red onion, minced
1 tablespoon salt-packed capers, soaked (page 84) and chopped
1 salt-packed anchovy, rinsed, filleted, and soaked (page 84) and then chopped
½ cup white wine, preferably full-bodied or off-dry

6 bruschette (page 93)

To prepare the artichokes, fill a large bowl with cold water and squeeze in the juice of the lemon halves. Place the lemon halves in the bowl. This will stop the artichokes from oxidizing as you work.

Working with 1 artichoke at a time, snap off and discard the tough outer leaves until you reach the pale green inner leaves. Trim the base of the stem, and then strip away the tough outer skin with a paring knife or a vegetable peeler, being careful to leave as much of the stem in place as you can (it is as tasty as the heart). Cut off the top 1 inch or so of the leaves, removing all of the prickly tips, and then slice the artichoke in half lengthwise. Using a spoon, scrape out the fibrous, feathery choke from each half. Rinse the halves in cold water to remove the remaining fibers, and then place them in the lemon water. Repeat with the remaining artichokes.

Bring a large pot of salted water to a boil. Add the artichoke halves and simmer until tender, about 30 minutes. Using a slotted spoon, remove the artichokes from the pot. When cool enough to handle, slice each half lengthwise into quarters.

In a wide, shallow pot, heat 1 tablespoon of the olive oil over medium heat. Stir in the *guanciale*, reduce the heat to medium-low, and cook, stirring occasionally, for about 3 minutes, or until it renders some of its fat. Add the onion and sweat, stirring occasionally, for about 4 minutes, or until translucent. Stir in the bay leaf, marjoram, and the remaining ¼ cup olive oil, bring to a simmer, and simmer for 1 minute. Stir in the artichokes and season the mixture with a couple of pinches of salt.

To prepare the chicken livers, rinse them, pat dry, and trim away any discolored areas. Season lightly with salt and set aside.

In a sauté pan, heat the olive oil over medium heat. Add the *guanciale* and cook, stirring occasionally, for about 3 minutes, or until it renders some of its fat. Add the onion and continue to cook, stirring occasionally, for about 5 minutes, or until the *guanciale* has rendered all of its fat and the onion is translucent. With a slotted spoon, transfer the *guanciale* and onion to a bowl, leaving the fat in the pan.

Increase the heat to high. When the fat is hot, add the livers and sear on each side for 1 to 2 minutes, until they no longer have any raw surface area. Add the capers and anchovy and sauté for about 30 seconds. Avoid overcooking the livers; they should still be pink at the center. Transfer the contents of the pan to the bowl holding the *guanciale* and return the pan to high heat.

Deglaze the pan with the wine, dislodging any browned bits from the bottom, and reduce the wine by half. Pour over the liver mixture and let cool to room temperature.

Puree the liver mixture in a food processor, then taste for seasoning and adjust with a pinch of salt if needed. Alternatively, for a more rustic preparation, finely chop the mixture by hand. If preparing the liver topping a day or two in advance of serving, top with olive oil to prevent oxidation, cover tightly, and refrigerate until needed. Bring to room temperature before serving.

Spread a spoonful of chicken livers on each bruschetta, and top with a spoonful of the artichokes. Serve immediately.

BRUSCHETTA WITH RICOTTA AND PEPERONATA

PAIR WITH FALANGHINA (CAMPANIA)
SERVES 6

I have been known to say this frequently about many dishes, but it is dead true about *peperonata*: it is one of my favorite things to eat. And it is even better when paired with fresh ricotta on a hot summer day.

6 bruschette (page 93)
1 ½ cups fresh ricotta, drained if necessary (page 76) and
 at room temperature
Kosher salt
2 cups peperonata (page 77)
Extra virgin olive oil

Taste the ricotta. If it seems bland, mix in a pinch of salt. Divide the ricotta evenly among the bruschette, and then top with spoonfuls of *peperonata*. Serve immediately.

CUCUMBER SALAD WITH RICOTTA, ALMONDS, AND BOTTARGA

PAIR WITH VERNACCIA DI ORISTANO (SARDINIA)
SERVES 6

This dish was born from a wine-pairing dinner. I was trying to figure out what the simple cucumber and almond salad needed when Shelley recommended adding ricotta. That addition made the salad a good match for Sardinia's Vernaccia di Oristano, a sherrylike white with a pronounced note of almond. The grated *bottarga* brings this salad one step closer to Sardinia, where dried mullet roe is a delicacy.

3 small to medium Persian cucumbers or 1½ English (hothouse) cucumbers
Kosher salt
2 tablespoons extra virgin olive oil
2 teaspoons freshly squeezed lemon juice, or as needed
2 cups fresh ricotta, drained if necessary (page 76)
¼ cup whole natural almonds, toasted (page 81) and coarsely chopped
1-ounce piece bottarga (page 74) for grating

Slice off a piece of cucumber and taste it. If the skin is bitter, peel the cucumbers. Otherwise, keep the peel. Halve the cucumbers lengthwise and remove the seeds with a spoon. Cut the cucumber halves crosswise. (If you are using an English cucumber, you will need to cut the halves crosswise into 2 or 3 pieces before quartering them.) Quarter each half lengthwise, then cut again into narrow, fingerlike wedges. They should be about 4 inches long. In a bowl, toss the cucumber wedges with ¼ teaspoon salt, the olive oil, and the lemon juice. Taste for seasoning and add more salt or lemon juice if needed. Set aside.

Taste the ricotta. If it tastes bland, mix in a pinch of salt. Place an equal amount of the ricotta, about ⅓ cup, in the center of 6 plates. Divide the cucumber wedges among the plates, arranging them around the ricotta. Sprinkle the almonds over the ricotta and cucumbers. Using a Microplane or other fine-rasp grater, grate a generous amount of *bottarga* over each salad. Serve immediately.

ROASTED BEET SALAD WITH FENNEL, BLACK OLIVES, AND PECORINO

PAIR WITH ASPRINIO DI AVERSA (CAMPANIA)
SERVES 4 TO 6

In this earthy salad, which works equally well as an antipasto and a vegetable side dish, the sweetness of the beets and fennel is balanced by the salty black olives. The time it takes to roast beets can vary depending on how old they are and their size, so be sure to monitor their progress.

2 bunches medium-sized red beets (about 8 total)
Kosher salt
⅓ cup extra virgin olive oil, plus more for
    roasting the beets
1½ fennel bulbs
⅔ cup black olives, pitted
2 tablespoons red wine vinegar
2 tablespoons freshly squeezed lemon juice,
    or as needed
Block of aged pecorino for shaving

Preheat the oven to 400°F.

Trim off the greens and the "tail" from each beet. (You can reserve the greens if they are in good condition and use them in the braised greens recipes on pages 230 and 232.) Place the beets in a roasting pan in which they fit snugly, and season with about 1 tablespoon salt and a drizzle of olive oil. Cover the pan and roast for 1 hour, or until the beets are tender when pierced with a wooden skewer or the tip of a paring knife.

Remove the beets from the oven, let them cool just until they can be handled, and then rub off the skins with your fingers or peel them with a paring knife. Slice the beets into ⅓-inch-wide wedges. Cool to room temperature.

Meanwhile, if still intact, cut off the stalks and feathery tops (reserve for another use) from the fennel bulbs. Cut the bulbs in half lengthwise, then cut away the core. Cut the halves lengthwise into ¼-inch-thick slices. Bring a medium pot of salted water to a boil. Add the fennel slices and blanch for about 2 minutes, or until they lose their raw bite. Drain, shock in ice water to halt the cooking, drain again, and set aside.

To make the vinaigrette, pulse the olives in a food processor until they form a chunky paste. Drizzle in the ¼ cup olive oil and the vinegar and pulse briefly to combine. Taste for seasoning and add more vinegar if needed.

In a bowl, toss together the fennel and the ¼ cup olive oil, coating the fennel evenly. Mix in the lemon juice and a pinch of salt, taste for seasoning, and adjust with more salt and/or lemon juice if needed.

In a separate bowl, combine the beets and olive vinaigrette and toss until the beets are thoroughly coated with the vinaigrette.

To serve, place the beets in a salad bowl or on a platter and top with the fennel. Using a vegetable peeler, shave curls of pecorino over the salad. Serve immediately.

ARUGULA SALAD WITH ALMONDS, GREEN OLIVES, AND TANGERINES

PAIR WITH BIANCOLELLA (CAMPANIA)
SERVES 6

One of the challenges of writing recipes for the dishes we serve is that they are never static. When Pixie tangerines start arriving in the late winter months, we like to pair the juicy segments with peppery arugula. But when the short winter Fuyu persimmon season is in full swing, we swap in shaved persimmons for the tangerine segments, exchange arugula for escarole, and use walnuts instead of almonds.

4 ounces arugula
¾ cup green olives, pitted and sliced
½ cup almonds, toasted (page 81) and coarsely chopped
¼ fennel bulb
4 tangerines, peeled and separated into segments
¼ cup extra virgin olive oil
1 tablespoon freshly squeezed lemon juice
Kosher salt
Freshly ground black pepper
Block of Ricotta Salata (page 76) for grating

Place the arugula, olives, and walnuts in a large bowl.

Cut the fennel quarter in half lengthwise, and then cut away the core. Using a mandoline or a sharp knife, shave the fennel lengthwise into paper-thin slices. Add the fennel slices and tangerine segments to the bowl. Drizzle the olive oil and lemon juice into the bowl, and season the salad with pinches of salt and pepper to taste. Using your hands, toss the salad gently, mixing well.

Transfer the salad to a large serving bowl. Using a Microplane or other fine-rasp grater, grate a generous amount of Ricotta Salata over the top. Serve immediately.

RAW ZUCCHINI SALAD WITH GREEN OLIVES, MINT, AND PECORINO

PAIR WITH VERDECA (PUGLIA)
SERVES 6

In this bright salad, zucchini is served raw with plenty of olive oil and lemon juice. The result will please even those raw-food skeptics out there—myself included.

1½ pounds zucchini (3 large or 6 medium)
Kosher salt
¼ cup extra virgin olive oil
2 tablespoons freshly squeezed lemon juice
1 cup green olives, pitted and sliced
⅔ cup loosely packed fresh flat-leaf parsley leaves, chopped
½ cup loosely packed fresh mint leaves, chopped
Block of aged pecorino for shaving
Freshly ground black pepper

Trim the ends of the zucchini. Using a mandoline or a sharp knife, slice the zucchini lengthwise into ⅛-inch-thick ribbons. Toss the ribbons with about 1 teaspoon salt, place in a colander set over a bowl, and set aside for 10 minutes. The zucchini will wilt and soften as the salt leaches out moisture.

Rinse the zucchini under cold running water, pat dry, and place in a large bowl. Add the olive oil, lemon juice, olives, parsley, and mint and toss to coat the zucchini evenly. Taste for seasoning and add more salt if needed. Be careful not to overseason, as the olives are salty.

Arrange the salad on a platter, distributing the olives evenly. Using a vegetable peeler, shave curls of pecorino over the salad. Finish with a grind of pepper and serve immediately—this salad becomes soggy if it sits too long.

ROASTED ASPARAGUS WITH WALNUT CREMA AND PECORINO TARTUFO

PAIR WITH PALLAGRELLO BIANCO (CAMPANIA)
SERVES 6

When we first paired roasted asparagus with a pureed walnut sauce, we had no idea it would become such a hit with the kitchen staff and our customers. Perhaps it is because there is a sense of indulgence surrounding this dish. No cream, butter, or eggs are used in the recipe, but the walnut *crema* adds a touch of decadence and the Pecorino Tartufo—a sheep's milk cheese with bits of black truffle—delivers a heady finish. If you cannot find Pecorino Tartufo, use any good aged pecorino. Buy the stoutest asparagus spears you can find and either roast them in the oven or grill them over a charcoal fire. Both methods concentrate their flavor, caramelize the outsides, and eliminate the need for blanching.

WALNUT CREMA
Kosher salt
1½ cups walnuts
½ cup plus 1 tablespoon extra virgin olive oil
1 small red onion, diced (about 1 cup)

ROASTED ASPARAGUS
Extra virgin olive oil
3 bunches jumbo asparagus (about 30 spears total)
Kosher salt
1 cup walnuts, toasted (page 81) and coarsely chopped
Sea salt
1 block Pecorino Tartufo for grating

To make the walnut *crema*, bring a pot of salted water to a boil. Add the walnuts and blanch for 8 to 10 minutes, or until tender in the middle. Drain the walnuts, reserving ¼ cup of the cooking liquid. Set aside separately.

In a sauté pan, heat the 1 tablespoon olive oil over medium heat. Add the onion and a generous pinch of salt and sweat for about 7 minutes, or until golden brown and tender. Remove from the heat.

In a food processor, combine the onion, walnuts, and reserved cooking liquid and process until creamy. Taste for seasoning and add more salt if needed. With the processor running, gradually add the remaining ½ cup olive oil, processing until creamy. The crema should have the consistency of creamy hummus. If it is too thick, add a little water. Transfer to a bowl and taste again for seasoning. Cover and keep at room temperature. (The *crema* can be made up to 3 days ahead and stored in a tightly covered container in the refrigerator; bring to room temperature before serving.)

Preheat the oven to 500°F, and lightly coat 2 baking sheets with olive oil. Or, prepare a medium-hot fire in a charcoal grill, spreading the coals evenly for direct-heat cooking.

Trim off the tough stems ends (about 1 inch) from the asparagus spears. Spread the asparagus in a single layer on the prepared baking sheets. Season with kosher salt and then coat each spear evenly with olive oil. Roast the asparagus for about 8 minutes, or until blistered and slightly charred and tender when pierced with a paring knife. Alternatively, season the spears with salt, coat with olive oil, place on the grill rack, and grill, rotating the spears as needed to ensure even browning, for about 6 minutes, or until evenly caramelized and tender when pierced with a paring knife.

In a small bowl, toss the walnuts with a pinch of sea salt and a drizzle of olive oil.

To serve, spoon the *crema* evenly across the bottom of a platter. Arrange the asparagus spears on top, and sprinkle the walnuts over the spears. Grate the Pecorino Tartufo on top and finish with a generous drizzle of olive oil. Serve immediately.

EGGPLANT PARMIGIANA

PAIR WITH MONICA (SARDINIA)
SERVES 6

This antipasto bears little resemblance to Italian-American eggplant parmesan. A little *prosciutto cotto* (imported Italian cooked ham; see Resources), a little mozzarella, a little tomato, all sandwiched between a pair of eggplant slices. Although it is tempting to serve them hot from the oven, they are meant to be served with the cheese slightly melted on the outside and still cool on the inside, a style Italians call *caldofreddo*.

The skin of the eggplant imparts a great bitter, smoky flavor to a dish, but it can also overwhelm the taste of the flesh, and it has a tendency to burn. We solve the problem by peeling away some of the skin before we slice the eggplant. Grilling is the fastest way to cook eggplant at home, but you can also bake it in a 400°F oven. Follow the instructions for preparing the eggplant up to the point where it goes on the grill, and then place the slices on a rimmed baking sheet lightly coated with olive oil, bake for about 8 minutes, flip the slices over, and continue to bake for about 7 minutes longer, or until they are cooked through but not so soft they fall apart.

1 large globe eggplant (about 1 pound)
Kosher salt
2 large beefsteak tomatoes (about 1½ pounds total)
Extra virgin olive oil
6 slices prosciutto cotto
6 ounces fresh mozzarella, cut into 6 equal slices
1 ounce grana, coarsely grated (about ¼ cup)
6 fresh basil leaves

Cut off the green top of the eggplant and trim both ends. Using a vegetable peeler, peel off lengthwise stripes of the skin so the finished surface is covered with alternating stripes of skin and flesh. Cut the eggplant crosswise into ¾-inch-thick slices. You need 12 slices total.

Place cooling racks on 2 baking sheets. Arrange the eggplant slices on the racks and season lightly with salt. Turn the slices over and season the second side. Set the slices aside for 20 minutes.

Prepare a medium fire in a charcoal grill, spreading the coals evenly for direct-heat cooking.

Meanwhile, slice the broadest part of each tomato into 3 thick slices, so you have a total of 6 slices. Season the slices lightly with salt and set aside. Cut the remaining tomato trimmings into chunks. In a food processor, combine the tomato chunks and a pinch of salt and pulse until the tomatoes are nearly smooth. Pour the tomatoes into a small bowl and top with a generous stream of olive oil. Taste the tomatoes and add more olive oil and salt to suit your taste. Set aside.

Pat the eggplant slices dry and brush both sides with olive oil. Place the slices on the grill rack and grill, turning once, for about 3 minutes on each side, or until the slices are cooked through and golden brown. Transfer to 1 or 2 platters, brush with olive oil again, and set aside to cool to room temperature.

Preheat the oven to 500°F.

To assemble the stacks, pair half of the eggplant slices with other eggplant slices of similar width. For each pair, use the larger slice as the bottom half. Top the bottom slice with a prosciutto slice, followed by a tomato slice, a mozzarella slice, a generous pinch of grana, and 1 basil leaf. Complete the stack with the matching eggplant slice.

To take the chill off the mozzarella, place the eggplant stacks in a single layer on a rimmed baking sheet and place in the oven for about 5 minutes, or until the eggplant is warm and the mozzarella is slightly melted on the edges. This dish should not be served bubbling hot from the oven.

Arrange the eggplant stacks on a platter. Spoon the reserved tomato sauce on top and drizzle it around the sides. Serve immediately.

TUNA CONSERVA FOUR WAYS

PAIR WITH FIANO DI AVELLINO (CAMPANIA) FOR ALL FOUR PREPARATIONS
MAKES ABOUT 2 CUPS FLAKED PRESERVED TUNA

While Naples and Bari have ready access to fresh seafood, many of the towns along the A16 *autostrada* are hill towns, where a regular supply of fresh seafood was once hard to come by. Resourceful home cooks solved the problem by preserving tuna in olive oil, a versatile and delicious preparation—so versatile, in fact, that it never leaves the A16 menu.

Look for ahi (yellowfin) tuna and ask the fishmonger to cut the piece with the grain. Thick pieces cut against the grain tend to flake apart as they poach. Ideally you want a piece 1½ to 2 inches thick. If the piece you buy is thin on one end and thick on the other, divide it in two and pull the thinner piece out of the poaching water the moment it is done, leaving the thicker piece in the pan.

Some recipes for tuna *conserva* call for poaching the fish slowly in olive oil, but we poach our tuna in water for two reasons. First, you have more control because you can monitor the temperature of the tuna more effectively, pulling it out of the water before it overcooks. (The carryover cooking time for fish cooked in oil—how long the fish continues to cook once it is removed from the oil—is longer than for water.) Second, the olive oil retains its flavor because it is never heated.

The four recipes that follow showcase how preserved tuna can be served throughout the seasons. At the peak of summer, it shares the spotlight with tomatoes, cucumbers, and bread, while it joins dried fava bean puree and dandelion greens—a traditional pairing in Puglia—in the cooler months. And any time of the year, you can put a chunk of leftover tuna on a piece of crusty bread, top it with a drizzle of chile oil (page 77) and a pinch of salt, cap it with another piece of bread, and then smash the bread slices together for just about the best tuna sandwich you can imagine.

The preparations also show how much you can do with a small amount of protein. True to the southern Italian tradition of frugal cooking, of making the most of what you have (and of eating plenty of vegetables), the tuna acts as a flavor accent, rather than a main component. If you do not want to make your own tuna *conserva*, you can use good-quality canned tuna packed in olive oil, drained, for the recipes that follow.

1-pound piece ahi tuna fillet
Kosher salt
½ fennel bulb, halved
½ red onion
1 celery stalk, halved
3 cloves garlic
1 lemon, halved
1 bay leaf
1 tablespoon black peppercorns
Generous amount of extra virgin olive oil

Season the tuna generously on all sides with salt. Cover and refrigerate for at least 2 hours but no more than 1 day.

In a medium pot, combine the fennel, onion, celery, garlic, lemon, bay leaf, and peppercorns and add water to cover by 2 inches. Bring to a simmer over medium heat, then carefully lower the tuna into the water. Adjust the heat to a gentle simmer and poach the tuna for about 8 minutes (or up to 15 minutes if using a very thick portion), or until medium-well done. It will firm up and change from red to brownish gray on the outside and to just slightly pink on the inside. Be careful not to let the water boil or the tuna will become tough. You can check on the progress by piercing the middle of the fillet with a knife and peeking at its color.

With a wire skimmer, carefully remove the tuna from the poaching liquid and place it on a plate. Discard the poaching liquid. Check the tuna for dark blood spots and skin and trim them off. Cover the tuna with a clean, damp kitchen towel and let cool to room temperature. Once the tuna is room temperature, taste a small piece. If it tastes bland, season it with more salt. Place the tuna in a container with a tight-fitting lid and add olive oil to cover completely—the smaller the container, the less oil you will need. Cover the container and refrigerate.

To use the tuna in the following recipes, remove a chunk from the container and scrape off the excess oil. Flake the tuna with a fork and then let it come to room temperature. Make sure the balance of the tuna is covered with oil before returning it to the refrigerator. It will keep for up to 2 weeks.

continued

TUNA CONSERVA WITH ROASTED FRIARELLI PEPPERS, CHILES, AND ANCHOVY

SERVES 6

A perfect match, preserved tuna and roasted peppers is lunchtime fare for vineyard workers in southern Italy. At A16, we use 2- to 3-inch-long, sweet green Friarelli peppers we buy from Mariquita Farm (page 226) in summer, roasting them whole, seeds and all, to highlight their incredible texture. If you cannot find them, look for any small, immature green pepper, such as the Padrón or Japanese Shishito pepper. Have crusty country bread nearby to sop up the extra olive oil.

¾ cup tuna conserva (page 105) or high-quality
    olive oil–packed tuna, drained
Extra virgin olive oil
3 tablespoons freshly squeezed lemon juice
2 Calabrian chiles (page 76), stemmed and chopped
1 salt-packed anchovy, rinsed, filleted, and soaked
    (page 84) and then chopped
Kosher salt
24 Friarelli peppers, 2 to 3 inches long

Prepare a hot fire in a grill, spreading out the coals evenly for direct-heat cooking, and ready a grill basket. Alternatively, use a large cast-iron skillet.

Put the tuna in a large bowl and mix in about 2 tablespoons olive oil and the lemon juice, chiles, and anchovy. Taste for seasoning and add a pinch of salt if needed. Set aside. In a large bowl, toss the peppers with about ½ teaspoon salt and enough olive oil to coat them.

Line the grill rack with a grill basket to prevent the peppers from falling through the rack. Put the peppers in the basket and grill the peppers, turning them a couple of times, for

about 5 minutes, or until they are blistered and softened on all sides. Alternatively, heat the skillet over high heat on the stove top. Working in batches, sear the peppers, turning them frequently, for about 4 minutes, or until they are blistered and softened on all sides.

Transfer the peppers to the bowl holding the tuna mixture, and toss until the peppers are evenly coated with the mixture.

To serve, pile the tuna and peppers mixture on a plate, carefully scraping any tuna clinging to the bowl onto the plate. Serve immediately.

TUNA CONSERVA WITH DRIED FAVA BEAN PUREE, DANDELION GREENS, AND CROCCANTINI

SERVES 6

Dried fava beans are a traditional Mediterranean pantry staple. In Puglia, they are mixed with braised dandelion greens in the classic dish *incapriata*. We add tuna to the combination to round out the flavors. The dried fava beans we buy are peeled, so there is no need to soak them overnight. If the ones you purchase have the skins intact, soak them in cool water to cover overnight, peel them (the skins should slip right off), and then cook them as you do dried peeled favas. The slightly bitter, yet creamy dried fava puree also makes a great vegetarian dip on its own, as our servers will tell you. They regularly spoon it onto bread and top it with a drizzle of olive oil for after-hours snacking. The puree recipe doubles easily and will keep, tightly covered, in the refrigerator for about a week.

1 cup peeled dried fava beans
4 cups water
Kosher salt
¾ cup extra virgin olive oil, plus more for finishing
3 cloves garlic, smashed with the side of a knife
1 pound dandelion greens, coarsely chopped
¼ teaspoon dried chile flakes
1½ cups tuna conserva (page 105) or high-quality olive oil–packed tuna, drained
1 Calabrian chile (page 76), stemmed and minced
1 tablespoon freshly squeezed lemon juice
Croccantini (page 79)

Put the beans in a medium pot and add the water and about 1 teaspoon salt. If the water does not cover the beans, add an additional cup of water to ensure the beans stay covered as they cook. Bring the beans to a boil over high heat, skimming off the surface foam with a ladle. Adjust the heat to a simmer and cook, uncovered, for about 1 hour, until the beans are very tender.

Drain the beans, reserving about 1 cup of the cooking liquid. Pass the beans through the medium disk of a food mill or pulse in a food processor until they form a nearly smooth puree and set aside.

Give the pot a quick scrub, dry well, and add ½ cup of the olive oil. Heat over medium heat, stir in 2 of the garlic cloves, and cook, stirring occasionally, for about 3 minutes, or until the garlic softens. Stir in the bean puree and simmer, stirring frequently to prevent scorching, for about 5 minutes, or until the oil melds with the bean puree into a creamy paste with a consistency slightly looser than hummus. If the puree is too dry, stir in the reserved cooking liquid, ¼ cup at a time, until the mixture is creamy. Taste the puree for seasoning and add more salt if needed. Keep warm.

Bring a large pot of salted water to a boil. Add the greens and boil for about 4 minutes, or until soft. Drain the greens well in colander, pressing out the excess water with the back of a wooden spoon.

In a large sauté pan, heat the remaining ¼ cup olive oil over medium-low heat. Add the remaining garlic clove and cook, stirring occasionally, for about 3 minutes, or until the garlic softens. Add the chile flakes and cook for 1 minute more. Stir in the greens, increase the heat to medium, and cook for about 3 minutes to blend the flavors. Remove the pan from the heat, taste for seasoning, and add more salt if needed. Keep the greens warm.

In a small bowl, mix the tuna with the Calabrian chile and the lemon juice. Taste for seasoning, adding salt if needed.

To serve, place the fava bean puree in the center of a platter. Top with the dandelion greens. Arrange the tuna evenly over the greens, and finish with a drizzle of olive oil. Serve the *croccantini* on the side.

TUNA CONSERVA WITH POTATOES, RADICCHIO, GREEN OLIVES, AND ALMONDS

SERVES 6

While radicchio tends to grow small and bitter in the summer, it comes into its own in the winter, when cold weather releases its natural sugars and mellows its flavor. Here, it is paired with briny green olives, rich tuna, and creamy potatoes in an antipasto that also makes a satisfying light lunch.

6 round white or red boiling potatoes
   (about 2 pounds total)
Kosher salt
1 head radicchio, cored, leaves separated,
   and torn into large bite-sized pieces
½ cup green olives, pitted and sliced
1½ cups tuna conserva (page 105) or high-quality
   olive oil–packed tuna, drained
½ cup extra virgin olive oil
3 tablespoons freshly squeezed lemon juice
⅓ cup whole natural almonds, toasted (page 81)
   and coarsely chopped

Place the potatoes in a 3- or 4-quart pot, cover with cold water by about 2 inches, and add 1 tablespoon salt. Bring to a boil over high heat, adjust the heat to a simmer, and cook, uncovered, for about 30 minutes, or until the potatoes are tender when pierced with a fork but have not started to split. Drain the potatoes and let cool to room temperature. Cut the potatoes into 1-inch wedges.

In a large bowl, combine the radicchio, olives, tuna, and potatoes. Drizzle the olive oil along the sides of the bowl, followed by the lemon juice and a generous pinch of salt. With your hands, gently mix the salad, ensuring that the olive oil and lemon juice are evenly distributed. Taste a piece of radicchio to check the seasoning, adding more olive oil, salt, or lemon juice to suit your taste.

Arrange the salad on a platter. Sprinkle with the almonds to finish. Serve immediately.

TUNA CONSERVA WITH TOMATOES, CUCUMBERS, CAPERS, AND BREAD

SERVES 6

Not to be confused with thick Sicilian caponata made with eggplant, Neapolitan caponata originated with local sailors who tossed tomatoes and a dash of seawater with the ship's store of hardtack. We have added cucumbers and capers to this simple tomato and bread salad, using baked leftover pizza dough torn into bite-sized chunks, and accented the flavors with tuna. Toasted crusty bread also makes a fine salad, but it's worth keeping this recipe in mind when you have extra dough after a pizza-making frenzy.

½ pound country bread or baked pizza dough
¾ cup extra virgin olive oil
2 Persian cucumbers or 1 English (hothouse) cucumber
1 pound tomatoes, cored and quartered
1 tablespoon salt-packed capers, soaked (page 84) and chopped
5 basil leaves, coarsely torn
Kosher salt
1 tablespoon red wine vinegar
¾ cup tuna conserva (page 105) or high quality olive oil–packed tuna, drained

Preheat the oven to 350°F.

Tear the bread into large bite-sized pieces. In a large bowl, toss the bread with about ½ cup of the olive oil, coating the bread evenly. Spread the pieces in a single layer on a rimmed baking sheet and toast for about 10 minutes, or just enough for the bread to turn slightly golden but not as crunchy as croutons. Remove from the oven and let cool.

Slice off a piece of cucumber and taste it. If the skin is bitter, peel the cucumbers. Otherwise, keep the peel. Halve the cucumbers lengthwise and remove the seeds with a spoon. Cut into chunks about the same size as the tomatoes.

Place the tomatoes and cucumbers in a large bowl, add the capers and basil, and season with a pinch of salt. Drizzle the remaining ¼ cup olive oil and the vinegar over the mixture and toss thoroughly. Add the tuna and bread and toss again just until incorporated.

Arrange the salad on a platter and serve immediately.

PIZZA

Naples is a city of faded glory, of hard luck and notorious corruption. Hotel proprietors warn travelers to tuck away jewelry and to guard handbags from thieves who whiz by on motor scooters. Taxi drivers charge more for a three-minute cab ride than restaurants charge for a three-hour meal. Driving yourself through the traffic-clogged one-way streets is even worse. Many travel guides acknowledge the city's historical significance, then suggest skipping it altogether for higher ground, notably the surrounding hills, the Amalfi coast, or the island of Capri. But I think what saves Naples from its demons is its food, particularly its pizza.

Neapolitan pizza is a beautiful thing. Toppings are sparse and traditional, with few signs that the California "gourmet" pizza revolution ever happened. The legendary Pizzeria Da Michele, open since 1870, offers just two choices: the marinara, raw tomato sauce topped with garlic and oregano, and the Margherita, the same sauce dotted with basil and mozzarella. Judging by the crowd that gathers there every night, the limited menu has not been bad for business.

At A16, we stay true to two key elements on which Neapolitans insist: we use imported canned San Marzano tomatoes for our raw tomato sauce and "00" flour from Caputo, the same brand used by Da Michele and dozens of other Neapolitan pizzerias, for our crust. Yet we also deviate from tradition. While it might seem sacrilegious to drizzle any oil other than olive oil on the top of a just-baked pizza, most pizzerias, including Da Michele, use vegetable oil to save money. I instead opt for a mild extra virgin olive oil, the same one I use to dress salads. And with about seven pizzas on the menu each day, our selection is broader than what is typically found in Naples. We have also been known to drape strips of prosciutto on top of a pizza on request. (In fact, such an addition is not wholly foreign in Naples, where trendier pizzerias will add prosciutto if asked.)

Pizza should be fun, and while I think it is hard to beat a classic marinara or Margherita, I also like to experiment.

We are responsible for our share of outrageous creations, including the infamous widow maker, a favorite among our dishwashers and cooks: it calls for piling on cheese, sausage, and pancetta and then seasoning them with garlic, dried chile flakes, and a hefty pour of chile oil—total overkill.

On busy nights, diners who sit at the bar in front of our wood-fired oven have an uninterrupted view of the pizza-making theatrics. But before any pizza is made, the stage is set so every topping the *pizzaiolo* (pizza maker) might need is prepared and ready to be used. Containers of mozzarella, grated Grana Padano, basil leaves, peeled garlic cloves, dried oregano, sliced anchovies soaked in olive oil, dried chile flakes, tomato sauce, and olive oil are all within reach. When the order comes in for the first pizza of the night, the *pizzaiolo* dusts the marble with flour and sets to work, patting the dough into a flat disk, then stretching it into a large, thin round. The shaping and baking processes happen quickly, since the longer the dough sits with tomato sauce before baking, the greater the chance it will fall apart before reaching the oven.

For the recipes that follow, assemble your own spread of ingredients before you start to form your pizzas. Have tomato sauce ready to go with a ladle; bowls of cheeses, seasonings, and other toppings; and a bottle of olive oil all within an arm's length.

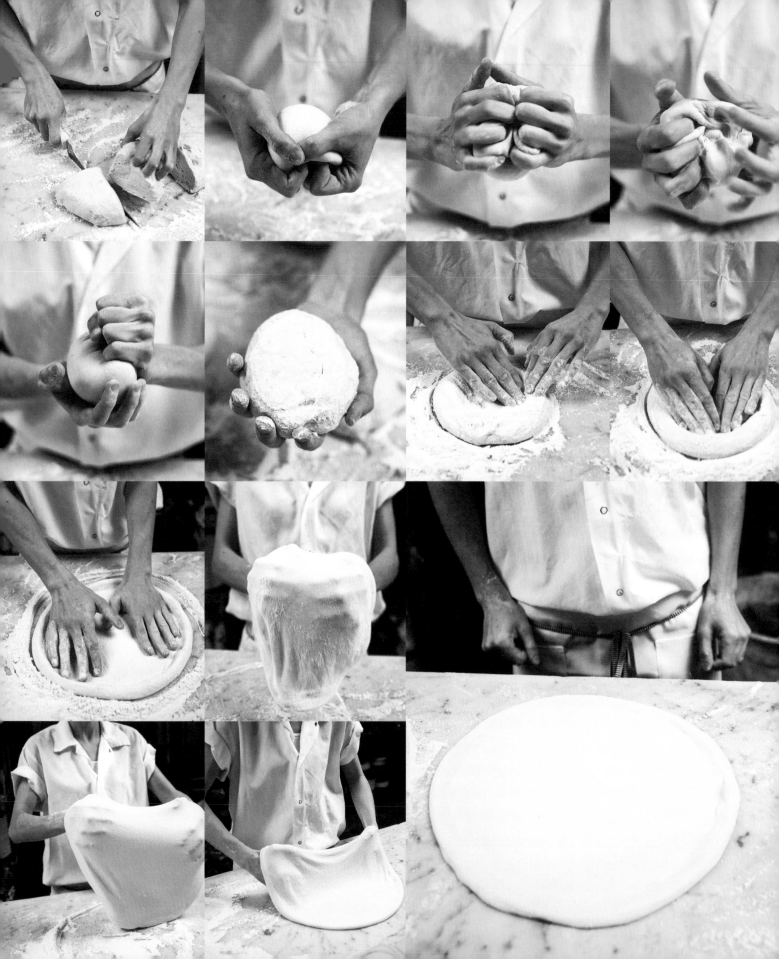

NEAPOLITAN-STYLE PIZZA

MAKES 4 (9- TO 10-INCH) PIZZAS

More than the toppings, a good pizza demands a light, sturdy, flavorful crust. While pizzas bake quickly—an experienced *pizzaiolo* will transform a round of raw dough into a blistered pie in less than three minutes—making the dough is a slow process. After eating pizzas at several pizzerias in Naples, I noticed that the crust at Da Michele had the deepest flavor. A handful of visits later, I figured out why: a bit of older, fermented dough is added to each fresh batch, giving the crust more complexity and a slight tang. A similar effect can be achieved by allowing for a long fermentation time. This not only gives the crust that tang but also provides an added benefit: as the dough ferments, it also becomes stronger and easier to work with. With this in mind, we use a small amount of yeast relative to the flour and let the dough develop flavor gradually as it ferments and proofs for two to three days.

Yet dough is unpredictable. Heat and humidity affect fermentation times; so do salt and yeast. That's when practice is important. Some people have a natural feel for the dough, but with enough practice, anyone can learn how to make a decent crust. If you are not used to handling pizza dough, make one with a little less water (say, a cup) and a little more olive oil. Drier dough with more fat is easier to handle and manage. If you prefer to make the dough from start to finish in a few hours, add double the amount of yeast to speed up the rising time. Try several batches until you become comfortable, and hold off inviting friends over for a pizza night until you have the technique and rhythm down.

Three of the pizzas that follow call for fresh mozzarella. Because the cheese has a high water content, never top a pizza with more than 3 ounces. If more is used, the pizza will be soggy, a problem we encounter when we receive orders for pizzas with extra mozzarella. Also, not all fresh mozzarellas melt the same. If you find that your mozzarella browns too quickly and hardens before the crust has finished baking, experiment with adding the mozzarella halfway through the baking process. Ideally, the mozzarella will melt into the tomato sauce, staying creamy rather than becoming chewy.

DOUGH

¼ teaspoon active dry yeast
1½ cups warm water (100˚ to 105˚F)
2 teaspoons extra virgin olive oil
2 teaspoons salt
4 cups "00" flour (page 79) or all-purpose flour

Toppings of choice (recipes follow)
Extra virgin olive oil

To make the dough, in a small bowl, sprinkle the yeast over the warm water and let proof for 10 minutes. If the yeast has not dissolved into a soft, frothy paste in that time, hunt down a fresher batch and repeat the process. Stir in the olive oil and salt.

In the bowl of a stand mixer fitted with the dough hook, combine the flour and yeast mixture and mix together on low speed for about 2 minutes, or until the dough is shaggy and most of the water has been absorbed. Knead on medium-low speed for about 10 minutes, or until the dough pulls away from the sides of the bowl and looks smoother. Cover the bowl with a damp kitchen towel and let rest for 5 minutes. Knead on medium-low speed for an additional 10 minutes, or until the dough is very smooth, soft, and warm to the touch.

Lightly coat a large bowl with olive oil. Transfer the dough to the bowl, turn the dough so that both sides are lightly coated in oil, cover with plastic wrap, and refrigerate overnight.

The next day, punch down the dough with your fist, then fold over the sides and turn the dough over in the bowl. Re-cover and return to the refrigerator for at least 4 hours or up to 24 hours.

Remove the dough from the refrigerator and place it on a floured work surface. Divide the dough into 4 equal pieces. One at a time, cup the pieces in your hands and tuck under

continued

the sides until you have formed a smooth ball. Place the balls on the floured work surface, providing plenty of room between the balls, and cover with a damp kitchen towel. Let the balls proof for 1½ to 2 hours, or until doubled in volume. Keep a water-filled spray bottle handy, and if you see a skin forming on the surface of the dough, spray the surface to dissolve the skin. The skin will prevent the dough from rising properly and will make shaping the dough difficult.

To make your oven pizza ready, place a pizza stone on the lowest rack and preheat the oven to its maximum temperature (typically between 500° and 550°F) for at least 30 minutes.

To shape a ball of dough into a pizza base, place it on a well-floured work surface. Using the tips of your fingers, pat down the ball, flattening it into a disk. Place the palm of one hand in the center of the dough and gently but firmly press down. At the same time, with the other hand, pull the dough outward while rotating it clockwise to form a flat circle with a slightly raised edge, or *cornicione*. If the dough feels resistant as you stretch it, set it aside, covered with a damp kitchen towel, while you work on a second ball of dough. This will give the gluten a chance to rest, making the dough more pliable once you return to it. The entire time you are working on the dough, maintain a thin layer of flour underneath it to prevent it from sticking. If you don't feel

confident handling pizza dough, try starting with a rolling pin to ensure you begin with an even circle, and then return to hand stretching. Continue to stretch the dough, allowing time for it to relax as needed, until it is 10 to 12 inches in diameter.

Generously dust a pizza peel or a rimless baking sheet with flour. Slide the pizza base onto the peel, and then immediately shake the peel to ensure the dough isn't sticking to it. Dress the base with the selected toppings. To transfer the pizza to the pizza stone, place the peel over the stone and quickly jerk it back. The pizza should slide smoothly off the peel onto the stone in one piece. It is important to bake the pizza immediately after putting the toppings on it, or the dough will soften and stick to the peel. If you are grilling the pizza, follow the instructions below, making sure not to add any of the toppings until the base has been brushed with olive oil, grilled on the first side, and flipped over.

Bake the pizza for 6 to 7 minutes, or until the dough is crisp and golden brown and the top is bubbling. Take care not to open the oven door often to maintain the high oven temperature. Using the peel or baking sheet, remove the pizza from the oven, drizzle with olive oil, and cut into 4 pieces with a knife or pizza cutter. Serve at once. Repeat with the remaining 3 balls.

PIZZA ON THE GRILL

At A16, we are lucky to have a wood-burning oven for baking our pizzas. Reaching temperatures above 800°F, it cooks pizzas insanely fast, allowing the dough to stay moist inside while it blisters on the outside. It is unlikely that you have the same setup at home—I sure don't—but a standard charcoal grill with a lid comes fairly close to mimicking the floor of a wood-burning oven, even though the technique is different.

Grilling pizza works best when a low to medium fire is maintained. Once you have shaped the dough but before

you put the toppings on it, brush both sides of the round with olive oil and place it on the grill (a pizza peel or floured baking sheet is not needed here). When the bottom begins to brown, after about 3 minutes, use tongs to flip the round over, add your toppings, and cover the grill. You will get those great blisters on the outside while the inside stays moist, a textural contrast difficult to achieve in a home oven. If the grill is too hot, you will need to transfer the pizza to the oven after it has been flipped so that the toppings will bake without the bottom burning.

SAN MARZANO TOMATO SAUCE

Neapolitans always use a raw tomato sauce for pizza, which means it is easy to make. At A16, we need to make large batches, so we pass canned San Marzano tomatoes (page 86) with their liquid through the medium disk of a food mill. But when you are working with a smaller amount, it is just as effective to put the tomatoes and their liquid in a large bowl, don an apron, and squeeze the tomatoes into small pieces with your hands. Do not puree the tomatoes in a food processor, as it will add too much air to the sauce, and you will lose the slightly rustic texture that is desirable for Neapolitan pizza.

If the can of tomatoes appears watery, which tends to be the case with domestic Roma tomatoes, drain off some of the water before preparing the sauce. One 28-ounce can of San Marzano tomatoes, seasoned with 1 or 2 teaspoons kosher salt, makes 3 cups sauce, or enough for 9 pizzas. The sauce freezes well and can be used as a braising sauce for Monday Meatballs (page 213) or any recipe that calls for canned tomatoes.

PIZZA MARINARA

PAIR WITH PIEDIROSSO (CAMPANIA)
MAKES 1 (9- TO 10-INCH) PIZZA

Believed to be one of the earliest pizzas eaten in Naples, this classic has greeted *marinai*, or "sailors," landing in the port of Naples for centuries. The more I make pizza, the more I appreciate the simplicity of a good marinara.

⅓ cup San Marzano tomato sauce (left)
1 Neapolitan-style pizza base (page 117)
1 fresh basil leaf
½ clove garlic
Pinch of dried oregano

Using the bottom of a ladle, spread the tomato sauce evenly over the surface of the pizza base, leaving a ½-inch border uncovered along the edge. Place the basil leaf in the center. With a sharp paring knife or a mandoline, slice the garlic into paper-thin slices and distribute them evenly over the pizza. Then sprinkle the oregano evenly on top. Bake as directed.

PIZZA MARGHERITA

....

PAIR WITH NERO D'AVOLA (SICILY)
MAKES 1 (9- TO 10-INCH) PIZZA

This patriotic pizza, named after a nineteenth-century Italian queen, waves the red, white, and green banner with its toppings of tomatoes, mozzarella, and basil. It is also the most popular pizza at A16.

⅓ cup San Marzano tomato sauce (page 119)
1 Neapolitan-style pizza base (page 117)
⅓ cup coarsely grated grana
3 ounces fresh mozzarella, sliced into
   ¼-inch-thick disks
5 large fresh basil leaves

Using the bottom of a ladle, spread the tomato sauce evenly over the surface of the pizza base, leaving a ½-inch border uncovered along the edge. Evenly sprinkle the grana over the tomato sauce. Judiciously distribute the mozzarella and basil leaves over the grana. Bake as directed.

PIZZA ROMANA

....

PAIR WITH FALANGHINA (CAMPANIA)
MAKES 1 (9- TO 10-INCH) PIZZA

Despite its name, this pizza is purely Neapolitan, and is, in fact, called *pizza napoletana* in Rome. The bold flavors from the garlic and anchovies, combined with the chile oil added at the end, make this the most assertive pizza on our menu.

⅓ cup San Marzano tomato sauce (page 119)
1 Neapolitan-style pizza base (page 117)
½ clove garlic
2 salt-packed anchovies, rinsed, filleted, and soaked
   (page 84) and then cut crosswise into ½-inch pieces
   and tossed in olive oil
15 to 20 black olives, pitted
Pinch of dried oregano
Calabrian chile oil (page 77)

Using the bottom of a ladle, spread the tomato sauce evenly over the surface of the pizza base, leaving a ½-inch border uncovered along the edge. With a sharp paring knife or a mandoline, slice the garlic into paper-thin slices and distribute them evenly over the pizza. Then scatter the anchovies, olives, and oregano evenly over the pizza. Bake as directed. Drizzle with the chile oil (instead of olive oil) just before serving.

PIZZA BIANCA

PAIR WITH MONTEPULCIANO (ABRUZZO)
MAKES 1 (9- TO 10-INCH) PIZZA

This is a great reminder that not every pizza needs tomato sauce. Briny green olives and dried chile flakes cut through the richness of the cheese.

½ cup coarsely grated grana
1 Neapolitan-style pizza base (page 117)
5 fresh basil leaves
5 to 10 green olives, pitted
Pinch of dried chile flakes
½ clove garlic
3 ounces fresh mozzarella, cut into
   ¼-inch-thick disks

Evenly scatter the grana over the surface of the pizza base, followed by the basil leaves, olives, and chile flakes. With a sharp paring knife or a mandoline, slice the garlic into paper-thin slices and distribute them evenly over the pizza. Judiciously distribute the mozzarella over the top. Bake as directed.

PIZZA POMODORO WITH RICOTTA

PAIR WITH MONICA (SARDINIA)
MAKES 1 (9- TO 10-INCH) PIZZA

Perfect for the height of summer when you have too many tomatoes on your counter, this pizza is the most delicate one we make. The recipe calls for a beefsteak tomato, but the pizza is also terrific with a handful of halved cherry tomatoes.

1 beefsteak tomato (about 4 ounces)
Kosher salt
½ cup fresh ricotta, drained if necessary (page 76)
½ cup coarsely grated grana
1 Neapolitan-style pizza base (page 117)
1 clove garlic
½ teaspoon dried chile flakes
5 fresh basil leaves

Core the tomato, cut into ¼-inch chunks, and place in a small bowl. Sprinkle with salt to taste, toss gently, and set aside at room temperature for at least 30 minutes or up to 2 hours. Place the ricotta in a separate small bowl, add ½ teaspoon salt, or to taste, and mix well.

Evenly scatter the grana over the surface of the pizza base. With a sharp paring knife or a mandoline, slice the garlic into paper-thin slices and distribute them evenly over the pizza. Sprinkle with the chile flakes and basil leaves, and judiciously distribute the tomato and ricotta over the top. Bake as directed.

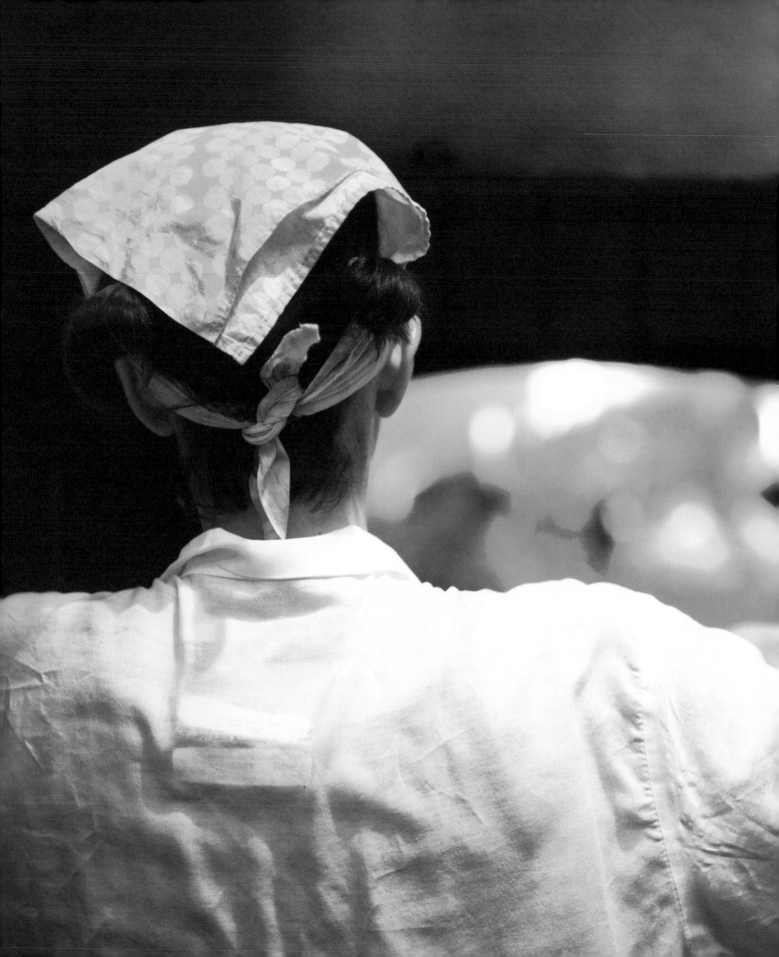

PIZZA SALSICCIA WITH SPRING ONIONS

PAIR WITH CASAVECCHIA (CAMPANIA)
MAKES 1 (9- TO 10-INCH) PIZZA WITH LEFTOVER SALSICCIA

Countless dishes are improved with the addition of pork in some guise, in this case, *salsiccia*, or "sausage." This recipe is a variation of the *salsiccia* we stuff into casings (page 211). For the best result, put the meat grinder or the food processor bowl and blade in the freezer for about 15 minutes to chill before you grind the meat and fat. The recipe yields about 1½ cups *salsiccia*, enough for topping 2 or 3 pizzas. Any leftover cooked sausage will keep for a week in the refrigerator; reheat it and add to pasta, such as Penne with Eggplant, Tomatoes, Black Olives, and Basil (page 163).

SALSICCIA

1 pound boneless pork shoulder, cut into 1-inch cubes and ground in a meat grinder or finely chopped in a food processor

4 ounces fatback, cut into 1-inch cubes and ground in a meat grinder or chilled for 15 minutes in the freezer and then finely chopped in a food processor

3 to 4 Calabrian chiles (page 76), stemmed and minced

2 cloves garlic, minced

1 tablespoon kosher salt

½ teaspoon fennel seeds

1 tablespoon extra virgin olive oil

4 ounces (½ bunch) spring onions, roots and stalks trimmed and halved lengthwise, or ¼ red onion, sliced

Extra virgin olive oil

Kosher salt

½ cup coarsely grated grana

1 Neapolitan-style pizza base (page 117)

½ teaspoon dried chile flakes

3 ounces fresh mozzarella, cut into ¼-inch-thick disks

If using the spring onions, place a pizza stone on the lowest rack and preheat the oven to 350°F. If using the red onion, preheat the oven to the maximum temperature as directed in the pizza dough recipe.

While the oven is heating, make the *salsiccia*. In a large bowl, combine the pork shoulder, fat back, chiles, garlic, salt, and fennel seeds and mix well. In a large sauté pan or a medium pot, heat the olive oil over medium-low heat. Add the pork mixture and cook, stirring occasionally and breaking up any clumps with a wooden spoon, for about 10 minutes, or until the meat is cooked through. Remove from the heat. Resist the temptation to drain the fat from the *salsiccia*; it adds flavor and richness to the pizza.

If using the spring onions, place in a bowl, drizzle with olive oil, and toss to coat evenly. Season with salt and toss again. Spread the onions in a single layer on a baking sheet and place in the center rack of the oven. Roast for about 18 minutes, or until soft. Remove from the oven and increase the oven temperature to its maximum. If using the red onion, in a sauté pan, heat a little olive oil over medium-high heat, add the onion, and sauté for about 3 minutes, or until softened and slightly caramelized. Remove from the heat.

Evenly scatter the grana over the surface of the pizza base, followed by ½ cup of the *salsiccia*. Drape a few pieces of roasted spring onion, or scatter the red onion, on top. Sprinkle with chile flakes and judiciously distribute the mozzarella over the pizza. Bake as directed.

ZUPPA

Melito Irpino, in the Campanian province of Avellino, is not a glamorous town. Most of its structures are plain and modern, the product of hasty rebuilding following a devastating earthquake that shook the region in 1980. But one taste of restaurant DiPietro's *minestra maritata*, brimming with braised greens and meat, and I forgot the nondescript surroundings. I am not sure what impressed me more: the rich, simple, old-world flavors endemic to such an unassuming spot, or chef Enzo DiPietro, who has prepared this soup all of his life.

Like Enzo, who preserves the culinary customs of the Irpinian hills, Italian soup is both soulful and traditional. In the south, it is commonly served as a first course, if pasta is not on the menu, yet it can also be a satisfying meal on its own, with just bread and a salad, perhaps with some cheese or *salumi* on the side. It might be a thick, filling *zuppa*, made with octopus and chickpeas or mussels and *borlotti* beans, or a brothy *minestra*. But in every case, it draws on regional ingredients.

Water, rather than the flavorful stock of northern European kitchens, is often used for the liquid, an approach that allows the bright flavors of the soup's vegetables to shine. Or, Campanian cooks will use the liquid drained from simmered dried beans to add body and a mild bean flavor. When broth is used, it has typically been prepared from an accumulation of trimmings, such as the prosciutto *brodo* (page 75) and cheese *brodo* (page 74) we make at A16. In these cases, the distinctive flavor of the cured ham or the cheese never dominates the other ingredients in the soup.

The soups in this chapter are versatile. They fit well into a menu of multiple courses and can also be served in larger portions as the centerpiece of a simple meal.

SUMMER VEGETABLE CIANFOTTA

PAIR WITH FRAPPATO/NERO D'AVOLA BLEND (SICILY)
SERVES 8 AS A FIRST COURSE, OR 4 TO 6 AS A MAIN COURSE

To make the *cianfotta*, a traditional vegetable stew of Campania, local cooks braise countless combinations of vegetables in a generous helping of fat, be it lard, olive oil, or prosciutto trimmings. The *zuppa* comes into its own in summer, when eggplants and zucchini are plentiful. *Fiorelli* are the buds that grow into blossoms on squash plants. If you have a prolific zucchini or other squash plant in your yard and want to reduce its productivity, pluck off the buds and use them for this soup and in squid ink *tonnarelli* (page 145). If you don't have access to *fiorelli*, look for squash blossoms at a farmers' market or specialty-produce store and give them a quick slice before you add them to the soup.

While the prosciutto *brodo* adds richness to the soup, you can substitute water to make a vegetarian rendition. Because *cianfotta* is naturally thick, you can use the leftovers for making bruschette (page 93), topping them with a few leaves of wild arugula for a peppery bite.

1 globe eggplant, trimmed and diced (about 4 cups)
4 summer zucchini or squashes, trimmed and diced (about 4 cups)
Kosher salt
1 fennel bulb
2 cups extra virgin olive oil
5 cloves garlic, smashed with the side of a knife
4 sprigs marjoram
1 bay leaf
3 Yukon Gold potatoes, cubed (about 2 cups)
1 cup prosciutto brodo (page 75)
1 cup water
1 cup fiorelli or thinly sliced squash blossoms
1 cup cherry tomatoes, stemmed and halved
Block of aged pecorino for shaving

Preheat the oven to 300°F.

Evenly distribute the eggplant and zucchini on a rimmed baking sheet and sprinkle with about 1 teaspoon salt. Let stand for 20 minutes.

Meanwhile, cut off the stalks and feathery tops (reserve for another use) from the fennel bulb, halve lengthwise, and then cut away the core. Cut the halves lengthwise into ¼-inch-thick slices. You should have about 2 cups.

In a 6- to 8-quart heavy-bottomed pot, combine the olive oil, garlic, marjoram, and bay leaf over medium heat and sweat, stirring occasionally, for about 3 minutes, or until the garlic begins to soften. Stir in the fennel and 1 teaspoon salt, and cook gently for about 2 minutes, or until the fennel begins to soften. Stir in the potatoes and cook, stirring occasionally, for a few minutes more.

Pat the zucchini and eggplant pieces dry and add them to the pot. Stir the vegetables to ensure they are coated evenly and generously with the oil. Cover the pot, place in the oven, and cook, stirring gently every 10 to 15 minutes, for about 40 minutes, or until the vegetables are tender but not falling apart.

Remove from the oven and drain off most of the olive oil from the vegetables (you can reserve the oil in the refrigerator for a future batch of *cianfotta*). Add the *brodo* and water to the vegetables, place over medium-high heat, bring to a simmer, and cook for 5 minutes. Add the *fiorelli* and tomatoes and simmer for a minute or two more. Check for seasoning and season cautiously if needed because the brodo is salty.

Divide the soup among warmed bowls. Using a vegetable peeler, shave a few pecorino curls over the top of each serving. Serve immediately.

MINESTRA MARITATA

PAIR WITH FIANO DI AVELLINO (CAMPANIA)
SERVES 6 AS A FIRST COURSE, OR 4 AS A MAIN COURSE

This hearty soup—a marriage of meat and greens—is served both as an everyday meal and for special family gatherings. The two broths impart a rich, savory quality that melds seamlessly with the braised greens.

    For an even sturdier version of this soup, roast some spicy pork meatballs (page 213) and add them to the pot a few minutes before serving.

Kosher salt
4 ounces (½ bunch) dandelion greens, coarsely chopped
1 bunch rapini (6 ounces), tough stems removed and coarsely chopped
2 cups coarsely chopped cabbage (about ¼ head)
¼ cup extra virgin olive oil, plus extra for finishing
2 celery stalks, diced
2 cloves garlic, smashed with the side of a knife
1 bay leaf
¼ teaspoon dried chile flakes
1 ounce pancetta, diced (about ¼ cup)
2 cups cheese brodo (page 74)
1 cup prosciutto brodo (page 75)

Preheat the oven to 400˚F. Coat 2 baking sheets with olive oil.

Bring a large pot of salted water to a boil. Add the dandelion greens and cook for 3 minutes, or until wilted. Scoop out the greens with a wire skimmer and drain well. Add the rapini to the same boiling water and cook for 3 to 5 minutes, or until soft. Scoop out the rapini with the wire skimmer and drain well. Add the cabbage to the same boiling water and cook for about 3 minutes, or until wilted, and then drain well. Set all of the greens aside.

In a large, heavy-bottomed pot, heat the olive oil over medium heat. Add the celery, garlic, bay leaf, and chile flakes and sweat, stirring occasionally, for about 3 minutes, or until the garlic begins to soften. Add the pancetta and cook, stirring occasionally, for about 3 minutes, or until it renders its fat and is lightly browned and crisp. Stir in the greens and all of the *brodo* and simmer for about 10 minutes, or until the greens are tender and have begun to absorb the flavors of the *brodo*. Taste for seasoning and cautiously adjust with more salt if needed (the prosciutto brodo contributes a good dose of salt).

Ladle into warmed bowls. Garnish each bowl with a drizzle of olive oil and serve immediately.

BORLOTTI BEAN AND MUSSEL ZUPPA WITH ZUCCHINI AND GRILLED BREAD

PAIR WITH CANNONAU (SARDINIA)
SERVES 6 AS A FIRST COURSE, OR 4 AS A MAIN COURSE

When a local farmer stepped into the restaurant and asked me to take forty pounds of fresh *borlotti* beans off his hands, I agreed. Then came the challenge of figuring out how to use up all of the red-speckled shelling beans. After many variations, the kitchen staff landed on this winning combination: a bean soup with diced zucchini, shucked mussels, dried chile flakes, and plenty of olive oil.

If you can't find fresh *borlotti* beans, substitute 1 cup dried *borlotti* or cannellini beans, picked over for broken pieces and pebbles, rinsed, soaked overnight in water to cover, and drained. Cook the dried beans until tender, about 1½ hours.

1½ pounds borlotti beans in their pods
Kosher salt
1½ pounds mussels
Extra virgin olive oil
2 cloves garlic, smashed with the side of a knife
1 zucchini, trimmed and diced
¼ teaspoon dried chile flakes
6 slices country bread, ½ inch thick
2 tablespoons chopped fresh basil

Shuck the beans and rinse under cold running water. You should have about 2 cups. Place in a pot, add water to cover by about 2 inches, and bring to a gentle simmer. Cook for about 45 minutes, or until tender. Season the beans lightly with salt and remove from the heat. Let the beans cool in their cooking liquid.

Scrub the mussels under cold running water and pull away their fibrous beards (which are usually quite small or absent on cultivated mussels). Discard any mussels with broken shells or mussels that don't close to the touch. Place in a colander, cover with a damp towel, and set aside to drain.

Prepare a medium-low fire in a grill, spread the coals evenly for direct-heat cooking, or preheat the oven to 450°F.

In a large, heavy-bottomed pot, heat 2 tablespoons olive oil over low heat. Add the garlic and sweat, stirring occasionally, for about 3 minutes, or until golden. Raise the heat to medium-high, stir in the zucchini, and cook, stirring occasionally, for about 2 minutes, or until lightly browned on the edges.

Add 2 more tablespoons olive oil and the chile flakes to the pot. Add the mussels, cover with a tight-fitting lid, and cook over medium-high heat for about 5 minutes, or until they open. Using the slotted spoon, lift out the mussels, pausing briefly to allow any liquid to drain back into the pot, and transfer to a bowl. Shuck the mussels, discarding any that failed to open.

Return the mussel meats to the pot over medium heat. Add the beans with their cooking liquid, season with salt, and bring the mixture to a simmer. Simmer for 5 minutes to blend the flavors.

Meanwhile, brush both sides of each bread slice with olive oil. If using a grill, place the slices on the grill rack and grill for about 3 minutes, or until golden brown. Flip them over and grill for 2 minutes. If using an oven, arrange the slices on a baking sheet and toast for 5 to 7 minutes, or until golden brown. Flip them over and toast for an additional 5 minutes. Cut each bread slice in half on the diagonal.

Ladle the soup into warmed bowls. Top each serving with a drizzle of olive oil and a scattering of basil. Serve immediately with the grilled bread.

OCTOPUS AND CECI BEAN ZUPPA WITH ESCAROLE, GARLIC, AND CHILES

PAIR WITH GAGLIOPPO (CALABRIA)
SERVES 8 AS A FIRST COURSE, OR 6 AS A MAIN COURSE

Octopus comes with its own braising liquid: just put it in a pot on the stove top, turn on the heat, and a couple of inches of water will soon appear at the bottom of the pot. It is a great little secret that a dish that appears so exotic is actually quite simple. Of course, any Neapolitan will tell you that the only octopus worth eating come from the Tyrrhenian Sea, and finding a Tyrrhenian octopus in California is a tall order. But we do have access to fresh octopus from the Pacific, which are a treat. If you cannot find fresh octopus, frozen ones are more widely available. Sometimes you will see frozen cooked octopus for sale, which are not the best option for this soup, though they will do. If you do use precooked octopus, decrease the braising time to 30 minutes and add about 2 cups water to the pot (the cooked octopus won't release sufficient liquid). And if you buy only octopus tentacles, you will also probably need to add water to the pot. Finally, I make this soup with the 4-pound specimens we get at A16, so if you can only find 2-pound octopus, you will need to buy a pair of them. Don't worry if they look large. They will shrink up as they release their water.

½ cup dried ceci beans (chickpeas)
Kosher salt
⅔ cup extra virgin olive oil, plus more for finishing
6 cloves garlic, smashed with the side of a knife
Rind of ½ lemon, zested into strips using a
    vegetable peeler
2 bay leaves
1 (3- to 4-pound) octopus, defrosted, if frozen,
    and rinsed
1 head escarole (about 12 ounces), cored
3 celery stalks, thinly sliced
3 to 4 Calabrian chiles (page 76), stemmed
    and minced

Pick over the beans, removing any broken pieces and pebbles, and rinse well. Place in a bowl, add water to cover generously, and let soak for at least 2 hours or up to overnight.

Drain the beans, place in a pot, and add water to cover by about 2 inches. Bring the beans to a boil over high heat, adjust the heat to a slow simmer, and cook, uncovered, for 1 to 1½ hours, or until tender. Season with 1 teaspoon salt and remove from the heat. Let cool completely, transfer the beans and their liquid to a storage container, and refrigerate overnight. Drain the beans, reserving their liquid. You should have 1 to 2 cups liquid, and you will need 2 cups for this recipe. If you have less than 2 cups, add water to the cooking liquid to bring it to 2 cups.

In a large, heavy-bottomed pot, heat ⅓ cup of the olive oil over medium heat. Stir in 3 of the garlic cloves, the strips of lemon zest, 1 bay leaf, and 2 teaspoons kosher salt and cook, stirring occasionally, for 3 minutes, or until the garlic begins to soften. Add the octopus, stir to coat it with the oil, and then weight it down with a plate or lid to ensure it does not begin to float once it starts releasing its water. Cover the pot and adjust the heat to a gentle simmer. The octopus should start slowly releasing its water, creating its own braising liquid.

Cook for about 30 minutes and check to see how much braising liquid is in the pot. If it is about 1 cup or less (unlikely if you are using an uncooked whole octopus), add 1 cup of water. Check the tenderness and continue to cook for 30 to 50 minutes longer, or until almost completely tender. The octopus will dramatically decrease in volume. Remove the pot from the heat and allow the octopus to cool in the braising liquid for 1 hour.

continued

Meanwhile, bring a large pot of salted water to a boil. Add the escarole and cook for about 3 minutes, or until tender. Drain well and when cool enough to handle, chop the leaves coarsely and set aside.

Place a colander over a large bowl. Once the octopus has cooled for 1 hour, transfer it to the colander. Strain the braising liquid through a fine-mesh strainer into a measuring pitcher. Add any extra liquid that has drained from the octopus into the bowl to the braising liquid. You will need 1 cup for the zuppa. Give the pot used to cook the octopus a quick wash and return it to the stove.

Transfer the octopus to a large cutting board. Starting at the thickest point of the tentacle, slice into ¼-inch-thick pieces, increasing the thickness of the pieces as the tentacle becomes narrower. Halve the head, then cut it into ¼-inch strips. Set aside.

To prepare the *zuppa*, heat the remaining ⅓ cup olive oil in the cleaned pot over medium heat. Add the remaining 3 garlic cloves, the celery, the chiles, and the remaining bay leaf and stir well. Stir in the beans and the reserved cooking liquid. Stir in the octopus and the reserved braising liquid. Heat until hot and then taste for seasoning, adding more salt if needed. Stir in the escarole and simmer for a few minutes more.

Ladle the soup into warmed bowls. Top each serving with a drizzle of olive oil. Serve immediately.

TRIPPA ALLA NAPOLETANA

PAIR WITH AGLIANICO (CAMPANIA)

SERVES 8 AS A FIRST COURSE, OR 4 TO 6 AS A MAIN COURSE

Tripe can be a challenging ingredient for many, but for the discerning few, it is the first thing they order from our menu. This recipe will definitely please tripe aficionados, while the pleasant trio of tomato, egg, and cheese that finishes the stew may win the dish some converts. It is also one of the only recipes we make that calls for both onion and garlic, ingredients that many Campanian cooks believe cancel each other out when used together. Here, each adds needed piquancy and sweetness to the dish.

It is not easy to prepare tripe in small batches, so if this recipe makes more than you anticipate serving, you can freeze a portion of the tripe in its sauce without the addition of the egg and cheese. Then, when you want to serve the tripe, simply defrost it, place it in a pot with a splash of water, bring it to a simmer, and add a couple of tablespoons each of beaten egg and grated cheese.

2 pounds honeycomb tripe

¼ cup distilled white vinegar

Kosher salt

½ cup extra virgin olive oil, plus more for finishing

½ red onion, diced (about 1 cup)

½ cup coarsely chopped fresh flat-leaf parsley

3 cloves garlic, thinly sliced

¼ teaspoon dried chile flakes

¼ cup tomato paste

¾ cup dry white wine

2 cups canned San Marzano tomatoes with juice, coarsely chopped

2 cups water

1 egg

¼ cup grated grana

¼ cup fresh bread crumbs, toasted (page 74)

Rinse the tripe well under cold running water. Place it in a large, heavy-bottomed pot and add the vinegar, a few healthy tablespoons of salt (it is important the water is salty), and water to cover by several inches. Bring slowly to a boil, adjust the heat to a simmer, and skim off any foam from the surface with a ladle. Cook the tripe, uncovered, for about 2 hours, or until it can be easily pierced with a fork. Remove from the heat and let the tripe cool in its cooking liquid.

Using tongs, transfer the cooled tripe to a large cutting board, and discard the cooking liquid. Cut the tripe into 2-inch-wide ribbons, and then slice the ribbons crosswise into thin ¼-inch-wide strips. Set aside.

In a large, heavy-bottomed pot, heat ¼ cup of the olive oil over medium heat. Add the onion, parsley, garlic, chile flakes, and about 1 teaspoon salt and cook, stirring frequently, for about 5 minutes, or until the onion has softened. Stir in the tomato paste and continue to cook for 5 minutes, or until the tomato paste changes from bright red to brick red. Pour in the wine and deglaze the pot, dislodging any browned bits from the bottom and reducing the mixture until it is almost dry. Add the tripe, tomatoes and their juice, and water and bring to a simmer. Continue to simmer, uncovered, for about 30 minutes, or until the tripe has absorbed the flavor from the sauce and is very tender.

At this point, the tripe should have the consistency of a thick soup. If it is too thick and has a consistency more like oatmeal, add a splash of water to loosen it up. It will thicken further once you add the egg and the cheese. Taste for seasoning and add more salt if needed.

In a small bowl, beat together the egg and grana until blended. Stir the mixture into the tripe stew and heat, stirring a few times, for about 1 minute, or just until the stew thickens.

Spoon the tripe into warmed bowls. Top each bowl with a drizzle of olive oil and a scattering of bread crumbs. Serve immediately.

PASTA

Clockwise from top left:
Ricotta gnocchi, maccaronara, squid ink tonnarelli, cavatelli

Pasta did not figure into the early menu drafts for A16, but when we discovered a pasta cooker in the restaurant space we found, we took it as a sign. Today the pasta station has grown to be one of the busiest on the line, serving both dried and fresh pastas paired with slowly cooked ragùs or sautéed seafood.

The southern Italian regions of Campania (particularly the cities of Naples and Gragnano), Abruzzo, and Puglia are the country's best-known centers of dried pasta production. The manufacture of dried pastas in Naples dates back to the Renaissance. By the eighteenth century, the industry had become an important part of the local economy, supplying the famine-prone city with a shelf-stable foodstuff. In hard times, pasta was served simply boiled, and when fortunes improved, pasta remained on the menu, dressed up with vegetables, fish, or meat.

Northern Italy is celebrated for its fresh pastas, particularly its ribbonlike tagliatelle, but cooks in the south also make some intriguing fresh pastas. The primary difference between the two styles is the amount of egg used. Frugal southern Italian cooks have traditionally saved eggs, a prized source of protein, to feature in other dishes, preferring to make pasta with mostly water and flour. In keeping with the southern practice of using a smaller measure of egg, we make the dough for the soft, chewy *maccaronara* with only four eggs per four-pound batch. In northern Italy, a cook would easily use more than twice as many eggs for a similar amount of dough.

No matter how much I like a particular sauce, I have to remind myself that it plays a supporting role to the pasta. The shapes and compositions of different pastas—their "cling factor" in particular—determine the sauce that accompany them. *Cavatelli*, a short fresh pasta that resembles curled gnocchi, grabs onto our *ragù bianco*, while *bucatini*, a long, hollow noodle, sops up the olive oil and garlic when tossed with oven-dried tomatoes. It is particularly important to consider the surface texture when purchasing dried pastas. Pastas made by extruding the dough through bronze dies, such as those produced by Rustichella d'Abruzzo, have porous surfaces that absorb sauces easily. Cheap dried pastas extruded through Teflon dies have slick surfaces that don't carry sauces as well.

FRESH PASTA

On days when *maccaronara* is on the prep list, our morning prep cook gets an early start, setting up a large portion of the kitchen for pasta production. First, he mixes the dough in the large Hobart mixer, pinching it now and again to assess its moisture content. He then lets the dough rest to develop gluten, during which time it softens notably. After the dough has rested, he rolls it into resilient sheets with the pasta machine, and then he sends the sheets through the machine's cutter attachment, and the sheets fall into noodles. Finally, he curls equal portions of the noodles into nests around the palm of his hand, lines them up on a baking sheet lightly dusted with flour, and freezes them to await dinner service.

As with any craft, it takes time to develop a feel for the dough, and a knack for operating the pasta machine. But the results are satisfying, particularly when making pasta that is rarely seen outside of Campania. Making the white, chewy *maccaronara* noodles at home is a way to extend Campanian handcrafted tradition to your kitchen. While skinny *tonnarelli* made with squid ink is a popular pasta in Abruzzo, it is often made throughout the south, with and without squid ink. Our short pastas, the ricotta gnocchi and the *cavatelli*, are also unique and very different from each other. While the gnocchi strives for lightness, the *cavatelli* is a dense, chewy pasta.

Each pasta has its own flavor characteristics and method of preparation. Pasta machines, particularly those such as KitchenAid attachments that don't require hand cranking, have made it easier to make fresh pasta noodles. I recommend using them for our *maccaronara* and *tonnarelli* recipes. *Cavatelli* and ricotta gnocchi require only your hands and a bit of patience.

We often start a pasta dough with less flour than we will ultimately need to complete the dough. That's because it is easier to add flour to a pasta dough than it is to add water. So, if the dough you are working with feels wet, just mix in a little more flour. Freezing fresh pastas on a baking sheet protects their shape from softening before they are cooked. This is especially true for softer pastas such as *maccaronara* and gnocchi. Because *cavatelli* are a little more durable, you can put them on a baking sheet, cover the sheet with a kitchen towel, and leave them on a kitchen counter for a few hours. To lighten your workload the day you plan to serve fresh pasta, make the pasta the day before and freeze it on a baking sheet, separating the layers with parchment paper. Or, for longer storage, freeze the pasta on a baking sheet as directed, then transfer it to resealable plastic freezer bags and tuck the bags away in the freezer for future use. The pasta will keep for up to 3 weeks. These freezing instructions are especially handy for the *cavatelli*, *maccaronara*, and *tonnarelli* recipes, all of which make twice as much pasta as you will need for the recipes that follow.

There are times when you will be too busy to make fresh pasta. To accommodate those occasions, I have recommended dried pastas that will make fine substitutes.

COOKING PASTA

To cook the pastas in this chapter, fill a large pot with water and add 1 generous tablespoon kosher salt per gallon of water. Bring to a boil, stir in the pasta, and cook as directed in individual recipes. For dried pasta, I recommend boiling it for less time than specified on the package so the pasta can finish cooking in the sauce. Drain the pasta a minute before it is done cooking (it should still have a toothsome bite to it), reserving some of the cooking water, toss it with the sauce, and then cook the two elements together for the final minute. If the pasta seems dry, add a splash of the cooking water and continue to cook. The sauce should cling to the pasta without the pasta drowning in it.

CAVATELLI

MAKES ABOUT 2½ POUNDS

The shape of *cavatelli*—a hollow, curled pasta a little longer than gnocchi—looks trickier to make than it is. But all it requires is a cleared space on a counter or kitchen table and your fingertips. It can take a while to make a whole batch, though, so recruit a few extra hands to help if possible. It is quite all right if every piece does not look exactly the same.

6 cups "00" flour (page 79) or all-purpose flour, plus more as needed
2 teaspoons kosher salt
1 ½ cups water

In the bowl of a stand mixer fitted with the dough hook, combine the flour and the salt. On low speed, drizzle in the water and mix just until combined. Knead the dough on medium-low speed for 3 minutes. At this point, the dough should feel slightly tacky but not sticky. If the dough sticks to your fingers, add ¼ cup more flour. Continue to knead the dough for 10 to 12 minutes. At this point, the dough should feel warm and a little stiff. Wrap the dough in plastic wrap and let it rest for about 30 minutes at room temperature to allow the gluten to relax, which will make shaping the *cavatelli* easier.

After 30 minutes, the dough should feel strong but more malleable than when it was first removed from the mixer. On a lightly floured work surface, flatten the dough into a disk about ½ inch thick. Using a pizza cutter or bench scraper, cut off a thin strip of dough about the width of your index finger. Pressing down on the dough lightly with your fingertips, roll the dough back and forth into a long, slender log about ¼ inch in diameter. If you need more traction to roll out the dough, sprinkle a little water on your work surface. Cut the log crosswise into 1-inch pieces. Working with 1 piece at a time, press down on it firmly with your fingertips and drag it toward you until it curls up. It should have the imprint of 2 or 3 fingertips and be hollow in the center. Repeat with the remaining dough.

Once shaped, spread the pasta on a floured baking sheet, cover with a kitchen towel, and set aside. At this point, the pasta can be boiled or stored (left).

MACCARONARA

MAKES ABOUT 2½ POUNDS

An iconic Campanian pasta, *maccaronara* is made from a soft, stretchy dough that yields a delightfully chewy noodle. At the restaurant, we always serve it tossed with a little ragù because the simple preparation highlights its distinctive, resilient texture. Most pasta machines have settings for tagliatelle and *tonnarelli*. *Maccaronara* is somewhere in between. The pasta sheets for it are thicker than the sheets for tagliatelle, but the noodle is narrower, though not as narrow as *tonnarelli*. Unless you have a model that allows for cutting the ⅛-inch-wide noodles described in the recipe, I suggest you cut the noodles by hand.

6 cups "00" flour (page 79) or all-purpose flour, plus more as needed
2 teaspoons kosher salt
1½ cups water
1 egg, lightly beaten

In the bowl of a stand mixer fitted with the dough hook, combine the flour and salt. On low speed, drizzle in the water and egg and mix just until combined. Knead on medium-low speed for 3 minutes. Check the consistency of the dough. It should feel slightly tacky but not sticky. If the dough sticks to your fingers, add ¼ cup more flour. Continue to knead the dough for 10 minutes to build up its strength. At this point, the dough should feel warm and a little stiff, yet softer than a pasta dough made with semolina (such as *tonnarelli*). If it is very soft and feels more like a pizza or bread dough, add more flour and continue to knead. Divide the dough into 4 equal pieces, wrap each piece tightly in plastic wrap, and let rest for about 30 minutes. The dough will soften as it rests.

Clear off a large area of the counter or kitchen table and prepare a well-floured work surface. If using a hand-cranked pasta machine, attach it to the counter or table next to the floured surface, and fit the machine with the rollers on the widest setting (these are smooth rollers that will transform the dough into long, thin strips for cutting later). If using

an attachment for a stand mixer, set the machine up to the side of the work surface and attach the rollers.

Unwrap a piece of the dough and transfer it to the work surface. With a rolling pin, flatten the dough into a rectangle ½ inch thick and no wider than will fit comfortably through the rollers (typically less than 6 inches wide). Guide the dough through the first setting of the pasta machine, then return it to the work surface and dust it lightly with flour. Fold the dough strip into thirds (like a business letter), flatten with the rolling pin, and send the piece through the machine again on the first setting. Repeat two more times, then switch to the next narrower setting. Guide the dough through the second setting twice, dusting with flour after each pass, and then switch to the next narrower setting and guide the dough through the third setting twice. The dough will become longer, thinner, and more even with each pass. If at any point it becomes too long to handle easily, cut it in half. Continue to pass the dough through the rollers, adjusting to narrower settings, until the dough is about ⅛ inch thick.

Cut the pasta sheet(s) into 10-inch-long rectangles while retaining its width (about 5 inches). Sprinkle each piece generously with flour, and then stack the rectangles to clear space so you can work. Repeat with the remaining dough pieces.

Select a baking sheet or pan that will fit in your freezer and line it with parchment paper or dust with flour. To cut the dough sheets into noodles, starting from a narrow end, roll up a rectangle into a cylinder. Then, using a very sharp knife, cut the cylinder crosswise into ⅛-inch-wide strips to create noodles 10 inches long and ⅛ inch wide. Dredge the noodles through flour so they don't stick together, divide into 4-ounce portions, and curl each portion around your fingers to form a nest. Place the noodle nests on the prepared pan and repeat with the remaining rectangles. At this point, the noodles can be boiled or stored (page 142).

SQUID INK TONNARELLI

··

MAKES ABOUT 2½ POUNDS

Tonnarelli are fine, square-cut noodles from Abruzzo, usually cut on the narrowest setting on a home pasta machine. We serve them frequently in the summer, adding squid ink to the dough to give the noodles a striking color and a briny flavor. While we buy large frozen blocks of squid ink, a little goes a long way, and it's unlikely that you'd want to buy the same quantity. Instead, call your local fishmonger. Some sell squid ink in frozen, 1-ounce portions. Italian or Spanish specialty stores often carry the ink in packets containing about 1 tablespoon of the ink (see Resources); four of those packets should give you the amount you need for this recipe. As you work with the dough, you will discover that the ink temporarily stains your hands. You can wear gloves to avoid this, although the ink is harmless. The dough itself is firm and dry, making it a challenge to knead it by hand or in a stand mixer. But those same qualities make it easy to roll out on a pasta machine and give the *tonnarelli* a chewy, toothsome texture.

2 ounces squid ink

1⅔ cups water

3 cups semolina flour

2 cups "00" flour (page 79) or all-purpose flour, plus more as needed

1 tablespoon kosher salt

In a small bowl, dissolve the squid ink in the water and set aside.

In the bowl of a stand mixer fitted with the dough hook, combine the semolina and "00" flours and salt. On low speed, drizzle in the squid ink mixture and mix just until combined. Knead on medium-low speed for 3 minutes. Check the consistency of the dough. If it feels soft, add a little more "00" flour; if it is very dry, drizzle in 1 tablespoon of water. Continue to knead for 1 minute to incorporate the additional flour or water. Halve the dough and knead each half for 10 minutes to build up its strength. At this point, the dough should feel warm and stiff. If the dough is sticky and soft, add a little more "00" flour and continue to knead

until the flour is incorporated. Divide each dough half into 3 equal pieces, wrap each piece tightly in plastic wrap, and let rest for about 30 minutes. The dough will soften as it rests.

Clear off a large part of the counter or kitchen table and prepare a well-floured work surface. If using a hand-cranked pasta machine, attach it to the counter or table next to the floured surface, and fit the machine with the rollers on the widest setting (these are smooth rollers that will transform the dough into long, thin strips for cutting later). If using an attachment for a stand mixer, set the machine up to the side of the work surface and attach the rollers.

continued

Unwrap a piece of the dough and transfer it to the work surface. With a rolling pin, flatten the dough into a rectangle ½ inch thick and no wider than will fit comfortably through the rollers (typically less than 6 inches wide). Guide the dough through the first setting of the pasta machine, then return it to the work surface and dust it lightly with flour. Fold the dough strip into thirds (like a business letter), flatten with the rolling pin, and send the piece through the machine again on the first setting. Repeat two more times, then switch to the next narrower setting. Guide the dough through the second setting twice, dusting with flour after each pass, and then switch to the next narrower setting and guide the dough through the third setting twice. Switch to the next narrower setting and pass the dough through the fourth setting twice. The dough will become longer, thinner, and more even with each pass. If at any point it becomes too long to handle easily, cut it in half. Continue to pass the dough through the rollers, adjusting to narrower settings, until the dough is about 1/16 inch thick.

Cut the pasta sheet(s) into 12-inch rectangles while retaining its width (about 5 inches wide). Sprinkle each piece generously with flour, and then stack the rectangles to clear space so you can work. Repeat with the remaining dough pieces.

Select a baking sheet or pan that will fit in your freezer and line it with parchment paper or dust with flour. To cut the dough sheets into noodles, fit the pasta machine with the 1/16-inch cutters (these might be called *tonnarelli*, depending on the manufacturer). One at a time, slowly feed the sheets through the cutter. As the noodles emerge from the machine, grasp them with your hands and dredge them through flour so they don't stick together. Divide the noodles into 3-ounce portions, and curl each portion around your fingers to form a nest. Place the noodle nests on the prepared pan and repeat with the remaining rectangles. At this point, the noodles can be boiled or stored (page 142).

RICOTTA GNOCCHI

MAKES 4 (4-OUNCE) SERVINGS OR 8 (2-OUNCE) SERVINGS

These featherlight gnocchi were the first pasta that our chef de cuisine, Liza Shaw, added to the A16 menu. They appropriately debuted on our annual celebration of Italy's Festa della Donna (Woman's Day), which falls on March 8, and quickly became a menu favorite.

When making gnocchi, be patient; it takes time to develop a feel for the dough. The key to making light ricotta gnocchi is to start with a good-quality fresh ricotta that has been drained of excess water and whey. Too much liquid means you have to use a heavier hand with flour, which makes denser gnocchi. Even though I have called for one beaten egg in this recipe, I use only half of it and save the other half in case the dough needs more strength. These gnocchi freeze well, and they are great to have on hand for a quick and easy meal. Tossed simply in pesto, they make a delicious weekday meal.

2 cups fresh ricotta, well drained (page 76)
2 tablespoons olive oil
Kosher salt
1 egg yolk
1 egg, lightly beaten
1 cup "00" flour (page 79) or all-purpose flour,
　plus more as needed
About ½ cup semolina flour, plus more as needed

In the bowl of a stand mixer fitted with the whisk attachment, combine the ricotta, olive oil, and a couple of pinches of salt (about ¾ teaspoon). Taste the mixture. The ricotta should taste salty; it will mellow once it is mixed with the egg and flour. On medium-high speed, mix the ricotta for about 2 minutes, or until the curds have just started to break up and the mixture looks smooth. Whisk in the egg yolk and half of the beaten egg and mix for about 1 minute more, or until the batter is just combined.

Clear off a large part of the counter or kitchen table for a work surface and coat with ½ cup of the "00" flour. Spread the ricotta batter on top, and cover with most of the remaining flour. Using a bench scraper, fold the flour into the ricotta mixture gently by cutting through the ricotta and folding it over. Continue to mix in this manner just until the dough begins to come together. Be careful not to overwork the dough, or the gnocchi will be tough. At this point, the dough should feel tacky to the touch, but it should not stick to your fingers. If it does, add more flour and knead the dough until it stays together. The dough is ready if it springs back slightly when touched but still feels soft.

To test the dough for seasoning and structure, bring a small pot of salted water to a boil. Pinch off a few 1-inch-long and ½-inch-wide pieces of the dough, drop them into the boiling water, and boil for 3 minutes after the gnocchi begin to float. Taste the sample gnocchi for salt and adjust the batter if necessary before shaping the rest of the gnocchi. If the gnocchi fall apart, mix the remaining half of the beaten egg into the remaining dough as a binder.

Lightly dust the work surface with "00" flour and divide the dough into 6 equal pieces. Pressing down lightly with your fingertips, roll the dough back and forth into a long, slender log, gently pulling the dough outward to stretch it as you would for a baguette. Continue until the piece is about ½ inch in diameter and 18 inches long. Repeat with the remaining pieces.

Select a baking sheet or pan that will fit in your freezer and coat it with the semolina flour. Roll the logs in the semolina and then return them to the work surface. Cut the logs into 1-inch-long pieces (a pizza cutter works well) and dust the pieces with semolina to prevent them from sticking together. Arrange the gnocchi in a single layer on the prepared pan. At this point, the gnocchi can be boiled or stored (page 142).

MACCARONARA WITH RAGÙ ALLA NAPOLETANA AND RICOTTA SALATA

PAIR WITH AGLIANICO (CAMPANIA)
SERVES 4 AS A MAIN COURSE, OR 6 AS A FIRST COURSE

It is with trepidation that I share a recipe for ragù, something so connected to southern Italian family traditions that no single right way to prepare it exists. In general, what separates a Neapolitan ragù from northern Italy's bolognese, with which it is so often compared, is that Campanian cooks serve the braised meat as a separate course, helping to extend one dish into two courses.

But we depart from Campanian tradition as well. We braise different meats, we use olive oil rather than lard, and we don't serve the meat as a main course because it doesn't work well in a restaurant setting. We do, however, save the braised shredded shoulder meat and belly for our Pork and Tomato Soffritto (page 229).

We like to use pig's feet (trotters) in the ragù because the skin and bones add body to the sauce, as does the prosciutto. Trotters can be hard to find, but pork belly makes a fine substitute. If you are saving the braised meat for Pork and Tomato Soffritto, or if you use some in the sauce, discard the remaining prosciutto; the dry and salty meat will become drier and saltier as it braises.

This recipe yields about 5 cups sauce, enough for several batches of pasta. It also pairs well with *cavatelli* and provides a rich accompaniment to chestnut polenta and eggs (page 150).

RAGÙ ALLA NAPOLETANA

1 pound boneless pork shoulder, cut into large chunks
1 pig's trotter, left whole, or 8 ounces pork belly, cut into chunks
Kosher salt
½ cup extra virgin olive oil
1 red onion, halved
2 (28-ounce) cans San Marzano tomatoes with juices
8 ounces prosciutto end pieces with skin intact, cut into large chunks

Kosher salt
½ recipe maccaronara (page 144)
Handful of fresh basil leaves
Extra virgin olive oil
Block of Ricotta Salata (page 76) for grating

To make the ragù, season the pork shoulder and pig's trotter with salt and refrigerate overnight.

In a Dutch oven or other large, heavy-bottomed pot, heat the olive oil over medium-low heat. Add the onion halves, cut sides down, and brown gently, ensuring the onion does not stick to the bottom of the pot or burn. Continue to cook the onion halves for about 20 minutes, or until they are deep golden brown. Remove the onion and save for another use or discard. (The onion is used here only to flavor the oil.)

Place the canned tomatoes and their juices in a large bowl, season with a few pinches of salt, and squeeze into chunks with your hands. Add the tomatoes, pork shoulder, pig's trotter, and prosciutto to the pot and bring to a boil, stirring frequently to prevent the tomatoes from burning. Adjust the heat to a very low simmer—you want the occasional bubble to rise to the surface—and cook, uncovered, at a lazy simmer for about 4 hours, or until the meat has given all of its richness to the sauce. As the sauce cooks, a lot of fat will rise to the surface, but do not skim it off. The fat is what will give the sauce a rich, velvety texture. Remove from the heat and let the meat cool in the sauce to room temperature.

Remove the meat from the sauce and set aside for use in another preparation. Taste the ragù and add more salt if needed. If you want a more uniform texture, pass the sauce through the medium disk of a food mill. You should have about 5 cups. Set aside 1½ cups for finishing the pasta, and store the remainder in a tightly covered container in the refrigerator for up to 1 week or in the freezer for up to 3 months.

Bring a large pot of salted water to a boil. Add the pasta and cook for about 5 minutes (longer than you think for fresh pasta), or until the raw bite is gone.

Meanwhile, put the 1½ cups ragù in a small saucepan, add the basil and a splash of water, and bring to a simmer.

When the pasta is ready, drain it, reserving 1 cup of the cooking water, and return the pasta to the large pot over medium heat. Add the ragù to the pasta and toss well, adding some of the reserved pasta water if needed to loosen the sauce. Cook, stirring occasionally, for about 1 minute, or until the sauce loosely clings to the noodles. Taste for seasoning, adding more salt if needed.

Serve the pasta in a warmed large bowl, family style. Drizzle with olive oil, grate Ricotta Salata over the top to finish, and serve immediately.

CHESTNUT POLENTA WITH RAGÙ ALLA NAPOLETANA, EGGS, AND RICOTTA SALATA

PAIR WITH AGLIANICO (CAMPANIA)
SERVES 4 AS A MAIN COURSE, OR 6 AS A FIRST COURSE

Eggs poached in a slow-cooked ragù with smoky chestnut polenta is deliciously decadent. Italians call this preparation *uova al purgatorio*, or "egg in purgatory," but there is nothing halfway about it. We use coarse-ground polenta from Anson Mills, an artisanal producer in Columbia, South Carolina. It has a toothsome texture and pronounced corn flavor. The only drawback is that it takes more than twice as long to cook as most polentas. Since Anson polenta is only available in select markets (and online; see Resources), we have called for standard coarse-grind polenta in this recipe. If you use Anson's version, follow the instructions on the package, then add the chestnut flour for the last 5 minutes of cooking.

1 cup coarse-grind polenta
4½ cups water
1 teaspoon kosher salt
¼ cup chestnut flour (page 79)
2 cups ragù alla napoletana (page 148)
Handful of fresh basil leaves
4 to 6 eggs
Extra virgin olive oil
Block of Ricotta Salata (page 76) for grating

To cook the polenta, combine the polenta, 4 cups of the water, and the salt in a medium pot. Bring to a simmer and whisk the polenta continuously for a few minutes until the mixture begins to come together and has returned to a boil. Adjust the heat to a slow simmer, switch to a wooden spoon, and stir the polenta frequently for about 30 minutes, or until the grains have lost their raw bite. If the mixture has become thick but the grains of polenta still taste raw, add a little more water and continue to cook until the raw texture disappears. Once the polenta is cooked, stir in the chestnut flour and cook for a few minutes more. Remove from the heat, cover, and keep warm.

In a large sauté pan, combine the ragù, basil, and the remaining ½ cup water and bring to a simmer over medium heat. Crack the eggs and distribute them evenly on top of the ragù. Give the pan a shake to ensure the eggs are not sticking to the bottom, cover with a lid, and cook for about 10 minutes, or until the eggs have set.

Divide the polenta among warmed bowls. Scoop up an egg with some ragù and place on top of each serving of polenta. Drizzle the eggs with olive oil and grate Ricotta Salata over the top to finish. Serve immediately.

CAVATELLI WITH RAGÙ BIANCO, WILD MUSHROOMS, AND PECORINO

PAIR WITH CASAVECCHIA (CAMPANIA)
SERVES 4 AS A MAIN COURSE, OR 6 AS A FIRST COURSE

This ragù is completely different from our *ragù alla napoletana*, and we often have both on our menu. It does not cook as long, though it still needs ample time to braise for the flavors to meld. You will need a meat grinder to grind the chicken thighs. Or, you might find the meat already ground at your butcher shop, or ask you butcher to grind the meat to order. If you buy ground thigh meat, mince the livers and the pancetta and mix them into the thigh meat. You can use 12 ounces dried *orecchiette* or penne in place of the *cavatelli*.

1 pound boneless, skinless chicken thighs, trimmed of
    sinew and cut into ½-inch cubes
4 ounces chicken livers, rinsed, patted dry, any
    discolored areas trimmed, and cut into small chunks
2 ounces pancetta, cut into small pieces
1 teaspoon salt
Extra virgin olive oil
1 red onion, diced
½ fennel bulb, cored and diced
½ cup dry white wine
½ cup prosciutto brodo (page 75) or water
1 bay leaf
1 sprig rosemary
4 ounces chanterelle or porcini mushrooms, cleaned
    and quartered
½ recipe cavatelli (page 143)
Block of aged pecorino for grating

To grind the chicken, first chill the grinder, its coarse plate, and a bowl in the freezer for 15 minutes. Place the chicken, livers, and pancetta in another bowl and season with salt. Set up the grinder and pass the meats through the grinder into the chilled bowl.

In a pot, heat 2 tablespoons olive oil over medium-low heat. Add the onion and fennel and sweat, stirring occasionally, for about 5 minutes, or until the vegetables are soft and translucent. Stir in the ground meat mixture and continue to cook over medium heat, stirring often, for about 10 minutes, or until the meat mixture is cooked through. Pour in the wine and deglaze the pan, dislodging any browned bits from the bottom, and cook for about 5 minutes, or until the wine has evaporated.

Stir in the *brodo*, bring to a simmer, and add the bay leaf and rosemary. Adjust the heat to low and cook, stirring often, for 40 to 60 minutes, or until the fat has been rendered from the pancetta and the flavors have melded together. If the mixture becomes dry as it simmers, add a little water to the pot and continue to simmer. Taste for seasoning and add more salt if needed (the prosciutto *brodo* is salty, so season cautiously).

To prepare the mushrooms, heat 1 tablespoon olive oil in a large sauté pan over high heat. Add the mushrooms, season with a pinch of salt, and sauté for about 5 minutes, or until cooked through and slightly caramelized. Stir the mushrooms into the ragù.

Meanwhile, bring a large pot of salted water to a boil. Add the *cavatelli* to the boiling water and cook for about 3 minutes, or until the raw bite is gone. Drain the pasta, reserving 1 cup of the cooking water, and return the pasta to the large pot over medium heat. Add the ragù and toss well, adding some of the reserved pasta water if needed to loosen the sauce. Cook, stirring occasionally, for about 1 minute, or until the sauce loosely clings to the pasta. Taste for seasoning, adding more salt if needed.

Serve the pasta in a warmed large bowl, family style. Drizzle with olive oil, grate pecorino over the top to finish, and serve immediately.

SQUID INK TONNARELLI WITH CALAMARI, FIORELLI, TOMATOES, AND WHITE WINE

PAIR WITH GAGLIOPPO (CALABRIA)
SERVES 4 AS A MAIN COURSE, OR 6 AS A FIRST COURSE

Revelatory in its tender freshness, squid is a must-have food when traveling along the Amalfi coast or visiting the islands of Ischia or Capri. Caught earlier in the day, the squid is prepared simply, grilled and served with a lemon wedge or fried in olive oil. At A16, we like serving fresh squid with squid ink pasta because the salinity of the ink subtly enhances the flavor of the squid. Fresh squid is more tender than the cleaned, sliced squid available frozen (or thawed) at grocery stores and some fish markets. If you can find fresh, cleaned squid, it will save you time on this recipe. If you are buying fresh whole squid, allow plenty of time to clean them.

When making this recipe from start to finish (including the *tonnarelli*), it is best to make the *tonnarelli* and freeze the noodles well before you prepare the sauce. Then clean and marinate the squid in the morning of the day you plan to serve the pasta. If you are using freshly cleaned and sliced squid, you can put this dish together quickly with 12 ounces dried pasta such as *bucatini*.

4 pounds whole squid or 3 pounds cleaned squid bodies
Kosher salt
½ teaspoon dried chile flakes
½ cup extra virgin olive oil, plus more for finishing
2 cups fiorelli (page 130) or sliced squash blossoms
6 cloves garlic, smashed with the side of a knife
½ cup tomato paste
¾ cup dry white wine
½ recipe squid ink tonnarelli (page 145)

If using uncleaned whole squid, rinse the squid well. Working with 1 squid at a time, cut the tentacles from the body and set the tentacles aside. Using the blunt edge of a knife, run it from the tip of the body sac to the open end to force out the entrails and the quill and discard. If the quill remains in the body, reach inside and pull it out with your fingers. Pull off the mottled purple skin covering the body and discard. Rinse the inside of the body under cold running water and pat dry. Slice into rings and place in a bowl. If the hard beak is at the base of the tentacles, force it out with your fingers. Cut the tentacles in half lengthwise and add to the bowl with the squid rings. If using already-cleaned squid bodies, cut into narrow rings. Sprinkle about ½ teaspoon salt over the squid, and then add the chile flakes and ¼ cup of the olive oil and toss to mix. Cover and refrigerate for at least 1 hour and up to 6 hours. Remove from the refrigerator and bring to room temperature before you begin cooking the sauce.

Bring a large pot of salted water to a boil. Add the *fiorelli* and cook for 1 minute, or until soft. Using a slotted spoon or a skimmer, remove the *fiorelli* and set aside. Return to a boil. You will use this water to cook the pasta.

To make the sauce, in a large sauté pan, heat the remaining ¼ cup olive oil over medium heat. Add the garlic and cook for about 3 minutes, or until soft and golden. Stir in the tomato paste and cook, stirring continuously, for about 5 minutes, or until the paste has turned from bright red to brick red. Pour in the wine and deglaze the pan, dislodging any browned bits from the bottom, and cook for about 1 minute, or until the wine has almost evaporated. Adjust the heat to low while the pasta cooks. If at any point the sauce reduces too much and the tomato paste starts to stick to the bottom of the pan, add some water to loosen.

Add the pasta to the boiling water and cook for 2 to 3 minutes, or until the raw bite is gone. At about the same time, stir the squid and *fiorelli* into the sauce.

When the pasta is ready, drain it, reserving about 1 cup of the cooking water, and return the pasta to the large pot over medium heat. Add the sauce and stir well, adding the reserved pasta water if needed to loosen the sauce. Cook, stirring occasionally, for about 1 minute, or until the squid cooks through and the sauce loosely clings to the noodles.

Taste for seasoning and adjust with salt if needed. Serve the pasta in a warmed large bowl, family style. Drizzle with olive oil to finish and serve immediately.

RICOTTA GNOCCHI IN BRODO WITH PEAS AND SPICY PORK MEATBALLS

PAIR WITH NERO DI TROIA (PUGLIA)
SERVES 4 AS A MAIN COURSE, OR 6 AS A FIRST COURSE

Juxtaposing delicate ricotta gnocchi, pea shoots, and peas with hearty meatballs and chile oil, this dish is our tribute to spring. Pea shoots are the delicate new growth—young leaves and thin, curly shoots—of the snow pea plant. They are sold seasonally at farmers' markets and at Asian produce stores. If you can't find them, just double the amount of peas.

Before you begin making the meatballs, read through Meatballs 101 on page 213.

MEATBALLS
1 pound boneless pork shoulder, cut into 1-inch cubes and ground in a meat grinder or finely chopped in a food processor
4 ounces fatback, cut into 1-inch cubes and ground in a meat grinder or chilled for 15 minutes in the freezer and then finely chopped in a food processor
2 eggs, lightly beaten
½ cup fresh bread crumbs (page 74)
2 Calabrian chiles (page 76), stemmed and minced
2 teaspoons kosher salt

SAUCE
Kosher salt
1 pound English peas in the pod, shelled (about 1 cup)
12 ounces pea shoots (about 2 cups)
1 recipe ricotta gnocchi (page 147)
1½ cups cheese brodo (page 74)
1 cup water
¼ cup Calabrian chile oil (page 77)

Preheat the oven to 400°F. Coat 2 rimmed baking sheets with olive oil.

To make the meatballs, in a large bowl, combine the pork shoulder, fatback, eggs, bread crumbs, chiles, and salt and mix with your hands just until all of the ingredients are evenly distributed. Form the mixture into balls each weighing about 1 ounce and ½ inch in diameter, and place on the prepared baking sheets.

Bake the meatballs for 18 to 20 minutes, or until lightly browned and cooked through. Remove from the oven.

To make the sauce, bring a large pot of salted water to a boil. Add the peas and blanch for about 1 minute or until the peas float to the top of the water. Using a wire skimmer, remove the peas from the water and shock immediately in ice water. Drain well and set aside.

Separate the very young and tender pea shoots from the more mature, tougher, thicker shoots and larger leaves. When the water returns to a boil, add the more mature shoots and blanch for 1 minute. Using a wire skimmer, remove the shoots and shock immediately in ice water. Blanch the young pea shoots for about 30 seconds. Using the skimmer, remove the shoots and shock immediately in ice water.

Return the water to a boil. Add the gnocchi, adjust the heat to maintain the water at a simmer, and cook for about 1 minute after the gnocchi float.

Meanwhile, in a large pot, combine the brodo and water over medium-high heat and add the meatballs, peas, and pea shoots.

When the gnocchi are ready, drain, reserving about 1 cup of the cooking water. Add the gnocchi to the pot holding the brodo mixture and simmer for about 30 seconds to meld together the flavors. This pasta is properly served with broth in the bottom of the bowl; it is not meant to be dry. Add as much of the reserved cooking water (or water from the tap if you need additional water) as needed until the broth is the correct consistency. Taste for seasoning, adding more salt if needed.

Divide the gnocchi and meatballs evenly among warmed bowls. Spoon the sauce over the top. Finish each bowl with a drizzle of chile oil and serve immediately.

PACCHERI WITH FRESH SARDINES, OLIVES, CAPERS, GARLIC, AND BREAD CRUMBS

PAIR WITH NERELLO MASCALESE (SICILY)
SERVES 4 AS A MAIN COURSE, OR 6 AS A FIRST COURSE

This is an eccentric dried pasta, not so much for its shape as for its size. *Paccheri* are large tubes—like oversized rigatoni—named for the supposed slap they make when pierced with a fork. More than 2 inches long and 1 inch wide when dry, they are great for stuffing and baking but more often are boiled and tossed with a sauce. When cooked with fresh sardines, olives, capers, and garlic, thick, chewy *paccheri* absorb and mellow the assertive Mediterranean flavors. If you can't find *paccheri*, smaller tube pastas, such as penne or rigatoni, can be used their place.

1½ pounds fresh sardines, scaled and gutted
Kosher salt
½ cup black olives, pitted
½ cup salt-packed capers, soaked (page 84)
Extra virgin olive oil
2 cloves garlic, smashed with the side of a knife
¼ teaspoon dried chile flakes
½ cup dry white wine
1 cup canned San Marzano tomatoes with juices, broken up into chunks with your hands or the back of a wooden spoon
¼ cup fresh bread crumbs, toasted (page 74)
1 pound paccheri
¼ bunch fresh flat-leaf parsley, coarsely chopped (about ⅔ cup)

If the fresh sardines you buy have not been scaled or gutted, it is easy to do. First, using a sharp paring knife, make a slit along the belly of the fish. Pry the fish open and scrape and rinse out its innards. Next, lay the fish, flesh side down, on a work surface. Grasping the tail and working from tail to head, drag the blunt edge of the knife the length of the fish to remove the scales. Rinse the fish well, pat dry, and repeat with the remaining fish, then clean your work surface before proceeding.

Working with 1 fish at a time, remove the head. Gently pry open the belly to expose its backbone. Place the fish, skin side up, on a work surface and run the palm of your hand along the spine to loosen it, then trim off the back fin. Turn the sardine over. Starting at the head end, pull the backbone toward the tail in a single motion. The tail should come off with the backbone. Rinse the sardine under cold running water, checking for any loose bones, and then pat dry. Repeat with the remaining fish. Divide the sardines into fillets, and cut the fillets crosswise into 1-inch pieces. Lay the sardine pieces in a single layer on a baking sheet, season with salt, and set aside.

In a food processor, combine the olives and capers and pulse until coarsely combined. In a large sauté pan, heat about ¼ cup olive oil over medium heat. Add the garlic and cook, stirring occasionally, for about 3 minutes, or until it begins to soften. Stir in the chile flakes, followed by the olive-caper mixture, and continue to cook for 1 minute. Pour in the wine and deglaze the pan, dislodging any browned bits from the bottom, and cook for about 2 minutes, or until the wine has evaporated. Stir in the tomatoes and their juices and cook for about 8 minutes, or until the tomato liquid is reduced by half. Taste for seasoning and cautiously adjust with more salt if needed (the capers and olives are salty). Set the sauce aside and keep warm.

Meanwhile, in a small sauté pan, heat 1 tablespoon olive oil over medium heat. Stir in the bread crumbs and sauté, stirring often, for about 1 minute, or until the bread crumbs begin to brown and crisp. Remove from the heat and transfer the bread crumbs to a plate lined with a paper towel. Set aside.

Bring a large pot of salted water to a boil. Add the pasta and cook for about 1 minute less than specified on the package.

When the pasta is about 1 minute from being ready, bring the sauce to a simmer over medium heat. Add the sardines and parsley and continue to simmer.

When the pasta is ready, drain it, reserving 1 cup of the cooking water, and return the pasta to the large pot over medium heat. Add the sauce and toss well, adding some of the reserved pasta water if needed to loosen the sauce. Cook over medium heat, stirring occasionally, for about 1 minute. The sauce should be loose enough to barely pool at the bottom of the pot, but not too watery. The pasta tubes will have partially collapsed and will look like broad, flat noodles. Taste for seasoning, adding more salt if needed.

Serve the pasta in a warmed large bowl, family style. Drizzle with olive oil, top with the fried bread crumbs, and serve immediately.

ORECCHIETTE WITH RAPINI, CALABRIAN CHILES, AND PECORINO

PAIR WITH NEGROAMARO (PUGLIA)
SERVES 4 AS A MAIN COURSE, OR 6 AS A FIRST COURSE

Round, concave orecchiette (little ears) nicely complement chunky pasta sauces, such as this one featuring rapini. In the world of pasta, homemade orecchiette, which are always fashioned by hand, are not difficult to shape. Rosanna Petrozziello, a busy mom who runs I Favati winery in Avellino, makes them and then leaves the pasta to dry a bit on semolina-dusted baking sheets while she prepares the rest of her meal. But you also can buy high-quality dried orecchiette, which guarantees you the al dente bite that comes with dried pasta. You will notice we have ignored the Italian "no cheese with fish" rule in this recipe. We use a little anchovy because it gives the rapini a depth of flavor, but it is subtle enough not to interfere with the pecorino. And if you can't find rapini, you can make this pasta with a head of broccoli. Cut the top into small, uniform florets, peel the tough skin from the stem and slice it into thin rounds, and then blanch the broccoli as directed for the rapini.

Kosher salt
Extra virgin olive oil
2 cloves garlic, smashed with the side of a knife
2 to 3 Calabrian chiles (page 76), stemmed and minced
1 salt-packed anchovy fillet, soaked (page 84) and then minced (optional)
1½ pounds rapini, coarsely chopped
1 cup water
12 ounces orecchiette
Block of aged pecorino for grating

In a large sauté pan, heat a generous few tablespoons of olive oil over medium heat. Add the garlic and cook, stirring occasionally, for about 3 minutes, or until softened. Stir in the chiles, anchovy, rapini, and water and bring to a simmer. Braise, stirring occasionally, for 20 minutes, or until the rapini is very tender.

Meanwhile, bring a large pot of salted water to a boil. Add the pasta and cook for about 1 minute less than specified on the package. If the rapini starts to dry out while the pasta is cooking, add a few tablespoons of pasta cooking water to the pan.

Drain the pasta, reserving about 1 cup of the cooking water, and return the pasta to the large pot over medium heat. Add the sauce to the pasta and toss well, adding some of the reserved pasta water if needed to loosen the sauce. Cook, stirring occasionally, for about 1 minute, or until the sauce is well integrated with the pasta. Taste for seasoning, adding more salt if needed.

Serve the pasta in a warmed large bowl, family style. Drizzle with olive oil, grate pecorino over the top to finish, and serve at once.

BUCATINI WITH FAVA BEANS AND PANCETTA

PAIR WITH PIEDIROSSO (CAMPANIA)
SERVES 4 AS A MAIN COURSE, OR 6 AS A FIRST COURSE

When the first crop of fava beans arrives through our front door in late spring, I make this simple pasta. Small and tender, early-season favas are perfect for this dish, with long, hollow *bucatini*, pepper, pancetta, and cheese playing supporting roles.

Kosher salt
2 pounds fava beans in the pod, shelled (about 2 cups)
Extra virgin olive oil
½ red onion, diced
4 ounces pancetta, finely diced
12 ounces bucatini
Freshly ground black pepper
Block of aged pecorino for grating

Bring a large pot of salted water to a boil. Add the fava beans and blanch for about 1 minute. If the fava beans are older and not as tender, they may require a minute more. Using a large skimmer or tongs, remove the fava beans from the water and shock immediately in ice water until cool. Drain again and peel off the tough outer skins. Set aside. Add more water to the pot if the water level has dropped and return to a boil. You will use this water to cook the pasta.

Meanwhile, heat about 1 tablespoon olive oil in a large sauté pan over medium heat. Add the onion and sweat, stirring occasionally, for about 3 minutes, or until translucent and soft. Stir in the pancetta and cook, stirring occasionally, 4 minutes, or until it renders its fat and is crisp.

Add the pasta to the boiling water and cook for about 1 minute less than specified on the package.

About 1 minute or so before the pasta is ready, add the fava beans to the sauté pan and ladle in about ½ cup of the pasta cooking water. Add a couple of generous pinches of black pepper and continue to simmer over low heat.

Drain the pasta, reserving about 1 cup of the cooking water, and return the pasta to the large pot over medium heat. Add the sauce to the pasta along with a couple of tablespoons of olive oil and toss well, adding some of the reserved pasta water if needed to loosen the sauce. If the sauce is too loose, turn the heat up to medium-high and cook down the sauce with the pasta. It should be loose enough to barely pool at the bottom of the pot, but not too watery. Taste for seasoning, adding more salt if needed.

Serve the pasta in a warmed large bowl, family style. Drizzle with olive oil, grate pecorino over the top to finish, and serve immediately.

BUCATINI WITH OVEN-DRIED TOMATOES, GARLIC, CHILES, AND BOTTARGA

PAIR WITH CAGNULARI (SARDINIA)
SERVES 4 AS A MAIN COURSE, OR 6 AS A FIRST COURSE

You cannot get any closer to a southern Italian summer than cooking up this simple pasta. Drying tomatoes in salt concentrates their flavors, but you could also do this dish with a handful of fresh cherry tomatoes for a sweeter effect.

Kosher salt
Extra virgin olive oil
2 cloves garlic, smashed with the side of a knife
¼ teaspoon dried chile flakes
2 cups oven-dried tomatoes (page 86), each tomato cut into thirds
12 ounces bucatini
1-ounce piece bottarga (page 74) for grating

Bring a large pot of salted water to a boil for the pasta.

Meanwhile, heat ¼ cup olive oil in a large sauté pan over medium-low heat. Add the garlic and chile flakes and sweat, stirring occasionally, for about 3 minutes, or until the garlic has softened. Stir in the tomatoes and cook for about 5 minutes, or until the tomatoes have plumped up. Taste for seasoning and add salt if needed, keeping in mind that the tomatoes are seasoned and the *bottarga* is salty, so you need to proceed cautiously.

Add the pasta to the boiling water and cook for about 1 minute less than specified on the package. Drain the pasta, reserving about 1 cup of the cooking water, and return the pasta to the large pot over medium heat. Add the sauce to the pasta along with a couple of tablespoons of olive oil and toss well, adding some of the reserved pasta water if needed to loosen the sauce. If the sauce is too loose, turn the heat up to medium-high and cook down the sauce with the pasta. It should be loose enough to barely pool at the bottom of the pot, but not too watery. Taste for seasoning, adding more salt if needed.

Serve the pasta in a warmed large bowl, family style. Grate the *bottarga* over the top to finish and serve immediately.

PENNE WITH EGGPLANT, TOMATOES, BLACK OLIVES, AND BASIL

PAIR WITH PRIMITIVO (PUGLIA)
SERVES 4 AS A MAIN COURSE, OR 6 AS A FIRST COURSE

Eggplant vies with zucchini for the distinction of Campania's most common summer vegetable, and its meaty texture is a natural for pasta. Toothsome penne tossed with chunky bits of eggplant, olives, and tomatoes is so hearty that I almost forget that this dish is vegetarian.

1 large globe eggplant (about 1 pound)
Kosher salt
Extra virgin olive oil
2 cloves garlic, smashed with the side of a knife
½ cup black olives, pitted
¼ teaspoon dried chile flakes
12 ounces penne
1 pint cherry tomatoes (about 12 ounces), halved
Handful of fresh basil leaves

Cut off the green top of the eggplant and trim both ends. Using a vegetable peeler, peel off lengthwise stripes of the skin so the finished surface is covered with alternating stripes of skin and flesh. Cut the eggplant into ½-inch cubes. Toss the cubes with about 1 tablespoon salt, place in a colander in the sink, and weight down the cubes with a heavy plate. Set aside for 20 minutes to 1 hour. This will leach out some of the water, giving the eggplant a better texture when it cooks.

Pat the eggplant dry. In a large sauté pan, heat about 2 tablespoons olive oil over high heat. Add about one-third of the eggplant, toss to coat with the oil, and cook, stirring occasionally, for about 5 minutes, or until the eggplant has browned and is nearly cooked through. Transfer the eggplant to a plate. Repeat with the remaining eggplant in 2 batches, using about 2 tablespoons oil for each batch and adding each batch to the plate.

Give the sauté pan a good wipe, return to medium heat, and add about ¼ cup olive oil. Stir in the garlic and cook, stirring occasionally, for about 3 minutes, or until softened. Stir in the eggplant, olives, and chile flakes and continue to simmer over medium heat.

Meanwhile, bring a large pot of salted water to a boil. Add the pasta to the boiling water and cook for about 1 minute less than specified on the package. When the pasta is about 2 minutes from being ready, add the tomatoes and basil to the eggplant and continue to simmer over medium heat.

When the pasta is ready, drain it, reserving 1 cup of the pasta water, return the pasta to the large pot over medium heat. Add the sauce and toss well, adding some of the reserved pasta water if needed to loosen the sauce. Cook, stirring occasionally, for about 1 minute. The sauce should be loose enough to barely pool at the bottom of the pot, but not too watery. Taste for seasoning, adding more salt if needed.

Serve the pasta in a warmed large bowl, family style. Drizzle with olive oil to finish and serve immediately.

SEAFOOD

On a given night, we have about five main courses on offer, only one of which is typically seafood. This isn't an indication of my personal bias toward meat and poultry. It is instead a reflection of the A16 itself, which cuts through the hilly, inland regions of Campania and part of Puglia. The *autostrada* runs between the ancient port cities of Naples and Bari, but the majority of its path is flanked by hill towns. The fresh squid and

octopus so frequently eaten in Naples, Ischia, and Capri were traditionally rare delicacies in the cities of Avellino and Benevento, where rabbit and lamb were more common. Even today, visitors in Naples asking for restaurants specializing in sausage and meat preparations will be directed east of the city limits and into the hills. While modern roads have made transporting fresh seafood easier, prices in southern Italy remain high for the best catch, thus limiting many preparations to special occasions.

Yet there is no denying how the proximity to the ocean has influenced southern Italian cooking. The use of *bottarga* (page 74) and preserved anchovies for seasoning dishes, by both coastal and inland cooks, is a reminder the sea is never far away. And when the A16 spills out of

Avellino toward Naples, fresh, simple seafood preparations begin to permeate restaurant menus.

To properly represent our namesake highway—and to reflect our own coastal location—I always keep one eye trained on the sea. Campanian cooking honors the notion that fresh seafood is best when prepared with just a few accent ingredients. Keeping this in mind, I carefully select the best local, sustainable seafood available (see Resources) and grill, roast, or simmer it to order, sometimes pairing it with a simple sauce or a vegetable. I frequently serve seafood in wide, shallow bowls with just its pan juices, a drizzle of good-quality olive oil, and a splash of fresh lemon juice—a simple, flavorful preparation that would be at home on any Campanian table.

GRILLED SHRIMP WITH PICKLED PEPPERS, PRESERVED MEYER LEMON, AND TOASTED ALMONDS

PAIR WITH CATARRATTO (SICILY)
SERVES 6

This bright, assertively flavored dish works well as an antipasto or main course. The sauce of pickled peppers and Meyer lemon is a versatile condiment to have on hand for both seafood and poultry dishes. And as our kitchen staff discovered, it also makes a great topping for deli sandwiches.

When buying shrimp, seek out fresh specimens with their heads attached for optimum flavor. If you cannot find fresh shrimp, look for flash-frozen head-on shrimp or headless shell-on shrimp. To prevent your dinner from slipping through the grill rack, buy medium-sized shrimp that average 16 to 20 per pound. While it is not difficult to devein shrimp, allow plenty of time for the task.

1½ pounds fresh or thawed shrimp in the shell, preferably head on (24 to 30 shrimp)

Kosher salt

1½ cups pickled peppers (page 78), coarsely chopped

1 tablespoon soaked and chopped preserved Meyer lemon rind (page 84)

½ cup extra virgin olive oil

2 tablespoons freshly squeezed lemon juice

⅔ cup natural whole almonds, toasted (page 81) and coarsely chopped

1 tablespoon chopped fresh flat-leaf parsley

1 tablespoon chopped fresh mint

In a bowl, toss the shrimp with a couple of generous pinches of kosher salt. Cover and refrigerate for at least 1 hour or up to 4 hours.

In a food processor, combine the pickled peppers and chiles and the preserved lemon and process until almost smooth. Transfer the mixture to a bowl and stir in the olive oil and lemon juice. Taste for seasoning and add salt or a splash of the pickling liquid if needed. Set aside.

Prepare a hot fire in a grill, spreading the coals evenly for direct-heat cooking.

To prepare the shrimp, peel away the middle section of the shell, leaving the head and tail segments intact, and trim off any long antennae. Make a shallow slit along the back, and lift out and discard the dark, veinlike intestinal tract.

When the fire is ready, arrange the shrimp on the grill rack and grill, turning them over once, for no more 4 minutes total, or until opaque.

Arrange the shrimp on a platter and drizzle generously with the pepper sauce. Sprinkle the almonds over the top, garnish with parsley and mint, and serve immediately.

ROASTED SARDINES WITH BREAD CRUMBS, GREEN GARLIC, AND MINT

PAIR WITH VERMENTINO (SARDINIA)
SERVES 6 AS AN ANTIPASTO, OR 4 AS A MAIN COURSE

Not only are sardines packed with flavor and easy to prepare, they are among the most sustainable species of fish. The addictive, crispy skin of these sardines, and the fresh flavors of green garlic and mint, come together for an inviting antipasto; or pair them with Roasted Potatoes and Cauliflower with Red Onion, Capers, and Chiles (page 238) for a light main course. Prepare this dish in spring, when green garlic starts to appear at farmers' markets. If you can't find green garlic, scallions make a good substitute.

12 (2-ounce) fresh sardines, scaled and gutted
Kosher salt
Extra virgin olive oil
4 stalks green garlic, trimmed and thinly sliced crosswise
½ cup coarse fresh bread crumbs, toasted (page 74)
1 tablespoon salt-packed capers, soaked (page 84) and minced
⅓ cup loosely packed fresh mint leaves, torn by hand
½ lemon

Preheat the oven to 500°F.

If the fresh sardines you buy have not been scaled or gutted, it is easy to do. First, using a sharp paring knife, make a slit along the belly of the fish. Pry the fish open and scrape and rinse out its innards. Next, lay the fish, flesh side down, on a work surface. Grasping the tail and working from tail to head, drag the blunt edge of the knife the length of the fish to remove the scales. Rinse the fish well, pat dry, and repeat with the remaining fish, then clean your work surface before proceeding.

Working with 1 fish at a time, remove the head. Gently pry open the belly to expose its backbone. Place the fish, skin side up, on a work surface and run the palm of your hand along the spine to loosen it, then trim off the back fin. Turn the sardine over. Starting at the head end, pull the backbone toward the tail in a single motion. (Part of the tail may come off with the backbone.) Rinse the sardine under cold running water, checking for any loose bones, and then pat dry. Repeat with the remaining sardines.

Arrange the butterflied sardines on a baking sheet, skin side up. Season both sides with salt, and brush both sides lightly with olive oil. Roast the sardines, skin side up, for about 5 minutes, or until they are cooked through and the skin begins to sizzle.

Meanwhile, in a small sauté pan, heat a few tablespoons olive oil over medium heat. Add the green garlic and sauté for about 1 minute, or until softened. With a slotted spoon, remove the green garlic and set aside. Over medium-low heat, replenish the sauté pan with a few additional tablespoons olive oil and sprinkle in the bread crumbs. Sauté for about 2 minutes, or until they crisp up and darken slightly. Remove from the heat, add the green garlic, stir in the capers and mint, and set aside until serving.

Transfer the sardines to a serving platter or divide among individual plates, and squeeze the lemon half over the top. Spoon the green garlic mixture over the sardines, and drizzle with olive oil to finish. Serve immediately.

SCALLOPS, SHRIMP, AND CLAMS IN ACQUA PAZZA

PAIR WITH GRECO DI TUFO (CAMPANIA)
SERVES 6

The term *acqua pazza*—"crazy water"—is catchy, enticing nearly any seafood fan to give it a try. It generally refers to water flavored with garlic, tomato, and olive oil, sometimes with a little heat from a chile, and is often used to cook whole fish. Yet variations abound. We use it to cook an assortment of shellfish for a flavorful, light main course. Serve crusty bread alongside.

¼ cup salt-packed capers, soaked (page 84)

½ cup small black olives, pitted

½ cup extra virgin olive oil

2 cloves garlic, smashed with the side of a knife

1 teaspoon dried chile flakes

2 cups dry white wine

2 cups juice and a little pulp from 2 (28-ounce) cans San Marzano tomatoes

2 cups water

2 pounds Manila clams, scrubbed and rinsed

1 pound shrimp (16 to 20), peeled and deveined

1 pound sea scallops

In a food processor, combine the capers and olives and pulse until coarsely blended. Set aside.

In a Dutch oven or other large, heavy-bottomed pot, heat the olive oil over medium heat. Add the garlic and cook, stirring occasionally, for about 3 minutes, or until it starts to soften. Add the chile flakes and wine and cook for about 10 minutes, or until the wine has evaporated. Stir in the tomato juice and cook for about 5 minutes, or until reduced by half. Add the caper mixture and water and bring to a simmer. The sauce should be the consistency of a thin tomato soup. If it looks more like a thick tomato puree, add a bit more water and taste for seasoning, adding salt if needed.

Add the clams and cover the pot tightly. Cook for 2 to 3 minutes, or until a few of the clams have opened. Uncover, stir in the shrimp and scallops, and continue to cook, uncovered, for 3 to 5 minutes more, or until all of the clams have opened. Pull out and discard any clams that did not open. Taste for seasoning and cautiously adjust with more salt if needed (the capers and olives are salty).

To serve, divide the scallops, shrimp, and clams evenly among warmed wide bowls. Ladle the cooking liquid over the top and finish with a generous drizzle of olive oil. Serve immediately.

GRILLED SWORDFISH WITH FENNEL AND TOMATO AGRODOLCE

PAIR WITH GRILLO (SICILY)
SERVES 6

Swordfish has a pleasantly acidic bite that makes it a good match with the natural sweetness of cherry tomato–fennel *agrodolce*, our summertime version of the sweet-and-sour Italian preparation made more frequently with cipollini onions. Before buying swordfish, check sources such as the Monterey Bay Seafood Watch for its sustainability status. If sustainable sources are not available, serve this *agrodolce* with grilled sausages or pork chops.

2½ pounds swordfish fillets, divided into 6 (6½-ounce) portions each about ½ inch thick

Kosher salt

½ cup extra virgin olive oil, plus more for marinating and finishing

1 red onion, diced

1 fennel bulb, cored and diced

1 teaspoon fennel seeds

5 whole allspice, coarsely crushed

¼ cup red or white wine vinegar

1 pint cherry tomatoes, stemmed

Season the fish portions evenly with a few generous pinches of salt, then coat lightly in olive oil. Cover and refrigerate for at least 1 hour or up to 4 hours.

Meanwhile, in a pot, warm the ½ cup olive oil over medium heat. Add the onion, diced fennel, fennel seeds, allspice, and a pinch of salt, adjust the heat to medium-low, and sweat gently, stirring occasionally, for about 6 minutes, or until the vegetables are tender but not browned.

Increase the heat to medium-high and deglaze the pan with the vinegar, dislodging any browned bits from the bottom. Cook for about 1 minute, or until the vinegar has evaporated. Stir in the tomatoes and cook over medium-low heat for about 2 minutes, or until the tomato skins begin to split and the tomatoes release their juices. Taste for seasoning and add salt if needed. Remove from the heat and set aside. The sauce can be served warm or at room temperature.

About 30 minutes before serving, remove the fish from the refrigerator and bring to room temperature. Prepare a hot fire in a grill, spreading the coals evenly for direct-heat cooking.

Arrange the fish pieces on the grill rack and grill, turning once, for 1 to 2 minutes on each side, or until both sides are marked by the grill with a slight char while the inside is cooked to medium, or to your liking.

Transfer the fish to a warmed platter and spoon the sauce on top of the fish and along the sides. Top with a generous drizzle of olive oil to finish and serve immediately.

BRAISED HALIBUT WITH PISTACHIOS, PRESERVED MEYER LEMON, AND CAPERS

PAIR WITH CARRICANTE (SICILY)
SERVES 6

One of my favorite simple ways to prepare firm-fleshed fish is to pair it with a mixture of nuts and herbs. Here, a paste of pistachios, preserved Meyer lemon, and parsley complements halibut, while in the next recipe a basil-almond mixture is matched with salmon. If you are fortunate enough to come across halibut cheeks, this dish is especially brilliant with them. If using halibut cheeks, remove the tough connective tissue on their underside before cooking them: slip the tip of a boning knife under the tissue—it will look similar to silver skin—and cut it off the cheek, leaving the cheek intact.

2½ pounds halibut fillet, divided into 6 (6½-ounce) portions, each about 1 inch thick
Kosher salt
1 cup unsalted shelled pistachios, lightly toasted (page 81)
1 tablespoon salt-packed capers, soaked (page 84)
2 wedges preserved Meyer lemon (page 84), pith and flesh removed, soaked, and minced
¼ teaspoon dried chile flakes
½ cup extra virgin olive oil, plus more for finishing
Leaves from ½ bunch flat-leaf parsley (about 2 cups loosely packed)
1 fresh lemon, cut into wedges

Season the fish portions evenly with a few generous pinches of salt. Cover and refrigerate for at least 1 hour or up to 4 hours.

About 30 minutes before serving, remove the fish from the refrigerator and bring to room temperature. Preheat the oven to 400°F.

Combine the pistachios, capers, preserved lemon, and chile flakes in a food processor or a mortar. Pulse a few times or crush with a pestle until coarsely blended. With the processor running, drizzle in the olive oil, or drizzle in the olive oil as you crush the ingredients with the pestle. Add the parsley and pulse a few more times or crush with the pestle just until combined. Taste for seasoning and add a pinch of salt if needed. The fish is seasoned and the preserved lemon and capers are salty, so you may not need to add any salt.

Place the fish pieces in a baking pan and divide the pistachio mixture evenly among the tops, covering each piece and pressing lightly so the topping adheres. Add enough water to the pan—about ½ cup—to come halfway up the sides of the fish, and transfer the pan to the oven. Braise the fish for 10 to 15 minutes, or until firm and just cooked through.

Using a slotted spatula, transfer the fish portions to a warmed platter. Taste the braising liquid and drizzle a few spoonfuls over the fish if desired. Finish with a generous drizzle of olive oil. Serve immediately with a side of fresh lemon wedges.

BRAISED SALMON WITH BASIL, ALMONDS, AND LEMON

PAIR WITH GAGLIOPPO (CALABRIA)
SERVES 6

The almonds and basil complement the rich pink flesh of local salmon, and also work well with similar fish such as arctic char and trout. Whole salmon sides with skin attached are often sold. While we portion our salmon ahead of time at the restaurant so we can cook it to order, you can braise a side of salmon whole, skin side down, and then portion it after it is cooked. Or, you can do as we do and remove the skin and portion it before you cook it. In either case, just be sure to remove the pin bones—or ask your fishmonger to do it for you—so your guests don't encounter them.

2½ pounds salmon fillet, whole side or divided into
   6 (6½-ounce) portions each about 1 inch thick,
   pin bones removed
Kosher salt
2 cups packed fresh basil leaves
½ cup extra virgin olive oil, plus more for finishing
½ cup whole natural almonds, lightly toasted
   (page 81) and coarsely chopped
1 lemon, cut into wedges

Season the fish with a few generous pinches of salt. Cover and refrigerate for at least 1 hour or up to 4 hours.

About 30 minutes before serving, remove the fish from the refrigerator and bring to room temperature. Preheat the oven to 400°F.

In a food processor, or in a mortar with a pestle, pulse or crush the basil until it forms a coarse paste. With the processor running, drizzle in the olive oil, or drizzle in the olive oil as you crush the ingredients with the pestle. Taste for seasoning and add a pinch salt if needed, keeping in mind the fish is seasoned.

Place the salmon in a baking pan and coat the top with the basil mixture. Add enough water to the pan—about ½ cup—to come halfway up the sides of the fish. Transfer the pan to the oven and braise the fish for about 10 minutes for portioned fish or 15 to 20 minutes for a whole side, or until done to your liking.

To serve, if using a whole side, remove it from the pan and skin and portion it. Or, using a slotted spatula, transfer the portions to a warmed platter. Taste the braising liquid and drizzle a few spoonfuls over the fish if desired. Sprinkle the almonds over the top, and finish with a generous drizzle of olive oil. Serve immediately with a side of lemon wedges.

POULTRY
AND MEAT

One of the most useful tools I have in the kitchen is a sturdy cleaver. A few gentle taps of its thick blade, followed by a forceful thwack, and I can divide a rabbit's rib cage into four pieces, portion lamb ribs, or cut through unwieldy spareribs. The cleaver's place in the kitchen, hanging from a peg on the wall, serves as a reminder of the importance of butchery. From my days in culinary school to the time I spent cooking

in Italy, I have always been drawn to butchery, striving to understand the anatomy of whole animals so that I could free myself from having to cook with prefabricated cuts. Now I pass the lessons I have learned to my staff, many of whom come to the restaurant on their days off to hone their skills, working with the whole lambs, goats, and pigs that are part of our regular deliveries.

By practicing the traditional craft of butchery, we are able to obtain superlative meat from a network of farmers and ranchers who raise animals humanely. Buying the whole animal also presents us with the creative challenge of preparing less typical cuts of meat, from tail to shank. And when we do work with more esteemed cuts, we follow the southern Italian tradition of making the most of them, whether they are the naturally tender chops and loins that we roast or the shoulder that we grind for meatballs and sausages. The term *stracotto*, "extra cooked," describes what we look for in such braised dishes as short ribs, in

which the meat is cooked long enough to coax out flavor and tenderness. Other meat, such as rabbit, benefits from quick cooking in a blast of direct heat from an open wood fire. Just as in Campania, all of our dishes are prepared simply and garnished sparingly, sometimes with nothing more than pan juices, extra virgin olive oil, or lemon.

While the raw ingredients we work with inspire our cooking, preparing the following recipes does not require a primer in butchery or a degree in animal husbandry. What the recipes require is enthusiasm, a sense of adventure, and a good butcher who can guide you through the tricky task of meat identification and acquisition. He or she will be able to special order meat that is difficult to locate, such as fresh rabbit and goat, or know someone who carries it. In Resources, we have included contact information for local and national meat purveyors to give you a start in finding products for these recipes and for the pork recipes in the following chapter.

ROASTED YOUNG CHICKEN WITH RADISHES AND SALSA VERDE

PAIR WITH CARRICANTE (SICILY)
SERVES 6

Known in France as *poussins*, young one-pound chickens are traditionally eaten in the spring. When we can get these tasty little birds, we serve them roasted with *salsa verde* and a refreshing radish salad. When we cannot get them, we use quail, which are about half the size of young chickens. The simple spice rub works equally well with a regular chicken, a Cornish hen, or a pheasant. When preparing any of these birds, season them a day or two before you cook them, first with salt, then with the spice rub. If using quail for this recipe, roast the quail for 5 minutes, rotate the baking sheets front to back, and roast for about 5 minutes more, or until the juices run clear when a thigh is pierced with a fork.

The chickens are also good grilled, so I have included grilling instructions at the end of the recipe.

3 tablespoons dried oregano
1 teaspoon aniseeds
1 teaspoon dried chile flakes
6 (1-pound) young chickens or 12 (8-ounce) quail, patted dry
Kosher salt
1 cup loosely packed fresh flat-leaf parsley leaves
½ teaspoon salt-packed capers, soaked (page 84)
½ cup fresh bread crumbs, toasted (page 74)
½ clove garlic, coarsely chopped
½ cup extra virgin olive oil
2 tablespoons freshly squeezed lemon juice
1 bunch red radishes, trimmed

In a spice grinder or in a mortar with a pestle, grind together the oregano, aniseeds, and ½ teaspoon of the chile flakes to a powder. Season the chickens' skin and cavities with about 2 tablespoons salt, followed by the spice rub. Cover and refrigerate at least overnight or up to 2 days.

Preheat the oven to 500°F. Bring the chickens to room temperature.

Meanwhile, make the *salsa verde*. In a food processor or mortar, combine the parsley, capers, bread crumbs, garlic, and the remaining ½ teaspoon chile flakes. Pulse a few times, or crush with a pestle, until coarsely blended. With the processor running, or while you continue to crush the mixture with a pestle, drizzle in the olive oil. Stir in the lemon juice and a pinch of salt. Taste for seasoning and add more lemon juice and salt if needed.

Using a mandoline or a sharp knife, carefully slice the radishes into thin slices. Toss the radishes with a pinch of salt and a couple of tablespoons of the *salsa verde*.

Roast the chickens on 2 rimmed baking sheets, rotating the pans front to back about halfway through cooking, for about 20 minutes, or until the birds are golden brown and the juices run clear when a thigh is pierced with a fork.

Serve the chickens on a warmed platter and spoon the radishes around the sides. Drizzle some of the *salsa verde* over the top of the birds. Pass the remaining sauce at the table.

continued

GRILLED YOUNG CHICKEN

....

You can grill the chickens instead of roasting them, with a few alterations to the main recipe. By searing the chickens over the hot coals and then finishing them on the cooler side of the grill, you are less likely to overcook the birds. If using quail, shorten the cooking time to 5 minutes on each side, or about 10 minutes' total cooking time.

Before seasoning the chickens, cut off the wing tips with kitchen shears or a boning knife, and then cut out the backbone. Place each chicken on the cutting board, breast side up, and press down with the palm of your hand to break the sternum. Season each side evenly with salt, followed by the spice mixture. Cover and refrigerate at least overnight or up to 2 days.

Prepare a hot fire in a grill, stacking the coals to one side so that you have two areas of heat, one with direct heat and one with indirect heat. Wipe off the excess spice rub from the chickens to prevent it from burning. Brush the chickens lightly with olive oil. Working in batches if necessary, place the chickens, skin side down, over the coals and grill for 3 to 4 minutes, or until the skin is lightly charred. Turn the birds over and continue to grill for an additional 3 to 4 minutes, or until lightly charred. Turn the birds over again and move to the cooler part of the grill. Grill over indirect heat, turning occasionally to ensure even cooking, for 7 to 10 minutes more, or until cooked through. Serve as directed for the roasted birds.

CHICKEN MEATBALLS WITH PEPERONATA

PAIR WITH NERO D'AVOLA (SICILY)
SERVES 6

The dark, tender meat of chicken thighs is the most flavorful part of the bird. We grind the thighs and form meatballs that are roasted in the oven. Unlike our Monday Meatballs (page 213), which are served in a tomato sauce, we serve the chicken meatballs plainly roasted, with *peperonata* on the side. They stay moist, especially with the addition of my secret weapon: pork fat. When peppers are out of season, serve the meatballs with Giardiniera (page 240).

Chicken thighs can be difficult to grind because they contain more sinew than, say, pork shoulder. For the best results, chill the grinder in the freezer for 15 minutes before using, and cut the thigh meat into small pieces before grinding, discarding any sinew you see. If you do not want to grind the chicken yourself, look for ground thigh meat at your butcher shop, or ask you butcher to grind both the chicken and the pork fat for you. If you are using thigh meat and pork fat that have been ground, place them in a large bowl with the spice mixture, parsley, wine, and garlic. Make your own fresh bread crumbs (page 74), add them to the bowl, and mix the ingredients with your hands just until combined. Add the eggs and proceed with the recipe. For more tips on making meatballs, see page Meatballs 101 on page 213.

Preheat the oven to 400°F. Coat 2 rimmed baking sheets with olive oil. Place a large bowl in the freezer to chill.

In a spice grinder, or using a mortar and pestle, grind together the fennel seeds and peppercorns. Combine the spices with the salt in a small bowl and set aside.

Pass the chicken through a grinder fitted with the coarse plate directly into a large, chilled bowl. Combine the spice mixture, fat, bread, parsley, and garlic. Pass the mixture through the grinder into the bowl holding the chicken. Add the wine and eggs and mix gently with your hands just until the eggs are incorporated. The mixture should feel tacky and wet. Pinch off a small nugget of the mixture, flatten it into a disk, and cook it in a small sauté pan. Taste it and adjust the seasoning of the mixture with salt if needed.

Form the mixture into 1½-inch balls each weighing about 2 ounces, and place on the prepared baking sheets.

Bake the meatballs, rotating the baking sheets front to back about halfway through cooking, for about 20 minutes, or until browned and fully cooked.

To serve, spoon the *peperonata* evenly on the bottom of a serving platter. Top with the meatballs and garnish with a generous drizzle of olive oil. Serve at once.

Extra virgin olive oil
2 teaspoons fennel seeds
1 teaspoon black peppercorns
1 tablespoon kosher salt
2 pounds boneless, skinless chicken thighs, cut into
  ½-inch cubes
6 ounces fatback, cut into ½-inch cubes
6 ounces day-old country bread, torn into chunks
1 cup loosely packed fresh flat-leaf parsley leaves,
  coarsely chopped
1 clove garlic, minced
2 tablespoons dry white wine
2 eggs, lightly beaten
3 cups peperonata (page 77), at room temperature

RABBIT MIXED GRILL: LOINS, RIBS, LEGS, AND BELLY MARINATED WITH BLACK OLIVES, PRESERVED LEMON, PARSLEY, AND CHILES

PAIR WITH CASAVECCHIA (CAMPANIA)
SERVES 6 TO 8

Rabbit is eaten all over Italy, but it is a specialty of the island of Ischia, which lies just off the coast of Campania. Rabbits once ran wild there (and were frequent targets of aristocrats' hunting expeditions). Nowadays, however, they are raised in dirt pits. Fed a diet similar to what rabbits eat in the wild, locals insist that these pit-reared rabbits have a flavor that closely resembles the meat of their wild cousins.

With practice, butchering a whole rabbit is easy. We portion the rabbit into pieces that can be grilled easily—boning the back legs, saving the belly flaps (tasty bits that are often overlooked in restaurant kitchens)—and then grill them and serve them with lemon wedges. We sometimes skewer the hearts and livers and grill them as well, or we use them in place of chicken livers for chicken liver puree (page 96).

Season and marinate the rabbits a day before you plan to cook them. Although you can grill the front legs with everything else here, you can also opt to save them for a braised dish. Grilled rabbit pairs well with Giardiniera (page 240) and Braised Green Beans with Pork and Tomato Soffritto (page 229).

2 (3- to 4-pound) rabbits
Kosher salt
½ bunch flat-leaf parsley leaves, coarsely chopped
1 ½ cups black olives, pitted
2 cloves garlic, coarsely chopped
2 wedges preserved Meyer lemon (page 84), pith and
    flesh removed, soaked, and coarsely chopped
½ teaspoon dried chile flakes
1 cup extra virgin olive oil, plus more for finishing
3 fresh lemons, cut in half crosswise and seeded

To butcher each rabbit, turn it back side down and remove each front leg by separating the muscle that attaches the leg to the shoulder and cutting it away from the body, much as you would a chicken leg. Set aside.

Turn the rabbit so that its back faces up. To remove each back leg, make an incision behind the hipbone to release the muscle that joins the hip to the leg, then cut down the backbone until the leg is completely detached. Ideally, you want the hipbone to stay attached to the backbone because it makes boning the leg easier. But if you overshoot and cut the backbone off with the leg, that's fine, too. You will just have to remove it from the thigh before boning it. Check the body cavity for the heart and liver and remove them; reserve for another use.

Turn the inside of each back leg so that it faces up. Cut the drumstick from each thigh and set aside. To bone each thigh, make an incision along the bone on the inside of the thigh, where the bone runs closest to the surface. Cut the meat away from the bone until the bone is completely

continued

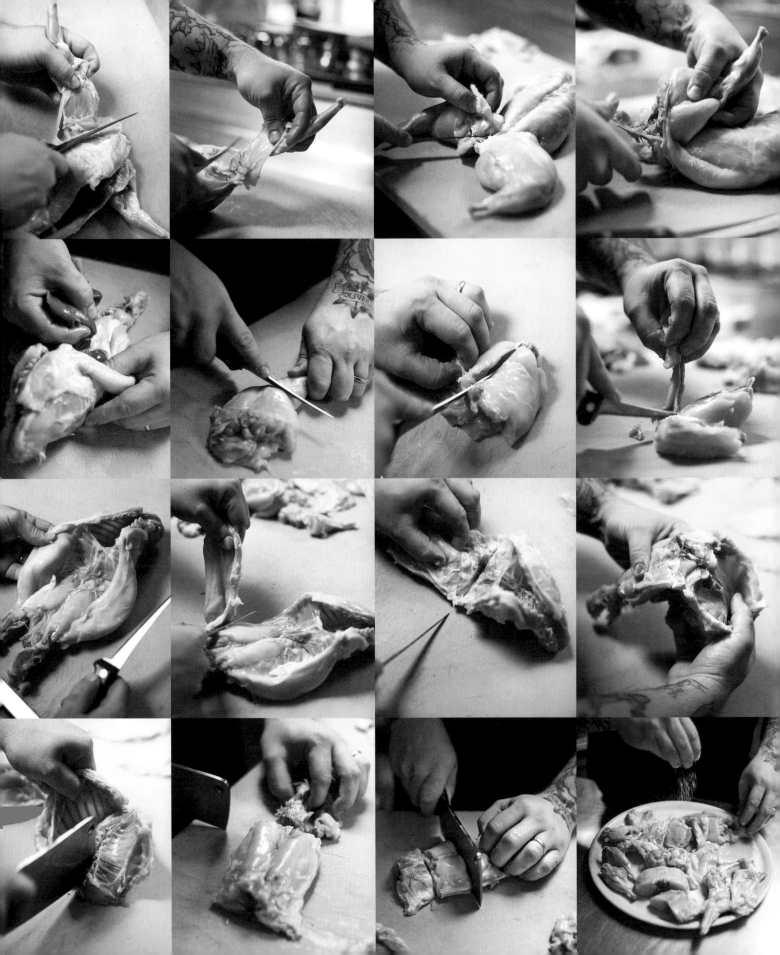

detached, much as you would for a chicken thigh. Set aside. Turn the body so that the back faces down. Cut off the thin flaps of belly that join the ribs to the loins and set aside. You should be left with the rib cage (the rack), the backbone, and the loins (the saddle). Make an incision along the last rib on both sides of the rib cage, separating the rib cage from the loins. At this point, the only thing keeping the rib cage connected to the loins should be the backbone.

Using sharp kitchen shears or a cleaver, cut through the backbone to detach the rib cage completely from the saddle. Using a cleaver or a heavy chef's knife, cut off the backbone attached to the rib cage. Using the kitchen shears or the cleaver, cut each rib-cage half crosswise along the ribs into 2 even pieces and set the pieces aside. Next, using the cleaver or chef's knife, remove the extra bit of backbone that was originally connected to the legs from the saddle. Finally, divide the saddle crosswise into 3 pieces with the cleaver or knife.

Evenly distribute the rabbit pieces over your work surface. For the mixed grill, you should now have 4 front legs, 4 drumsticks, 4 boned thighs, 4 belly flaps, 8 rib pieces, and 6 saddle pieces (freeze the remaining bones for a stock or stew). Season each piece evenly with salt, about 1 tablespoon per rabbit, and set aside.

For the marinade, combine the parsley, olives, garlic, preserved lemon, and chile flakes in a food processor or in a mortar. Pulse a few times or crush with a pestle until coarsely blended. With the processor running, drizzle in the olive oil, or drizzle in the olive oil as you crush the ingredients with the pestle. Taste for seasoning. The olives are salty and you have seasoned the rabbit, so you may not need to add salt. Place the rabbit pieces in a large storage container. Pour in the marinade, turn the pieces to coat evenly, cover, and refrigerate overnight.

The next day, prepare a hot fire in a grill, spreading the coals evenly for direct-heat cooking. Bring the rabbit pieces to room temperature.

To prevent some of the smaller pieces, such as the belly flaps, from falling through the grill rack, lay a piece of foil on part of the rack to serve as a safety net. Evenly distribute the rabbit pieces across the grill rack, putting the smallest ones on the foil. Grill the pieces, turning over once or twice to ensure even cooking. The pieces will finish cooking at different times, so pull them off the grill as soon as they are done, place them on a platter, and cover with foil to keep them warm. The belly flaps need only about 1 to 2 minutes to cook; followed by the rib pieces after about 4 minutes; the thighs, drumsticks, and the rack after about 7 minutes; and the front legs after about 10 minutes. The pieces are done when golden brown and the juices run clear when the thickest part of the meat is pierced with a fork.

Serve the rabbit pieces on the same platter. Finish them with a generous drizzle of olive oil, and then garnish the platter with the fresh lemon halves. Serve immediately.

BRAISED GOAT WITH TOMATOES, ROSEMARY, CINNAMON, AND WHITE WINE

PAIR WITH AGLIANICO (BASILICATA)
SERVES 6

A few years ago, at the home of my friend Andy Griffin of Mariquita Farm (page 226), I helped slaughter and butcher a goat Andy had raised. That experience gave me newfound respect for raising animals as a food source. Soon after that day, I put a goat special on the menu.

Goats thrive almost anywhere, their meat is highly flavorful, and nearly every part of the animal can be braised or slow roasted over a smoky fire. And finding goat meat is not as hard as you might think. Marin Sun Farms sells it at its Point Reyes Station butcher shop in west Marin County and at local farmers' markets. You can also buy it from Mexican grocers, who sell it as *cabrito*, and from halal butchers, who ensure a steady supply in Muslim communities. (See Resources for other suppliers around the country.) Goats are bony, so ask the butcher to cut the meat through the bone into 4- to 8-ounce pieces. But if you cannot find goat, you can use lamb shoulder or pork shoulder to make this dish. Serve with Braised Lacinato Kale with Tomato and Anchovy Soffritto (page 230).

5½ pounds bone-in goat shoulder or hindquarter, cut into 4- to 8-ounce pieces
2 tablespoons kosher salt
¼ cup extra virgin olive oil, plus more for finishing
3 cloves garlic, smashed with the side of a knife
2 cups dry white wine
2 sprigs rosemary
1 (28-ounce) can San Marzano tomatoes with juices
½ teaspoon ground cinnamon

Season the goat with the salt. Cover and refrigerate overnight.

Preheat the oven to 275°F.

In a heavy-bottomed pot, heat the olive oil over medium heat. Add the garlic and cook, stirring occasionally, for about 3 minutes, or until it softens and starts to turn golden. Add the wine and rosemary and boil for about 8 minutes, or until the wine has almost fully evaporated.

Meanwhile, place the tomatoes and their juices in a bowl and crush with your hands or the back of a wooden spoon. Once the wine has reduced, stir in the tomatoes with their juices and the cinnamon. Bring the sauce to a boil, then remove from the heat.

In a large roasting pan, evenly distribute the goat pieces. Carefully pour the sauce over the goat. Cover the roasting pan with aluminum foil and transfer to the oven.

Place the pot in the oven and braise the goat for about 3½ hours, or until the meat pulls away easily from the bone.

Remove the pot from the oven and let the meat cool in the braising liquid. Lift out the goat from the sauce, and pull the meat from the bones, removing it in large chunks if possible. It should come away easily from the bone and the connective tissue. Skim off most of the fat from the sauce, remove and discard the rosemary sprigs, taste for seasoning, and add more salt if needed.

To serve, return the meat to the sauce and bring to a simmer. Ladle the meat with some of the sauce into warmed bowls and finish with a drizzle of olive oil. Serve immediately.

LAMB AND RICOTTA CRESPELLE WITH TOMATO AND PECORINO

PAIR WITH CARIGNANO (SARDINIA)
SERVES 6

Lamb is the most commonly prepared meat in southern Italy, for good reason. Sheep are nimble animals and require less food and pastureland than cows, which are important traits in the rocky, dry terrain of Campania and surrounding regions.

The lambs we get from Don Watson of Napa Valley Lamb are milk fed, and their meat has a subtle flavor. The lightness of *crespelle* (Italian crepes), paired with ricotta, complements the richness of the lamb without overwhelming its nuanced flavor. When preparing this dish, make the *crespelle* batter and marinate the lamb the night before you plan to serve the dish. Since lamb shanks vary in their meatiness, you may be left with extra filling. Leftovers can be heated gently and tossed together with mint and peas to sauce pasta.

CRESPELLE

2 cups whole milk

1½ cups plus 1 tablespoon all-purpose flour

4 eggs, lightly beaten

4 tablespoons unsalted butter, melted

½ teaspoon kosher salt

LAMB AND RICOTTA FILLING

3 cloves garlic, minced

1 sprig rosemary, leaves picked and coarsely chopped

¼ cup extra virgin olive oil

2 pounds lamb shanks

Kosher salt

1 cup water

1 pound (about 2 cups) fresh ricotta, drained if very moist (page 76)

Leaves from 2 sprigs mint, torn into pieces

¼ teaspoon dried chile flakes

LAMB SAUCE

2 tablespoons extra virgin olive oil

2 cloves garlic, smashed with the side of a knife

¼ teaspoon dried chile flakes

⅓ cup dry white wine

1 (28-ounce) can San Marzano tomatoes with juices

Block of aged pecorino for grating

Extra virgin olive oil for finishing

To make the batter for the *crespelle*, in a bowl, whisk together the milk, flour, eggs, butter, and salt until well combined. Strain through a fine-mesh strainer, cover, and refrigerate overnight.

To make the filling, in a small bowl, combine the garlic, rosemary, and olive oil. Place the lamb shanks in a shallow dish, season them with about 2 teaspoons salt, and then coat them with the olive oil mixture. Cover and refrigerate overnight.

Preheat the oven to 250°F.

Transfer the shanks to a roasting pan or Dutch oven and pour in the water. Cover, transfer the pot to the oven, and roast for about 4 hours, or until the meat is completely tender and beginning to fall off the bone.

Remove the pot from the oven. Place a colander over a bowl, and transfer the shanks to the colander to rest. Let the braising liquid rest in the pot for 30 minutes to allow the fat to rise to the surface. Skim off most of the fat with a large spoon. Taste the liquid for seasoning and add salt if needed. Stir in any liquid that has drained from the resting shanks, and set the braising liquid aside. You should have about 1 cup.

continued

Once the meat is cool enough to handle, pull away the meat from the bones and shred it into bite-sized pieces with your fingers. In a bowl, combine the lamb, ricotta, mint, and chile flakes and mix well. Set the filling aside.

To make each *crespella*, heat an 8-inch nonstick sauté pan or crepe pan over medium heat. Brush the pan with butter, then ladle about ¼ cup of the batter into the pan. Swirl the batter in the pan until evenly distributed. Cook for 1 to 2 minutes, or until the bottom is golden and the top is almost dry. Using a spatula and a flick of the wrist, flip the *crespella* carefully and cook for 30 seconds on the second side, or until the bottom is lightly browned. Slide the *crespella* onto a plate and repeat until all of the batter has been used, brushing the pan with butter as needed and stacking the *crespelle* as you work. You should have 16 to 20 *crespelle*.

To make the lamb sauce, heat the olive oil in a pot over medium heat. Add the garlic and chile flakes and cook, stirring occasionally, for about 3 minutes, or until the garlic softens and starts to turn golden. Remove from the heat and gradually pour in the wine. Return to the stove, increase the heat to medium-high, and reduce for 3 minutes, or until the wine has evaporated. Add the braising liquid and cook for about 3 minutes more, or until reduced by three-fourths.

Meanwhile, place the canned tomatoes and their juices in a bowl and crush with your hands or the back of a wooden spoon. Once the sauce has reduced, stir in the tomatoes and bring the sauce to a boil. Remove from the heat and reserve.

Preheat the oven to 450°F. Lightly oil a roasting pan with olive oil.

To assemble the *crespelle*, lay a *crespella* flat on a work surface. Spread ⅓ cup of the filling horizontally along the center, fold the edge of the crespella closest to you over the filling, and then roll it up, securing the filling firmly inside. Place the *crespella*, seam side down, in the roasting pan. Repeat until all of the *crespelle* have been filled.

Place the pan in the oven and heat the *crespelle*, rotating the pan front to back after a couple of minutes, for about 5 minutes, or until evenly browned.

Meanwhile, reheat the sauce until hot. When the *crespelle* are ready, remove them from the oven. To serve, spoon the sauce into warmed bowls, dividing it evenly, and place the *crespelle* on top. Grate pecorino over the top of each serving, and then drizzle with olive oil to finish. Serve immediately.

RIB ROAST OF BEEF WITH MOSTO AND ROSEMARY

PAIR WITH MONTEPULCIANO (MOLISE)
SERVES 6 TO 8

This recipe provides a simple, complementary means to celebrate an exceptional cut of meat. My cut of choice is a boned rib roast tied with butcher's twine, which is called a rolled roast. When the same piece of meat is sold with the bone in, it is called a standing rib roast. (With some minor adjustments, this recipe can be prepared with a standing rib roast: put the roast, fat side up, on a rack set in a roasting pan and roast at 400ºF, rotating the pan front to back about halfway through the roasting time, for about 1½ hours for a 4-pound roast.) Serve the rib roast with a side of Roasted Carrots and Snap Peas with Green Garlic and Mint (page 237) and Chard Gratinata with Bread Crumbs and Grana (page 233).

1 (3- to 4-pound) rolled rib roast
Kosher salt
¼ cup extra virgin olive oil
Leaves from 2 sprigs rosemary
2 tablespoons mosto (page 87)

Season the rib roast evenly with about 2 tablespoons salt. Cover and refrigerate at least overnight or up to 3 days.

Two hours before roasting, remove the rib roast from the refrigerator and bring to temperature. Thirty minutes before roasting, preheat the oven to 400˚F.

Place the roast on a rack set in a roasting pan. Roast, rotating the pan front to back once or twice, until an instant-read thermometer inserted into the center of the roast reads 115˚F for rare (about 1 hour), 125˚F for medium-rare (about 1 hour and 20 minutes), or 135˚F for medium (about 1 hour and 30 minutes). Keep in mind that the meat will continue to cook—usually rising 10 to 15 degrees—as it rests. Allow the roast to rest for at least 20 minutes before slicing.

Meanwhile, heat the olive oil in a small pot over medium heat. Add the rosemary leaves and fry gently for about 1 minute, or until they pop. Immediately remove from the heat (the leaves burn easily), and strain the oil through a fine-mesh sieve into a heatproof bowl, reserving the rosemary. Let the oil cool and then return the rosemary to the oil.

Snip the strings and cut the meat into ¼- to ½-inch-thick slices. Arrange the slices on a warmed platter. Spoon the rosemary oil over the meat and along the sides of the slices, making sure that ample rosemary leaves are garnishing the slices. Drizzle the mosto around the sides of the slices. Serve immediately.

SHORT RIBS ALLA GENOVESE

PAIR WITH NEGROAMARO (PUGLIA)
SERVES 6

The name of this dish is thoroughly misleading. While it would lead you to think it was from Genoa, it is actually a traditional Neapolitan recipe that predates the arrival of tomatoes to the region. No one has been able to explain the connection to Genoa with certainty, as no similar sauce exists there, but one story suggests that it was made for visiting Genoese merchants, as both Genoa and Naples have long boasted bustling ports.

Neapolitans do, however, generally agree on what goes into the sauce. As with the classic *ragù alla napoletana*, *ragù alla genovese* is more about the sauce than the meat. In this case, onions take center stage, with a bit of carrot and celery playing supporting roles, accompanied by a small amount of meat. Traditionally, the sauce is served with pasta, and the meat follows as a second course. Campania has become more prosperous, however, so it is no longer unusual to see the meat served with the sauce, as we do at the restaurant. We serve chicken, duck, and octopus *alla genovese* as well, but these short ribs have evolved into an A16 classic. You can also cook this sauce without any meat and serve it with pasta for a so-called *finta genovese*, or "fake genovese."

When buying short ribs, look for thicker, meatier cuts that come from the chuck end. We braise 2- to 4-rib slabs, but you also can use individual ribs cut from the slab. If you use boneless short ribs, decrease the braising time to about 1¾ hours. Avoid short ribs cross-cut for Asian preparations (they are a thinner, more sinewy, less meaty cut). Season the short ribs with salt at least a day before you prepare the dish. Serve with Giardiniera (page 240), Braised Chard with Garlic, Anchovy, and Lemon (page 232), or Braised Cannellini Beans with Garlic, Marjoram, and Oregano (page 234).

5 pounds short ribs (about 6 ribs total)
Kosher salt
¼ cup extra virgin olive oil, plus more for finishing
1½ cups dry red wine
½ carrot, peeled and finely chopped
1 celery stalk, finely chopped
1 salt-packed anchovy, rinsed, filleted, and soaked (page 84) and then minced
2 cloves garlic, peeled but left whole
5 black peppercorns
4 red onions, thinly sliced
3 tablespoons red wine vinegar
1 sprig rosemary

Trim some of the fat from the short ribs, leaving the tough outer sinew and silver skin intact. Season the ribs evenly with about 2 tablespoons salt. Cover and refrigerate at least overnight or up to 3 days.

Preheat the oven to 275°F.

In a large Dutch oven or other heavy-bottomed pot, heat 2 tablespoons of the olive oil over medium-high heat. Working in 2 batches (so as not to crowd the pot), add the ribs and brown evenly on all sides. Transfer to a plate and set aside. Pour out the fat and check the pot for burned bits of meat. If the pan looks scorched, deglaze it with ¼ cup of water, dislodging any browned bits from the bottom. Strain the liquid through a fine-mesh sieve and taste it. If it tastes appealing, reserve it to add to the braising liquid. If not, discard it. Reserve the pot for the sauce.

Meanwhile, in a small pot, reduce the wine over medium-high heat to about ½ cup. Set aside.

continued

To make the sauce, add the remaining 2 tablespoons olive oil to the reserved pot and heat over medium-low heat. Stir in the carrot and celery and sweat slowly, stirring occasionally, for about 5 minutes, or until the vegetables begin to soften; lower the heat if needed to prevent the vegetables from burning or browning too quickly. Stir in the anchovy, garlic, and peppercorns and continue to cook for 3 minutes, or until the garlic begins to soften. Add the onions with a pinch of salt (the short ribs have been seasoned, so go light with seasoning the vegetables) and cook, stirring occasionally, for about 5 minutes, or until the onions are soft and translucent. Stir in the vinegar and the reduced wine and remove the pot from the heat.

Return the short ribs to the pot with the rosemary sprig and cover tightly with aluminum foil or a lid. Transfer to the oven and braise for about 2½ hours, or until the short ribs are tender when pierced with a fork

To serve, remove the rosemary sprig and transfer the ribs to a large, rimmed serving platter. Ladle the sauce on top, and drizzle with olive oil to finish. Serve immediately.

These ribs will be even better if cooled down completely, then refrigerated and served the following day. Before reheating, scrape off and discard some of the fat that has risen to the surface. To reheat, preheat the oven to 400°F. Remove the ribs from the braising liquid, bring to room temperature, place on a rimmed baking sheet, and roast in the oven for about 25 minutes, or until the outside sizzles and the inside is heated through. Heat the sauce in a medium pot over medium heat, and remove the sprig of rosemary. Place the ribs on a rimmed serving platter, ladle the sauce on top, and finish with a drizzle of olive oil.

THE PIG

Once a week, when the restaurant is closed for lunch, a white van pulls up at the entrance. A couple of our cooks wheel a rolling rack up to the van and out comes a foreshank, a shoulder, a belly, a loin, a back leg, and a head—a procession that provokes a few quizzical looks from bystanders on Chestnut Street. This delivery, a pig butchered into its primal cuts, is the principle source of my inspiration in the kitchen. It is what drives me to be creative, frugal, thoughtful, and ambitious. It is also what makes our pork dishes taste so good.

I started buying whole pigs to support sustainable producers who raise their animals under humane conditions. I have also found, not surprisingly, that the quality of pork improves tremendously when it comes directly from these small producers. Real pork, as opposed to cheap commodity pork, has flavor and fat, the result of pigs raised on a varied diet with room to roam. Bringing in a whole hog also keeps our cooking rooted in the traditions of Italy, where every region has its own distinctive sausages and where once-regional specialties, such as prosciutto and pancetta, have been embraced beyond their origins. Hog butchery has integrated itself well into the rhythm of our kitchen, and using the different cuts of pork provides me with an ongoing, stimulating challenge.

Buying a whole hog is a privilege that we don't take for granted. The rich source of flavor in much of our cooking can be traced back to the good pork we use in such dishes as our quickly grilled pork loin *spiedino* or our slowly braised pork shoulder served with green olives and chestnuts. Yet a whole pig gives us more than meat. I wish all cooks had pig's trotters in their freezers so they could use their amazing gelatinous properties to impart body to soups, braises, and stocks. Buying a whole pig also provides access to its highly valued fat, which includes both leaf fat and trimmings to render into lard and fatback to grind for juicy sausage and tender meatballs.

This chapter focuses on fresh pork recipes, both antipasti and main courses, plus a simple way to make

fresh pancetta, an A16 pantry staple. (I love curing pork, but the process merits its own book.) Some of the more ambitious projects, such as *ciccioli*, a terrine made with pork shoulder and skin anchored in place with pork fat; *coppa di testa*, Italian headcheese made by braising a pig's head; and *zampone*, a stuffed pork foreshank, illustrate how you can truly eat just about everything but the squeal.

Buying good pork—the alternative cuts in particular—requires some research. I spend a lot of time developing relationships with small producers who allow their pigs to roam free, root, and wriggle as they are naturally inclined to do. A good producer also supplies his or her charges with a varied diet of dairy, vegetable trimmings, and grains. To support these conscientious entrepreneurs and to eat great-tasting meat, it is worth visiting the meat vendors at your local farmers' market. If they don't raise pigs, they might know someone who does. Another good source are local butchers, who occasionally or typically buy whole pigs and thus often have such hard-to-acquire parts as the head or the liver. Strike up a conversation. Describe the part or the cut—bone-in shoulder with fatback and skin or a pig's foreshank—you are after. Finding producers who specialize in whole hogs, or a middleman who can connect you to them, is well worth the time. Not only will you be able to find the more obscure parts and cuts, but you will also have access to more flavorful pork for any recipe you prepare. See Resources for a selection of stores and online shops to help get you started.

SPECIALTY PORK

I am happy to see the growing excitement over heritage breeds, such as the black Berkshire, Red Wattle, and the curly-coated Mangalitza, among chefs and farmers. New York City–based Heritage Foods has been a leader in the heritage-breed movement, encouraging farmers to raise heritage breeds, and then connecting them with chefs and cooks interested in their products. The organization's hard work and extensive network means that pork lovers like me have a lot more to choose from.

At A16, we buy pigs from different farmers, depending on availability. I also seek out pork breeds with which I am unfamiliar. I have purchased a Duroc-Berkshire cross, two breeds that are known for their marbling. Durocs have especially juicy shoulder meat, and better-known

Berkshires have darker, well-marbled meat with a thick layer of fatback. Some producers are revitalizing breeds such as Yorkshire and Hampshire, which have been overbred for leanness for commodity pork production, while others are introducing the Mangalitza breed, a Central European variety prized for its fat.

Age also influences the taste and texture of the meat. At eight months old, with a live weight from 300 to 350 pounds, a pig still has tender meat but also has developed a good layer of fatback and plenty of marbling around the muscles. The meat from older, larger sows between 400 and 450 pounds has a stronger flavor, which is great for making *salumi*; but it is tougher, and the fresh cuts, such as loin, ribs, or chops, are quite large.

CICCIOLI

PAIR WITH PALLAGRELLO NERO (CAMPANIA)
SERVES 10 TO 12

The term *ciccioli* is used for pork cracklings packed in lard. In Campania, the mixture is sold in blocks by the kilogram, and home cooks use it to flavor soups or braised meat, or to spread on bread. We take the idea behind *ciccioli* and make it meaty enough to serve sliced, garnished with extra virgin olive oil and *mosto*, on a *salumi* platter or with pickled chiles. The recipe includes directions for using a 1½-quart mold or 4 miniature loaf pans. Well-wrapped smaller loaves or leftovers from the larger mold can be frozen for future use. They will keep for 1 week in the refrigerator and 2 months in the freezer. Plan on making this dish at least 1 day before serving.

2 pounds boneless pork shoulder, cut into 1-inch cubes
8 ounces pork skin, cut into 1-inch cubes
8 ounces fatback, cut into 1-inch cubes
1 tablespoon kosher salt
1 tablespoon minced garlic
1 teaspoon chopped fresh rosemary
1½ cups dry white wine
1¼ teaspoons freshly ground black pepper
Extra virgin olive oil
Mosto (page 87)

In a large bowl, combine the pork shoulder, skin, fat, salt, garlic, and rosemary and mix well. Cover and refrigerate overnight.

Preheat the oven to 275°F.

Evenly distribute the pork mixture in a roasting pan. Add the wine, cover the pan with aluminum foil or a lid, and place in the oven. Braise for about 3½ hours, or until the fat has rendered out of the pork and the meat is tender.

Meanwhile, line a 1½-quart loaf pan or terrine or 4 miniature loaf pans (3 by 6 by 2 inches) with plastic wrap, allowing a 2-inch overhang on the long sides.

When the pork is ready, drain it in a strainer, reserving at least ¾ cup of the liquid. Place the pork in the bowl of a stand mixer fitted with the paddle attachment and mix on low speed for about 3 minutes, or until the meat chunks have broken up. Add the pepper and continue to mix on low speed for 1 minute to combine. With the mixer running, gradually drizzle in ⅔ cup of the reserved liquid, mixing for about 4 minutes, or until completely incorporated. The mixture should be soft and moist but not soupy. If it seems stiff and dry (like clumpy oatmeal), drizzle in the additional liquid by the tablespoon until the correct consistency is achieved. The mixture will firm up as it cools.

Spoon the meat mixture into the prepared mold(s) and press down evenly to eliminate air pockets. Smooth the top, and then fold the overhanging plastic wrap over the top and press down to secure. Refrigerate overnight before serving. (It will keep in the refrigerator for about 1 week.)

To serve, lift the terrine from the mold(s) with the plastic wrap, invert it onto a cutting board, and peel away the plastic wrap. Cut crosswise into ½-inch-thick slices and lay the slices flat on a plate. Drizzle with olive oil and *mosto*.

LIVER TERRINA

PAIR WITH LATE-HARVEST FIANO (CAMPANIA)
SERVES 12

Pork liver is milder than beef liver and is creamier when pureed than chicken liver, yet it is rarely sold in butcher shops or at meat counters of grocery stores. The best way to secure a good source is to seek out a butcher who buys pigs whole or who is willing to special order the liver for you. Some ethnic grocery stores also carry pork liver. For the pork fat, ask your butcher for fat trimmed from chops or roasts. Fatback, cubed or ground, will also work. To render the fat, you can either cook it in water, as directed in the recipe, or you can speed up the process by grinding the fat before you start, which will shorten the rendering time to about 25 minutes.

Thin slices of the terrine are a popular antipasto at A16. Serve with Marinated Olives (page 91), Giardiniera (page 240), crostini, and assorted cured meats.

1 pound pork fat
2 pounds pork liver
1 tablespoon salt
7 black peppercorns
¼ teaspoon coriander seeds
Pinch of dried chile flakes
¾ cup heavy cream
¾ cup prosciutto brodo (page 75)
5 eggs, lightly beaten

In a medium pot, combine the pork fat with ¼ cup water over low heat. Cook uncovered, stirring occasionally, until the fat becomes completely soft, 1 to 1½ hours. Avoid heating the fat too quickly or it will scorch. Remove from the heat, let cool completely, and then cover and refrigerate overnight.

The next day, drain the fat of any remaining water. Transfer the fat to a blender and puree until smooth. You should have about 2 cups. You will need ⅓ cup fat for this recipe; cover tightly and refrigerate overnight. Reserve the remaining fat for searing meat or for braising vegetables for *cianfotta* (page 130). It will keep in the refrigerator for up to 3 months.

Meanwhile, clean the liver. Wipe it with a damp cloth, and then remove the thin outer membrane, the veins, and any signs of discoloration with a sharp paring knife. Cut the liver into 1-inch cubes and set aside. In a spice grinder, or in a mortar with a pestle, grind together the salt, peppercorns, coriander seeds, and chile flakes to a coarse blend. In a large bowl, toss the liver with the spice mixture, cover, and refrigerate overnight.

Preheat the oven to 300°F. Line a 1½-quart loaf pan or terrine or 4 miniature loaf pans (3 by 6 by 2 inches) with plastic wrap, allowing a 2-inch overhang on the long sides. In a pot, combine the cream and *brodo* and bring to a simmer. Mix in the ⅓ cup fat, stirring to combine, and remove from the heat. Place the liver in a food processor and add 1 cup of the cream mixture. Pulse until you have a coarsely combined mixture. Add the eggs and puree until smooth, adding the remaining cream mixture as necessary to achieve a mousselike consistency.

Spoon the mixture into the prepared mold(s), fold the overhanging plastic wrap over the top, and then cover with aluminum foil or a terrine lid. Place the mold(s) in a deep roasting pan and pour hot tap water into the roasting pan to come halfway up the sides of the mold(s). Bake until set and cooked through, about 1 hour for the 1½-quart loaf pan or terrine and 45 minutes for the miniature loaf pans. To test for doneness, uncover and insert an instant-read thermometer into the center of the terrine; it should register 165°F.

Remove from the oven and let cool completely. Refrigerate overnight, or until the terrine is firm enough to slice neatly. (Or, you can store the terrine in the refrigerator for up to 1 week or in the freezer for up to 3 months before serving.)

To serve, lift the terrine from the mold(s) with the plastic wrap, invert onto a cutting board, and peel away the plastic wrap. Heat a sharp knife under hot water, wipe it dry with a clean cloth, and slice the terrine into ½-inch-thick slices, reheating and drying the knife as needed to ensure neat slices. Arrange the slices flat on a plate.

COPPA DI TESTA

PAIR WITH TREBBIANO (ABRUZZO)
SERVES 10 TO 12

Like Ciccioli (page 205), this classic headcheese is molded in a terrine and bound together by gelatin and fat, but it has its own nuances. Thinly sliced ear and skin give it texture, and chunks of cheek give it rich, pure pork flavor.

The most challenging aspect of this recipe is locating a pig's head and then finding a pot big enough (but not too big) to hold it. The size of the pot is important. If it is too big, the braising liquid will be diluted, and thus lack the concentration of gelatin necessary to set the mixture. If this recipe yields more than you plan on serving within a week, the leftovers can be well wrapped and frozen for future use. They will keep for up to 3 months. The *coppa di testa* should be made at least a day before serving. Serve slices of it alongside Giardiniera (page 240).

1 pig's head (about 12 pounds), halved
About ½ cup kosher salt
1 tablespoon black peppercorns
2 teaspoons dried chile flakes
2 teaspoons fennel seeds
1 teaspoon whole allspice
1 teaspoon coriander seeds
2 red onions, quartered
2 carrots, halved
2 celery stalks, cut into chunks
2 heads garlic, halved
1 lemon, halved
About 1 cup red wine vinegar

Season the pig's head generously with the salt and refrigerate overnight.

Make a spice sachet by placing the peppercorns, chile flakes, fennel seeds, allspice, and coriander seeds on a square of cheesecloth, bringing the corners together, and tying securely with kitchen string. Set aside.

Place the pig's head in a deep stockpot in which it fits snugly. Add the onions, carrots, celery, garlic, lemon, spice sachet, ¾ cup of the red wine vinegar, and water to cover by about 2 inches (or 1 inch if the pot is very wide). Place over medium-high heat and bring to a boil, skimming any foam that forms on the surface with a ladle. Adjust the heat to a low simmer and cook the head, uncovered, for about 4 hours, or until the meat is tender and has started to pull gently away from the bone and the jaw is loose.

Meanwhile, line a 1½-quart loaf pan or terrine or 4 miniature loaf pans (3 by 6 by 2 inches) with plastic wrap, allowing a 2-inch overhang on the long sides.

Remove the head and any meat that detached from it from the pot and set aside to cool for about 30 minutes, or until it can be handled. At the same time, refrigerate a small plate, to use for testing the sauce for consistency. Strain the braising liquid through a fine-mesh strainer and reserve, discarding the contents of the strainer. Set the liquid aside.

When the head can be handled, pick through the warm meat, discarding all the bones and glands. Peel off the skin from the tongue, which should come off easily with the help of a paring knife, and discard it. Coarsely chop the tongue and place in a large bowl. Pull apart and coarsely chop the meat, and add to the bowl with the tongue. Coarsely chop the skin (which will have softened but will still be firmer than the meat) and finely chop the ears; add them to the bowl. Taste the meats for seasoning. If they taste underseasoned, sprinkle them with a pinch or two of salt.

Take the plate out of the refrigerator and spoon a shallow pool of the warm braising liquid on it. If the liquid firms up like Jell-O, it is ready to go. If it is runny, it needs to be reduced. Reduce it over high heat by one-fourth, then retest it on the chilled plate. Be careful when reducing the liquid. If you reduce it too much, you will muddy the flavors.

Once the braising liquid is sufficiently gelatinous, taste it for seasoning, adding salt and the remaining ¼ cup vinegar to taste if desired. Stir about 2 cups of the braising liquid into the meat mixture, and transfer the mixture to the prepared mold(s). Pour ¼ inch of the braising liquid on top to cover, and then fold the overhanging plastic wrap over the top and press down to secure. Refrigerate overnight before serving. (It will keep in the refrigerator for about 1 week.)

To serve, lift the *coppa di testa* out of the mold(s) with the plastic wrap, invert it onto a cutting board, and peel away the plastic wrap. Cut into ¼- to ½-inch-thick slices and lay the slices flat on a plate.

FRESH PANCETTA

MAKES ABOUT 4 POUNDS

We use pancetta so frequently that we started making a simple cooked version that is ready to use within just 4 days. It is especially good as a topping for pizza and bruschetta (even though it is cooked, it still has plenty of fat that renders out when it is cooked further), and it can also be used in any recipe calling for cured pancetta, *guanciale*, or bacon.

This recipe is for 4½ pounds of pork belly, but you can adjust the directions to fit the quantity of belly you have on hand. The most important element is the amount of salt, which is better to eyeball than to measure in advance. The salt should coat the pancetta thoroughly on both sides, almost like a light dusting of snow. In other words, the salt must be visible but not the thick coat you might apply if curing a side of salmon. After a day in the refrigerator, the salt will have nearly dissolved completely into the belly.

1 (4½-pound) slab pork belly, preferably skin on
About ½ cup kosher salt

Place the pork belly on a rimmed baking sheet. Generously sprinkle the belly on both sides with the salt, using about ¼ cup on each side, and then rub the salt evenly into the belly. Turn the belly, skin side up, and cover with plastic wrap. Refrigerate for 3 days.

Preheat the oven to 325°F.

Remove the belly from the baking sheet, and pat the belly and the baking sheet dry (water will have accumulated on the bottom). Return the belly, skin side up, to the baking sheet and place in the oven. Roast for about 1½ hours, or until cooked through and soft.

Remove from the oven and let cool slightly. When cool enough to handle but still hot, pull off the skin with your hands. Then let the belly cool completely.

Cut the cooled belly into 4 equal portions, each about 1 pound, and wrap each portion tightly in plastic wrap. The pancetta keeps for up 2 weeks in the refrigerator and up to 6 months in the freezer.

MIXING SAUSAGE FILLINGS AND STUFFING CASINGS

The day we get a whole pig in, one of our cooks will cube the fat and the meat for a batch of sausages, season the mixture, and then cover it and refrigerate it overnight. The next morning, the meat is ground through a meat grinder that attaches to our large stand mixer and then stuffed into casings with our piston-and-crank sausage stuffer. Dividing sausage making into a two-day process gives the meat time to absorb the seasoning and allows the fat to chill thoroughly, making it easier to grind and ensuring that it does not get too warm (grinding warm fatback compromises the texture of the sausage). With a little foresight and the right equipment, making sausage at home can be just as easy.

You will need a grinder and a sausage stuffer. A stand mixer with a food grinder attachment works well. For stuffing casings, I find a piston-and-crank sausage stuffer, which stands on its own and is operated by a hand crank, to be the best choice. Buying one is an investment, but if you make a lot of sausages, the cost is worth it. Or, you can use the stand mixer's sausage stuffer attachment. The website sausagemaker.com is a terrific place to explore various equipment and ingredients needed for making sausages.

Hog casings are the most common type of casing, and they are also the easiest to use. They can be purchased online or at butcher shops that make sausage (see Resources). I prefer salt-packed casings, though I also occasionally buy brine-packed casings, which I drain, rinse, pack in salt, and refrigerate for a few days before using. (Salt strengthens the casings, making them less likely to tear.) To prepare the casings for stuffing, soak them in warm water for at least 30 minutes (or overnight in the refrigerator), and then flush out the insides with cold running water before using. You can store extra casings in the refrigerator for up to a year if fully packed in salt.

While chilling the meat and fat overnight is an important step, so too is chilling your equipment before using it. Chill the grinder in the freezer for about 15 minutes before using.

SALSICCIA

PAIR WITH CASAVECCHIA (CAMPANIA)
MAKES ABOUT 16 SAUSAGES

Salsiccie, or "sausages," are commonly eaten in Campania's inland provinces. Sausages are a significant part of our menu as well. Because we deal with whole pigs, we have a lot of meat to use and a generous inventory of fatback, the key ingredient to tender, juicy sausages. This recipe is essentially the same as the one we use for our Pizza Salsiccia with Spring Onions (page 125), but we have adjusted it slightly to make it suitable for packing into casings. Grill these sausages and serve them with *peperonata* (page 77), some arugula, and a few lemon wedges. Or, for a simpler rendition that omits the stuffing procedure, form the sausage mixture into patties and pan-fry them.

4 pounds boneless pork shoulder, trimmed of sinew and cut into 1-inch cubes
1 pound pork fatback, cut into 1-inch cubes
6 Calabrian chiles (page 76), stemmed and minced
4 cloves garlic, smashed with the side of a knife and coarsely chopped
3 tablespoons kosher salt
2 tablespoons fennel seeds
12 feet hog casings, soaked and rinsed (left)

In a large bowl, combine the pork shoulder, fatback, chiles, garlic, salt, and fennel seeds. Cover and refrigerate overnight.

Before grinding the meat, put the grinder, outfitted with the coarse plate, and the bowl of a stand mixer in the freezer for about 15 minutes, or until well chilled. Then grind the meat mixture into the chilled bowl.

Fit the mixer with the dough hook and mix the ground meat on low speed for about 5 minutes, or until it starts to look sticky and leaves a white film along the sides of the bowl.

continued

To stuff the casings with a piston-and-crank stuffer, transfer the meat mixture to the sausage stuffer and pack it in tightly to prevent air pockets from forming as you fill the casing. Give yourself ample counter space. Here, it helps to have an extra set of hands to crank the stuffer, so you can concentrate on guiding the stuffing into the casing. Slide the entire casing over the stuffing tube, leaving about 1 inch of the casing hanging off the end, and tie the end into a knot.

Keeping a hand at the base of the feeding tube over the casing, slowly crank the sausage stuffer. As the meat mixture fills the casing, move your hand back and forth from the nozzle to guide the stuffing into the casing, and curl the filled casing into a coil on the counter. If the casing starts to feel dry, moisten it with a few drops of water; a dry casing is more likely to split when filled. If the mixture starts to come out too quickly, stop cranking or the casing could burst. If the casing does burst, twist the end of the casing and tie it right before the break. Reload the casing onto the stuffer and start again, continuing to crank the stuffer until the casing is filled. If you have extra filling, save it for topping pizza or use it to make sausage patties.

To stuff the casings using a stand mixer's stuffer attachment, remove the grinding plate from the grinder and attach the feeder tube. Transfer the meat mixture to the grinder. Slide the entire casing over the feeder tube attachment, leaving about 1 inch of the casing hanging off the end, and tie the end into a knot. Pass the mixture through the grinder and follow the instructions above for stuffing sausage with a sausage stuffer.

To twist the sausage into links, measure out about 6 inches, pinch the casing, and twist the sausage 3 times in one direction until it forms a 6-inch link. Measure out an additional 6 inches, pinch the casing, and twist the sausage 3 times in the opposite direction. You should now have two 6-inch sausage links. Continue twisting the sausage into links, alternating directions each time, until all of the sausage is portioned into 6-inch segments. If you see any air pockets, prick the casing with a sewing needle or a sausage pricker. At this point, the sausages can be cooked immediately, or they can be refrigerated for up to 3 days or frozen for up to 2 weeks.

To cook the sausages, cut apart the links. Prepare a medium-hot fire in a grill, stacking the coals to one side so you have two areas of heat, one with direct heat and one with indirect heat. Arrange the sausages over the coals and sear them on all sides for 1 to 2 minutes, or until well browned. Move the sausages to the cooler side of the grill and continue to cook gently over indirect heat for about 8 minutes, or until cooked through (150ºF on an instant-read thermometer).

Transfer the sausages to a platter or individual plates and serve immediately.

MEATBALLS 101

Here are a handful of helpful tips to keep in mind when making any recipe for meatballs:

Before you grind the meat and fat, put the grinder or the food processor bowl and blade in the freezer to chill for about 15 minutes. This ensures the meat is evenly and easily ground or minced.

Using lean meat produces an inferior meatball. If you buy preground pork, make sure that it is ground shoulder meat, and don't skip the pork fat called for in the recipes. Not only does the fat ensure a more tender meatball, but it also renders into the sauce, giving it body and flavor. Most butchers and grocers who make their own sausages grind shoulder meat and maintain an inventory of pork fat trimmings that you can grind yourself in a meat grinder or ask them to grind for you. If you use a food processor to grind the fat, first cube the fat and chill it in the freezer until firm but not frozen, about 15 minutes; then pulse in a food processor before mixing it with the meat. The same technique can be used for the prosciutto in Monday Meatballs (right). If you use a grinder, the fat should be cold, but it does not need to be chilled until firm in the freezer.

If you are braising the meatballs, egg and bread help to bind the meat and strengthen it for extended cooking. If you are roasting the meatballs (such as the chicken meatballs on page 185), less egg and bread are needed for binding. While many meatball recipes call for dried bread crumbs, I recommend using day-old bread, torn or cut into chunks, which you can then pulse in a food processor or grind along with the meat in a meat grinder. Fresh bread crumbs made right before mixing give the meatballs a better texture than dried bread crumbs.

Use a light hand when mixing. Overworking the meat with the eggs and bread crumbs will create tough, dry meatballs. The mixture should be moist and tacky. If the mixture sticks to your hands, moisten them with cold water before rolling the balls and keep a bowl of cold water nearby as you work.

MONDAY MEATBALLS

PAIR WITH AGLIANICO (CAMPANIA)
SERVES 6

What began one Monday night as a way to use up a growing inventory of beef and pork trimmings unexpectedly turned into an immensely popular weekly event. The attraction to this dish is understandable: these meatballs are at once simple and deeply satisfying.

Since the inception of Meatball Monday, the meatballs have evolved through experimentation. We added lamb on some occasions, omitted beef on others. We sampled different braising liquids, from various broths to San Marzano tomatoes. Then, when we started receiving a whole pig every week, pork became a core ingredient—particularly the shoulder meat, which makes a perfectly tender meatball.

One trait of our meatballs has remained consistent, however. We use significantly more bread in the mix than is typically called for in classic Italian American recipes. Lured by the cheap price of meat, Italian immigrants in America began to make denser meatballs with more meat and less bread than used in the old country. But you get a much lighter texture with a higher percentage of bread in the mixture.

If you are grinding the pork shoulder and beef at home using a meat grinder, the fat, prosciutto, and bread chunks can be ground together with the pork and beef. If you are using a food processor, they should be done separately. If you want to make the meatballs in advance, roast the balls and freeze them. Before braising, defrost the balls completely, and then braise in the oven as directed in the recipe. The meatballs will continue to improve if refrigerated overnight in their braising liquid.

continued

10 ounces boneless pork shoulder, cut into 1-inch cubes and ground in a meat grinder or finely chopped in a food processor

10 ounces beef chuck, cut into 1-inch cubes and ground in a meat grinder or finely chopped in a food processor

6 ounces day-old country bread, torn into chunks and ground in a meat grinder or finely chopped in a food processor

2 ounces pork fat, cut into 1-inch cubes and ground in a meat grinder or chilled in the freezer for 15 minutes and then finely chopped in a food processor

2 ounces prosciutto, cut into 1-inch cubes and ground in a meat grinder or chilled in the freezer for 15 minutes and then finely chopped in a food processor

1 cup loosely packed fresh flat-leaf parsley leaves, coarsely chopped

1 tablespoon plus 2 teaspoons kosher salt

2 teaspoons dried oregano

1½ teaspoons fennel seeds

1 teaspoon dried chile flakes

⅔ cup fresh ricotta, drained if necessary (page 76)

3 eggs, lightly beaten

¼ cup whole milk

1 (28-ounce) can San Marzano tomatoes with juices

Handful of fresh basil leaves

Block of grana for grating

Extra virgin olive oil for finishing

Preheat the oven to 400°F. Coat 2 rimmed baking sheets with olive oil.

In a large bowl, combine the pork, beef, bread, pork fat, prosciutto, parsley, 1 tablespoon of the salt, oregano, fennel seeds, and chile flakes and mix with your hands just until all of the ingredients are evenly distributed. Set aside.

In a separate bowl, whisk together the ricotta, eggs, and milk just enough to break up any large curds of ricotta. Add the ricotta mixture to the ground meat mixture and mix lightly with your hands just until incorporated. The mixture should feel wet and tacky. Pinch off a small nugget of the mixture, flatten it into a disk, and cook it in a small sauté pan. Taste it and adjust the seasoning of the mixture with salt if needed. Form the mixture into 1½-inch balls each weighing about 2 ounces, and place on the prepared baking sheets. You should have about 30 meatballs.

Bake, rotating the sheets once from front to back, for 15 to 20 minutes, or until the meatballs are browned. Remove from the oven and lower the oven temperature to 300°F.

Sprinkle the tomatoes with the remaining 2 teaspoons salt, and then pass the tomatoes and their juices through a food mill fitted with the medium plate. Alternatively, put the entire can of tomatoes in a large bowl, don an apron, and then squeeze the tomatoes into small pieces with your hands.

Pack the meatballs into 1 large roasting pan or 2 smaller roasting pans. Pour the tomato sauce over the meatballs, cover tightly with aluminum foil, and braise for 1 to 1½ hours, or until the meatballs are tender and have absorbed some of the tomato sauce.

Pull the pans out of the oven and uncover. Distribute the basil leaves throughout the sauce.

For each serving, ladle meatballs with some of the sauce into a warmed bowl. Grate grana over the top, drizzle with olive oil to finish, and serve immediately.

PORK LOIN SPIEDINO WITH PINE NUT, GARLIC, AND CURRANT SOFFRITTO

PAIR WITH MAGLIOCCO (CALABRIA)
SERVES 6

A *spiedo* is a kitchen spit over an open fire that is most often used for cooking whole animals, particularly chicken. *Spiedino*—literally "little spit"—refers to food cooked on skewers, which is how we like to prepare pork loin. Grilled briefly over a smoky fire, the meat takes on an addictive char that counterbalances the sweet, mellow *soffritto* of pine nuts, garlic, and currants. For a discussion of *soffritto*, see page 228.

2 pounds boneless pork loin, cut into 1-inch cubes
About 1 tablespoon kosher salt
½ cup dried currants
¾ cup pine nuts
½ cup plus 1 tablespoon extra virgin olive oil
⅔ cup garlic cloves, minced
3 ounces arugula

In a bowl, toss the pork with the salt. Cover and refrigerate for at least overnight or up to 3 days.

To make the *soffritto*, soak the currants in just enough warm water to cover for about 20 minutes.

Meanwhile, add the pine nuts and ½ cup of the olive oil to a small, heavy pot and place over low heat. Gradually bring to a low simmer, stirring frequently, and cook, stirring, for about 5 minutes, or until the pine nuts have started to brown. Stir in the garlic and continue to cook on low heat for about 8 minutes, or until the garlic is a light golden brown. Watch the *soffritto* carefully; the pine nuts and garlic will burn easily. Drain the currants, add them to the pot, and then remove the pot from the heat. Let the *soffritto* cool to room temperature. It will keep, tightly covered, in the refrigerator for 2 weeks.

About 30 minutes before cooking, remove the pork from the refrigerator. If using wooden skewers, soak them in water to cover to prevent them from scorching. Prepare a hot fire in a grill, stacking the coals to one side so you have two areas of heat, one with direct heat and one with indirect heat.

Drizzle the remaining 1 tablespoon olive oil over the pork and toss to coat evenly. Drain the skewers, and thread about 5 pieces of pork onto each skewer.

Place the skewers over the coals and grill for about 1 minute on each side, or until well seared. Move the skewers to the cooler side of the grill and continue to cook over indirect heat for 8 to 10 minutes, until cooked medium-well but still juicy.

Arrange a bed of arugula on a platter. Place the pork skewers on top. Drizzle some of the *soffritto* over the top of the pork and the arugula. Pass the remaining sauce at the table. Serve immediately.

GRILLED SPARERIBS WITH YOGURT AND LEMON

PAIR WITH CANNONAU (SARDINIA)
SERVES 4 TO 6

Sold in 4- to 5-pound strips, spareribs include both the lower section of the rib cage and the breastbone. This preparation is a great way to serve them. The long braising makes them tender, and then a relatively short time on the grill gives the meat a smoky flavor and crisp exterior. A 4- to 5-pound strip of spareribs will have a larger meaty end and a smaller, leaner, less meaty end. Each end cooks at a different rate, so cut the strip in half and monitor their cooking progress separately as they braise.

1 tablespoon fennel seeds
1 teaspoon coriander seeds
1 teaspoon dried chile flakes
1 (4- to 5-pound) strip pork spareribs
About 2 tablespoons kosher salt
¾ cup whole-milk plain yogurt
Extra virgin olive oil
1 lemon, cut into wedges

In a spice grinder, or with a mortar and pestle, grind together the fennel seeds, coriander seeds, and chile flakes until coarsely ground.

Place the ribs on a large cutting board and cut them in half, separating the larger end from the smaller end. Season the pieces on both sides with the salt. Transfer the rib pieces to a shallow dish large enough to accommodate them in a single layer (or use 2 dishes). Rub each rib piece on both sides with the spice mixture, and then coat on both sides with the yogurt. Cover and marinate in the refrigerator for at least 1 day or up to 3 days.

Preheat the oven to 275°F. Remove the ribs from the refrigerator.

Transfer the ribs to a roasting pan large enough to accommodate them in a single layer (or divide the ribs between 2 smaller roasting pans). Cover with aluminum foil or a lid and place in the oven. Braise the ribs for about 2 hours, or until the meat is tender, but not so tender that it starts to fall off of the bones. Remove from the oven and let the ribs cool slightly. At this point, you can cool the ribs completely in the liquid they have released in the pan and grill them the following day.

Prepare a medium-hot fire in a grill, spreading the coals evenly for direct-heat cooking. Remove the ribs from their braising liquid and discard the liquid. Lightly coat the ribs with olive oil and place on the grill rack. Grill, turning once, for about 4 minutes on each side, or until browned.

Cut the strips into individual ribs and arrange them on a warmed platter with the lemon wedges. Serve immediately.

BRAISED ZAMPONE WITH MOSTO

PAIR WITH BOVALE SARDO (SARDINIA)
SERVES 4 AS A MAIN COURSE, OR 6 AS AN ANTIPASTO

Zampone, a boned pig's trotter (foot) stuffed with a sausage filling, is a special-occasion dish served throughout Italy, often for holidays. Some Italian specialty stores carry ready-to-cook *zampone*, made with the whole trotter, foot attached. We choose to make it with the foreshank, or the lower section of the front leg. It is shorter, often there are no foot joints to contend with, and it has its own nice bit of meat that adds to the final dish. If you can find only hindshanks, they can be used in place of foreshanks, though they are a bit trickier to bone because they are smaller and have an extra knoblike protrusion.

Some butchers sell the whole trotter, the foot with the foreshank attached. If you come across this configuration, ask the butcher to saw off the foot (which you can use in *ragù alla napoletana*, page 148), leaving you with the foreshank for the *zampone*. And if he or she will bone the foreshank for you, it will save you a step. Boning a foreshank requires some practice, but the meat is forgiving. The most important thing is to avoid nicking the skin. Think of the skin as a sausage casing. In other words, you must keep it intact so it will contain the filling.

Start making the *zampone* a day or two before you plan to serve it. For the best result, put the meat grinder or the food processor bowl and blade in the freezer for about 15 minutes to chill before you grind the meat and fat. The amount of filling you will need to stuff the trotter will vary depending on how meaty the foreshank is after you have boned it. If you are left with extra filling, you can cook it up and use it to top our Pizza Salsiccia with Spring Onions (page 128), toss it with pasta, or freeze it for future use. If you make the *zampone* the day before you serve it, cool it in its braising liquid and refrigerate it. The next day, remove the shanks from the liquid, cut them as directed in the recipe, and heat in a 350°F oven until lightly browned. Heat the braising liquid separately, adjusting the seasoning as instructed in the recipe.

SAUSAGE FILLING

8 ounces boneless pork shoulder, cut into 1-inch cubes and ground in a meat grinder or finely chopped in a food processor

4 ounces fatback, cut into 1-inch cubes and ground in a meat grinder or chilled in the freezer for 15 minutes and then finely chopped in a food processor

2/3 cup loosely packed fresh flat-leaf parsley leaves, coarsely chopped

2 tablespoons dry white wine

1 clove garlic, minced

1 tablespoon kosher salt

2 teaspoons fennel seeds

1 teaspoon black peppercorns

1/4 teaspoon dried chile flakes

2 (5-inch-long) pig foreshanks, skin on

Kosher salt

2 cups dry red wine

1 cup mosto (page 87)

2 tablespoons red wine vinegar

Extra virgin olive oil for finishing

To make the sausage filling, in a large bowl, combine the pork shoulder, fatback, parsley, wine, garlic, salt, fennel seeds, peppercorns, and chile flakes and mix well. Cover and refrigerate until needed.

continued

To bone each foreshank, stand it upright, wide end facing up, on a cutting board. With a boning knife, make an incision between the bone and the meat surrounding the bone. Trace a circle around the bone, then follow your cuts, making small incisions deeper into the foreshank until you have released about half of the meat from the bone. While you are cutting along the bone, be sure to angle the blade toward the bone rather than toward the meat to make sure you don't cut through the skin or remove too much meat. While boning the trotter, you might hit additional bones from a joint. If you do, turn the foreshank over and approach this side in the same way, tracing a circle around the bone, then following your cuts, making small incisions deeper into the foreshank until you have released the meat from the bones.

Once you have released about three-fourths of the meat from the bone, you can turn the foreshank inside out so that the bone and the meat are exposed. Hold the bone in one hand and peel back the meat in the other hand. Once the meat and bone are exposed, continue to cut along the bone until you release it from the meat. Cut out the tendon and discard. If you see a large strip of silver skin that remained after you removed the bone, cut it off.

While the foreshank is still inside out, season the inside with salt. Return the foreshank to its original shape. Aside from the hollow center, it should look similar to how it looked before you removed the bone. Fill the center with ¾ to 1 cup

of the sausage filling. Repeat with the second foreshank. Transfer the foreshanks to a loaf pan, a small casserole, or any baking container that holds them snugly, such as a tall, porcelain soufflé dish.

In a measuring pitcher, mix together the red wine and *mosto* and pour enough of the mixture over the foreshanks just to cover them. (If you are using a larger cooking vessel, and the liquid doesn't cover, mix together equal parts red wine and water as needed to cover.) Cover the pan tightly with aluminum foil and refrigerate overnight.

The next day, preheat the oven to 250°F.

Place the covered pan in the oven and braise the foreshanks for 3 ½ hours, or until the skin is soft when pierced with a knife. Remove the trotters from the braising liquid and let cool slightly. Meanwhile, pour the braising liquid into a small pot and bring to a simmer on the stove top. Taste for seasoning and add salt if needed. Stir in 2 tablespoons vinegar to balance the sweetness from the *mosto*, then taste and adjust with more vinegar if needed.

To serve, cut each foreshank in half to serve 4 or into thirds to serve 6. Place the pieces in warmed bowls and ladle enough of the braising liquid over each piece to create a shallow pool of sauce around it. Drizzle with olive oil to finish and serve immediately.

BRAISED PORK SHOULDER WITH CHESTNUTS, OLIVES, AND HERBS

PAIR WITH AGLIANICO (CAMPANIA)
SERVES 6

Chestnut trees blanket the hills of Avellino, in central Campania, and the hilly town of Montella is particularly renowned for its chestnuts. With their ubiquity, chestnuts have become a staple of regional Campanian cooking. This dish, which debuted on our opening menu, is a classic, with the subtle sweetness of the chestnuts pairing effortlessly with the rich pork.

While the recipe is not difficult, it helps to work a few days ahead. The pork should sit at least overnight after being seasoned with salt. It also will improve in flavor if cooled completely in its braising liquid and served the following day. Since this dish only gets better when you work ahead, it is a good one to do for parties, as the last step only requires heating the braising liquid and roasting the pork to brown its fat.

When purchasing the pork shoulder for this recipe, request a skin-on boned shoulder with skin and fatback attached. While the skin and some of the fat will be trimmed off before the pork is served, braising the pork with them attached adds body and flavor to the braising liquid. It is not always easy to find pork shoulder with its skin, but a good butcher will special order it for you. If you are unable to find skin-on, boneless pork shoulder, make this recipe with skinned, boneless pork shoulder. Skip the steps requiring you to remove the skin and then brown the pork in the oven before serving, and just reheat the pork in the sauce.

Unsweetened shelled chestnuts are not always easy to find, but if you have ever tried shelling chestnuts, you know it is worth looking for them. We buy Italian dried shelled chestnuts, though frozen chestnuts are a good substitute. During the holidays, shelled, vacuum-packed chestnuts and shelled French chestnuts in cans are sometimes available in upscale markets. If you use them, just make sure they are unsweetened.

36 shelled whole chestnuts (see headnote)
2 tablespoons kosher salt, plus 1 teaspoon if using dried chestnuts
1 (4-pound) boneless pork shoulder, with fatback and skin intact
¼ cup extra virgin olive oil
2 cups green olives
1 head garlic, divided into cloves but not peeled
4 sprigs sage
2 sprigs marjoram
2 sprigs rosemary
1 bay leaf
1 cup dry white wine
1 cup water

If using dried chestnuts, place in a pot, add water to cover by 1 inch, and simmer for about 40 minutes, or until tender. Remove from the heat, season with 1 teaspoon salt, and let cool in the cooking liquid, then drain. If using frozen, vacuum-packed, or canned chestnuts, skip this step. Let the frozen chestnuts thaw, or drain the canned chestnuts. Vacuum-packed chestnuts are ready to use.

Place the shoulder, skin side down, on a cutting board. Slice in half lengthwise, and then slice each half crosswise into about 6 evenly sized pieces, with each piece including both fatback and skin. Season with the 2 tablespoons salt, transfer to a storage container, and refrigerate overnight.

Bring the pork to room temperature. Preheat the oven to 250°F.

Pat the pork dry with paper towels to absorb any extra liquid. Coat the bottom of a Dutch oven with 2 tablespoons of the olive oil and place over medium-high heat. Working in batches, sear the pork for about 3 minutes on each side, or until well browned. As each batch is ready, transfer it to a large plate. Pour off the excess fat from the pot, and then add a few tablespoons of water and deglaze the pot over high heat, dislodging any browned bits from the bottom.

Add the remaining 2 tablespoons olive oil to the pot and stir in the chestnuts, olives, garlic, and herbs. Place the browned shoulder pieces on top. In a small pot, combine the wine and water and bring to a boil. Pour the wine mixture over the pork. The liquid should come halfway up the sides of the shoulder pieces. If it comes up short, add more water.

Cover the pot and place in the oven. Braise, turning the meat over halfway through cooking to ensure both sides of each piece spend time in the liquid, for about 2½ hours, or until the meat is tender when pierced with a knife.

Remove the pot from the oven, uncover, and let the pork cool in the cooking liquid. As the dish cools, skim off some of the fat that surfaces and taste the braising liquid, adjusting with salt if underseasoned or adding water if it tastes too concentrated. The flavor of the dish will improve if it is refrigerated overnight and then finished the next day.

To serve the dish, preheat the oven to 500ºF. Remove the pork pieces from the braising liquid and pat them dry. Cut off the pork skin and part of the fat from each piece and discard, leaving a layer of fat about ¼ inch thick on each piece. Place the pieces in a roasting pan, fat side up, and roast for 15 to 20 minutes, or until the fat begins to brown and sizzle.

Just before the pork is ready, discard the bay leaf and herb sprigs from the braising liquid and bring the liquid to a simmer. For each serving, place 2 pieces of pork into a warmed bowl. Ladle enough of the braising liquid into each bowl to come about halfway up the sides of the meat. Then spoon a few olives, garlic cloves, and chestnuts over the pork. Serve immediately.

Right: Fresh chestnut

Overleaf: San Marzano vines at Mariquita Farm

VEGETABLES

"There's nothing lifestyle about being a peasant," Andy Griffin observed when a few members of the A16 kitchen staff visited Mariquita Farm's Hollister plot, operated by Andy and his wife, Julia, two hours south of San Francisco. Given the crops cultivated at Mariquita Farm—lacinato kale, San Marzano tomatoes, summer and winter squashes, Friarelli peppers— the farm would fit right into the Campanian countryside. Yet Andy,

a tall, hardworking farmer whose ruddy, bearded face shows a resiliency to hot Hollister summers, grows more tomatillos than he knows what to do with. And you get the feeling that he is probably more at home sitting down to a Oaxacan feast than an Italian one. The main reason for the farm's Italian leanings comes straight from the earth: vegetables and fruits favored by Italians flourish on the farm. Out of necessity, Italian peasants stuck with crops that grew well in the local soil and climate, Andy explains, and Hollister's hot and dry summers and evening maritime breezes resemble the growing conditions in parts of southern Italy.

In the winter, Andy harvests sweet, earthy beets, the best I have ever tasted. In the summer, the farm supplies us with a continual stream of pepper varieties. When we brought back Friarelli seeds from one of our research trips and asked Andy to grow them for us, he did not hesitate, even when the first batch of seeds did not produce a single surviving pepper. So we tried again, and the next time, the smuggled seeds took to the soil. Now, the peppers grow in neat rows next to a field of carrots that are going to seed (another one of Andy's experiments).

What we are able to achieve at A16 comes in large part from the raw materials we receive through our relationships with producers like Mariquita. So we give vegetables the attention that they deserve at the table, and by doing so, we honor Campania's long history of vegetable cookery. Well before a bowl brimming with pasta became emblematic of Neapolitan cooking, city residents were called *mangiafoglie*, "leaf eaters." And even after pasta made significant inroads into the local diet, vegetables

continued to accompany nearly every meal, garnishing pasta or served, with gusto, as *contorni*, the Italian side dishes that traditionally accompany the second course.

Our approach to cooking vegetables may differ from how you have prepared them in the past. In Italy, vegetables are occasionally quickly cooked, but more often they are braised or roasted for extended periods. Yet these long-cooked vegetables never taste overcooked. Cauliflower, basted with olive oil, takes on a crispy, addictive sweetness. Cannellini beans, braised in a generous amount of olive oil until they nearly lose their shape, make a creamy, hearty side dish. Green beans soak up flavor when allowed to cook beyond a crunchy, bright green al dente to a silky, rich *straccotto*, or "extra cooked." And we never skimp on olive oil.

In keeping with the Italian tradition of *contorni*, we let our guests choose the vegetable side dishes that accompany their main courses. When I compose a meal, I approach matching a vegetable dish to a main course like a wine pairing. Rich cannellini beans complement equally rich meatballs, and refreshingly acidic *giardiniera* brightens braised short ribs. When serving several vegetable side dishes together, I look for complementary ingredients, but avoid duplicating flavors. For example, the creamy chard *gratinata* complements the crunch of roasted carrots and snap peas accented with green garlic, and the nutty flavors of roasted potato and cauliflower balance out the deep tomato and anchovy flavors in braised lacinato kale.

Yet above all else, I look to what is in season to make my choice. When sweet, local yellow corn hits the market, I eat it with just about everything.

SOFFRITTO

The process of making a *soffritto* is integral to a number of our recipes, particularly vegetable dishes. We consider a *soffritto*, literally "underfried," in much the same way a food manufacturer thinks of a bouillon cube: a concentrated flavor enhancer. In our *soffritto*, aromatic ingredients are simmered in ample olive oil over low heat and then tossed with a vegetable, infusing it with a deep, slow-cooked flavor. Other times, the *soffritto* is used as a condiment, as we do with our pork *spiedino* (page 216), where the char from the roasted pork is accented by the sweet flavor and pungent aroma of slowly fried pine nuts, garlic, and currants. When we prepare our *ragù alla napoletana* (page 148), we start by gently searing onion halves in olive oil. These onion halves are removed before we cook the ragù, and the flavored oil left behind is the *soffritto*.

While a *soffritto* takes time to make, the technique is simple. For two of the following recipes, it helps to have a food mill on hand to smooth the *soffritto* into a paste. But a similar, though more rustic, effect can be achieved by smashing it with the back of a wooden spoon as it cools in the pot. And even though I have suggested a specific *soffritto* for a dish, you can use them interchangeably. Make more than you need, and store the leftovers in the refrigerator, covered with a layer of olive oil. The pork *soffritto* will keep for 1 week, and the tomato and anchovy *soffritto* and garlic and anchovy *soffritto* for 2 weeks. You can also freeze them, divided into ready-to-use portions, for up to 3 months.

BRAISED GREEN BEANS WITH PORK AND TOMATO SOFFRITTO

SERVES 6

The idea for this recipe came about when I wanted to find another use for the pork shoulder and belly braised, then removed, from our ragù (page 148). We had used it for the family meal too many times, and the staff was beginning to protest. So the tender meat, too good to discard, found its way into a *soffritto*, which we simmer with green beans until the beans soften and absorb its flavor.

I call for ground pork shoulder in this recipe, but if you have leftover braised pork from either the ragù or the braised pork shoulder (page 222), you can substitute 8 ounces of it for the ground pork. Just skip the instruction directing you to render the fat from the pork.

PORK AND TOMATO SOFFRITTO
1 tablespooon extra virgin olive oil
½ red onion, diced (about 1 cup)
1 teaspoon kosher salt
¼ cup tomato paste
8 ounces boneless pork shoulder, cut into
   1-inch cubes and ground in a meat grinder
   or finely chopped in a food processor
1 cup water

Kosher salt
2 pounds green beans, ends trimmed
1 tablespoon extra virgin olive oil

To make the *soffritto*, heat the olive oil in a large pot over medium heat. Add the onion, season with the salt, and cook, stirring occasionally, for about 3 minutes, or until tender. Stir in the tomato paste and continue to cook, stirring frequently, for about 2 minutes longer, or until the tomato paste changes from bright red to brick red.

Add the pork, adjust the heat to low, and cook gently, stirring occasionally, for about 5 minutes, or until the pork has rendered most of its fat and is cooked through. Taste for seasoning and add more salt if needed. Stir in the water and continue to simmer for about 5 minutes more, or until the mixture is nearly dry. You should have about 1½ cups *soffritto*.

Bring a large pot of salted water to a boil. Add the green beans and blanch for about 5 minutes, or until nearly tender. Drain well and lay the beans out on a towel-lined baking sheet. Taste a bean. If it tastes underseasoned, season the beans with more salt.

Give the pot you used for cooking the beans a quick rinse and return it to the stove. Add the olive oil and warm over medium heat. Stir in the *soffritto* and cook for about 3 minutes, or until it is sizzling. Stir in the beans, add a splash of water, adjust the heat to medium-low, and simmer the beans for about 6 minutes, or until they are soft and have absorbed the flavor from the *soffritto*. Taste for seasoning and add salt if needed.

Transfer the beans to a warmed serving bowl and serve immediately.

BRAISED LACINATO KALE WITH TOMATO AND ANCHOVY SOFFRITTO

SERVES 6

There are several other terms for this dark kale, with *cavolo nero*, black cabbage, Tuscan kale, and dinosaur kale among them. More important than its name is its role in Campania's culinary history. While Americans tend to treat this kale as a novelty, similar greens, boiled and seasoned with anchovy, have been eaten in and around Naples since the Middle Ages, predating pasta and pizza as classic Campanian dishes.

The key to braising the greens in this book is to blanch them long enough. If the kale is blanched adequately, you won't have to cook it for very long with the *soffritto*. If you have undercooked the kale in the blanching process, simply ladle in water and continue to cook the kale with the *soffritto* until the leaves are tender. If lacinato kale is unavailable, regular kale or chard is a fine substitute. The *soffritto*, which will keep in a tightly sealed container in the refrigerator for 2 weeks, is also delicious with green beans.

TOMATO ANCHOVY SOFFRITTO
⅓ cup extra virgin olive oil
½ red onion, thinly sliced (about 1 cup)
4 salt-packed anchovies, rinsed, filleted, and soaked (page 84)
½ cup tomato paste
⅔ cup water

2 pounds lacinato kale (about 3 bunches)
Kosher salt
¼ cup extra virgin olive oil

To make the *soffritto*, in a large sauté pan, warm the olive oil over medium-low heat. Stir in the onion and anchovies and sweat, stirring occasionally, for about 3 minutes, or until the onion has softened. Stir in the tomato paste and fry, stirring frequently, for about 7 minutes, or until the paste turns from bright red to a deep rust. You need to cook the tomato paste this long to develop the rich, full flavor of the *soffritto*.

Deglaze the pan with the water, dislodging any browned bits from the pan bottom. Adjust the heat to low and simmer, partially covered, stirring every 10 minutes, for about 30 minutes, or until the mixture develops a pastelike texture. If the mixture starts to brown too quickly, stir in a splash of water and continue to simmer.

Pass the *soffritto* through the medium or fine disk of a food mill into a bowl and set aside. Alternatively, smash the *soffritto* against the sides of the pan with the back of a wooden spoon. You should have about ¾ cup. Set aside.

Using kitchen shears or a sharp paring knife, remove the center ribs from the kale leaves. Cut the ribs crosswise into ½-inch-wide pieces and set aside. Stack 3 to 5 leaves, roll them up lengthwise, and cut crosswise to create 1-inch-wide ribbons. Repeat with the remaining leaves. Rinse the leaf pieces and rib pieces separately in several changes of water until the water is clear.

Bring a large pot of salted water to a boil. Add the rib pieces and blanch for about 12 minutes, or until tender. Using a wire skimmer, transfer them to a large, towel-lined baking sheet to drain. Working in batches, add the leaves to the boiling water and blanch each batch for about 8 minutes, or until tender, then transfer to the baking sheet.

Give the pot a quick rinse and return it to the stove. Add the olive oil and warm over medium heat. Stir in the *soffritto* and cook for about 1 minute, or until it is sizzling. Stir in the kale, add about ½ cup water, adjust the heat to low, and simmer the kale for about 5 minutes, or until it is very tender and has absorbed the flavor from the *soffritto*. If the kale is too dry, add a splash of water and continue braising. Taste for seasoning and add salt if needed.

Transfer the kale to a warmed serving bowl and serve immediately.

BRAISED CHARD WITH GARLIC, ANCHOVY, AND LEMON

SERVES 6

Like the lacinato kale recipe (page 230), this chard dish draws its flavors from a slow-cooked *soffritto*. This recipe makes about 1 cup *soffritto*, which is more than you need for the dish, but the remainder keeps in the refrigerator for 2 weeks. For a milder dish, use less *soffritto* and add olive oil to the chard.

GARLIC AND ANCHOVY SOFFRITTO
2 heads garlic
6 salt-packed anchovies, rinsed, filleted, and
    soaked (page 84)
¾ cup extra virgin olive oil, or as needed
½ cup water
1 teaspoon kosher salt

2 pounds chard (about 3 bunches)
Kosher salt
Juice of ½ lemon

To prepare the *soffritto*, break the garlic heads into cloves and soak the unpeeled cloves in water to cover for 5 minutes. (Soaking garlic cloves in water for a few minutes loosens their skins, which makes peeling them faster and easier.) Drain the garlic cloves, peel them, and place in a small pot. Add the anchovies, olive oil, water, and salt, place over low heat, and simmer gently for about 1 hour, or until the cloves are very soft.

Remove the garlic mixture from the heat and pass it through the medium or fine disk of a food mill to create a smooth paste. Alternatively, smash the garlic and anchovies against the sides of the pot with the back of a wooden spoon. Either way, be sure to mix the *soffritto* well before adding it to the chard. You should have about 1 cup. Set aside ½ cup for the recipe and store the remainder in the refrigerator for future use.

Using kitchen shears or a sharp paring knife, remove the center ribs from the chard leaves. Cut the ribs crosswise into ½-inch-wide pieces and set aside. Stack 3 to 5 leaves, roll them up lengthwise, and cut crosswise to create 1-inch-wide ribbons. Repeat with the remaining leaves. Rinse the leaf pieces and rib pieces separately in several changes of water until the water is clear.

Bring a large pot of salted water to a boil. Add the rib pieces and blanch for about 10 minutes, or until tender. Using a wire skimmer, transfer them to a large, towel-lined baking sheet to drain. Working in batches, add the leaves to the boiling water and blanch each batch for about 5 minutes, or until tender, then transfer to the baking sheet.

Give the pot used for cooking the chard a quick rinse, return it to the stove, and warm over medium heat. Stir the ½ cup *soffritto* and cook for about 1 minute, or until it is sizzling. Stir in the chard, add about ½ cup water, adjust the heat to low, and simmer the chard for about 5 minutes, or until it is very tender and has absorbed the flavor from the *soffritto*. If the chard is too dry, add a splash of water and continue braising. Stir in the lemon juice, taste for seasoning, and add more lemon juice or salt if needed.

Transfer the chard to a warmed serving bowl and serve immediately.

CHARD GRATINATA WITH BREAD CRUMBS AND GRANA

SERVES 6

Italians use *besciamella* (béchamel) as a binder for baked pastas, vegetables gratins, and other dishes. It is a particularly decadent component in a recipe for hearty greens, such as the chard used here.

2 pounds chard (about 3 bunches)
Kosher salt
4 tablespoons unsalted butter
¼ red onion, finely diced (about ½ cup)
¼ cup all-purpose flour
⅛ teaspoon freshly grated nutmeg
2 cups cold whole milk
1 bay leaf
Extra virgin olive oil
½ cup fresh bread crumbs (page 74)
¼ cup grated grana

Using kitchen shears or a sharp paring knife, remove the center ribs from the chard leaves. Cut the ribs crosswise into ½-inch-wide pieces and set aside. Stack 3 to 5 leaves, roll them up lengthwise, and cut crosswise to create 1-inch-wide ribbons. Repeat with the remaining leaves. Rinse the leaf pieces and rib pieces separately in several changes of water until the water is clear.

Bring a large pot of salted water to a boil. Add the rib pieces and blanch for about 10 minutes, or until tender. Using a wire skimmer, transfer them to a large, towel-lined baking sheet to drain. Working in batches, add the leaves to the boiling water and blanch each batch for about 5 minutes, or until tender, then transfer to the baking sheet.

Preheat the oven to 400°F.

To make the *besciamella*, melt butter in a pot over medium heat. Add the onion and a couple of pinches of salt and sweat the onion, stirring occasionally, for about 3 minutes, or until softened. Stir in the flour and nutmeg to form a roux and cook the roux, stirring frequently with a wooden spoon, for about 4 minutes, or until it turns a light blond. Remove from the heat and let cool for 1 minute.

Add ¼ cup of the milk to the roux, whisking constantly to create a smooth paste. Return the pot to medium heat and continue to add the milk in ¼-cup increments, whisking steadily, until all of the milk is incorporated. Gradually bring to a boil while stirring steadily. Lower the heat to a simmer, add the bay leaf, and cook, stirring steadily, for about 6 minutes, or until the mixture thickens and loses the gritty texture of flour on the tongue when tasted. The finished sauce, aside from the onion, should be smooth, and it should taste well seasoned.

Lightly coat a small baking pan (about 8 inches square) with olive oil, and then coat with ¼ cup of the bread crumbs, tapping out the excess. In a small bowl, mix together the remaining ¼ cup bread crumbs, the grana, and enough water (about 1 tablespoon) to moisten.

Remove the bay leaf from the *besciamella*, add the sauce to the chard, and stir to incorporate. Spoon the sauced chard into the prepared baking pan. Sprinkle the bread crumb mixture evenly over the top.

Bake the gratin for 20 to 30 minutes, or until the *besciamella* bubbles on the sides and the bread crumb topping has turned golden brown. Remove from the oven and let stand for a few minutes before serving.

BRAISED CANNELLINI BEANS WITH GARLIC, MARJORAM, AND OREGANO

SERVES 6

I like to call this recipe the Italian answer to refried beans. A lot of olive oil goes into these beans, and necessarily so: the dish is rich, with the beans and garlic cloves losing their shape in the olive oil. Pair these beans with Monday Meatballs (page 213), and if you find yourself with leftover beans, serve them the next day on bruschetta (page 94).

2 cups dried cannellini beans
2 teaspoons kosher salt
¾ cup extra virgin olive oil, plus more for finishing
2 cloves garlic, smashed with the side of a knife
1 bay leaf
¼ teaspoon dried oregano
1 tablespoon fresh marjoram leaves
¼ cup fresh bread crumbs, toasted (page 74)

Rinse the beans well in a colander, picking out any broken beans and pebbles. Transfer to a bowl, cover with plenty of cool water, and let soak for at least 2 hours or up to overnight.

Drain the beans, transfer to a 3-quart pot, and add water to cover by 1 to 2 inches. Place over high heat and bring to a boil, skimming off any foam that rises to the surface. Adjust the heat to a slow simmer and cook uncovered, skimming as needed, for 2 hours, or until tender. (It might be necessary to top off the beans with more water as they cook.) Remove from the heat, stir in the salt, and let the beans stand in their cooking liquid for 30 minutes. Drain the beans, reserving ¾ cup of the cooking liquid.

In a pot, heat the olive oil over medium heat. Add the garlic, bay leaf, and oregano and cook for about 3 minutes, or until the garlic begins to soften. Stir in the beans and the ¾ cup cooking liquid and simmer, stirring gently, for about 4 minutes, or until the beans achieve a creamy consistency. The beans should not be as thick as mashed potatoes, but they should just hold their shape if spooned onto a piece of bread. If the beans are too thick, stir in a little water and continue to cook. Stir in the marjoram, taste for seasoning, and add salt if needed. Remove from the heat. (At this point, the beans can be cooled, covered, and refrigerated for up to 1 week. Reheat gently before serving.)

To serve, pour the beans into a warmed serving bowl, or ladle them into warmed individual bowls. Top with the bread crumbs and a drizzle of olive oil to finish. Serve immediately.

Clockwise from top: Roasted potatoes and cauliflower, roasted squash with pancetta, and roasted carrots with snap peas

ROASTED BUTTERNUT SQUASH WITH PANCETTA AND CHILES

SERVES 6

Sweet squash and hot chiles make a happy match with salty pancetta. Ask your butcher to cut the pancetta into thick slices, which will render their fat better than thin slices for this recipe. If you like more heat, add an extra chile.

1 (3-pound) butternut squash
Kosher salt
3 tablespoons extra virgin olive oil
4 ounces pancetta, diced (about 1 cup)
2 Calabrian chiles (page 76), stemmed and chopped

Preheat the oven to 500°F.

Halve the squash lengthwise and scoop out the seeds. Peel the squash halves and slice crosswise into ½-inch-thick pieces You should have about 8 cups.

In a large bowl, toss the squash with a few generous pinches of salt and 2 tablespoons of the olive oil. Divide the squash between 2 rimmed baking sheets, spreading the pieces evenly over the pans. Roast the squash, rotating the pan front to back about halfway through cooking, for about 15 minutes, or until cooked through and golden.

Meanwhile, heat the remaining 1 tablespoon olive oil in a small pot over low heat. Stir in the pancetta and cook, stirring occasionally, for about 4 minutes, or until crispy. Stir in the chiles, remove from the heat, and set aside.

When the squash is ready, remove from the oven and let cool for a few minutes. Transfer to a large bowl, add the pancetta mixture, and toss to mix. Taste for seasoning and adjust with salt if needed. Transfer to a serving bowl and serve immediately.

ROASTED CARROTS AND SNAP PEAS WITH GREEN GARLIC AND MINT

SERVES 6

One of the many reasons I love cooking in San Francisco is the quality of the tender peas and earthy carrots I am able to serve, not only in the spring but all the way through summer. It is not uncommon to find fava beans, peas, and snap peas grown in cool, foggy Half Moon Bay, which lies just south of San Francisco, in July. At the same time, late winter and spring is the ideal time for Mariquita Farm's green garlic, which gives a fresh bite to these sweet vegetables.

The flavor of green garlic varies in intensity depending on how young the garlic is. For this recipe, look for very young green garlic, which looks similar to a scallion. Trim off the flimsy tops and thinly slice the whole stalk crosswise. Adding green garlic at the very end and roasting it briefly mellows its flavor. If green garlic is out of season, use scallions instead.

Kosher salt
4 cups (about 12 ounces) snap peas
1 pound carrots, peeled and sliced on the diagonal
   ¼ inch thick
Extra virgin olive oil
Freshly ground black pepper
2 stalks green garlic, trimmed and thinly sliced crosswise
¼ cup loosely packed fresh mint leaves, sliced

Preheat the oven to 450°F.

Bring a large pot of salted water to a boil. Meanwhile, string the peas by snapping off the stem and peeling away the stringy fiber. Add the peas to the boiling water and blanch for 2 minutes. Drain and shock immediately in an ice bath. Once cool, drain, pat dry, and slice in half on the diagonal.

Place the carrots in a bowl and toss to coat with olive oil. Season with salt and pepper to taste. Spread the carrots evenly in a single layer on a baking sheet. Roast for 20 minutes, stirring carrots every 5 minutes to ensure even browning.

Once the carrots are golden, add the snap peas and green garlic to the baking sheet and stir carefully to combine. Roast a few minutes more, until the peas are heated through and the garlic has lost a bit of its raw bite. Remove the vegetables from the oven and place in a serving bowl. Stir in the mint right before serving.

ROASTED POTATOES AND CAULIFLOWER WITH RED ONION, CAPERS, AND CHILES

SERVES 6

In this embellished version of the classic roasted potato *contorno*, cauliflower florets add a crispy, sweet element to the potatoes' buttery flavor. You also can serve the dish at room temperature with a few diced pickled peppers (page 78), in a variation on potato salad.

1 pound Yukon Gold potatoes, similar in size,
   cut into 1-inch pieces
Kosher salt
½ cup extra virgin olive oil
1 head cauliflower (about 2 pounds)
⅓ cup salt-packed capers, soaked (page 84)
½ teaspoon dried chile flakes
1 red onion, sliced
3 tablespoons red wine vinegar

Preheat the oven to 450°F.

In a large bowl, combine the potatoes with about 1 teaspoon salt and 2 tablespoons of the olive oil and toss to coat the potatoes evenly. Transfer the potatoes to a rimmed baking sheet, spreading them in an even layer. Reserve the bowl for seasoning the cauliflower. Roast the potatoes, rotating the pan front to back about halfway through cooking, for about 40 minutes, or until cooked through and golden.

Meanwhile, remove the core of the cauliflower and separate the head into florets. Cut the largest florets in half, so that all of the florets are uniform in size. Transfer to the same bowl used to season the potatoes, add about 1 teaspoon salt and ¼ cup of the olive oil, and toss to coat the florets evenly. The florets must be generously coated with olive oil to brown evenly.

Heat a large ovenproof sauté pan over high heat. Give the cauliflower a final toss in the bowl and then transfer to the sauté pan. Using a rubber spatula, scrape any oil remaining in the bowl into the pan. Cook the florets, stirring occasionally, for about 7 minutes, or until they begin to turn golden brown on the outside but remain firm on the inside. Transfer the sauté pan to the oven and roast the florets, stirring them a few times to ensure even cooking, for about 20 minutes, or browned but not completely soft.

While the potatoes and cauliflower roast, heat the remaining 2 tablespoons olive oil in a small pot over medium heat. Pat the capers dry with a paper towel and carefully add them to the oil (they may splatter). Fry the capers for about 2 minutes, or until they bloom and become crispy. Stir in the chile flakes and onion and cook for 3 minutes longer, or until the onion softens. Stir in the vinegar and remove from the heat.

When the potatoes and cauliflower are ready, remove from the oven and let cool slightly before combining. Then combine them in a large bowl, add the onion mixture, and toss gently until all of the ingredients are evenly distributed. Taste for seasoning and add more salt and vinegar if needed to balance the flavors. Serve hot or at room temperature.

POTATO TORTA

SERVES 6

Think of all of the rich, salty, creamy things you can think of (starting with mozzarella and ending with prosciutto) and you will find them in this *torta*. It is also one of the few savory recipes we make that calls for butter and cream. Perhaps then it comes as no surprise that the original name for the dish is *gatto*, from the French *gâteau*, or "cake" (rather than anything to do with a cat, the more common Italian translation). While this dish makes a hearty winter side dish, it also can be served as an antipasto, or with a salad for a light lunch.

1 pound large Yukon Gold potatoes
Kosher salt
5 tablespoons unsalted butter
½ cup fresh bread crumbs, toasted (page 74)
2 eggs
¾ cup heavy cream
8 ounces fresh mozzarella, chopped (about 1 cup)
¼ bunch Italian parsley, coarsely chopped (about ⅔ cup)
2 ounces prosciutto, finely diced
¼ cup grated aged pecorino
½ cup grated grana
Freshly ground black pepper

Position a rack in the upper third of the oven, and preheat the oven to 375°F.

Place the potatoes in a medium pot, cover with cold water by about 2 inches, and season generously with salt. Bring to a boil over high heat, adjust the heat to a simmer, and cook, uncovered, for about 30 minutes, or until the potatoes are tender when pierced with a fork but haven't started to split. Drain the potatoes. Once the potatoes are cool enough to handle, peel them and pass them through the medium disk of a food mill or a potato ricer into a bowl.

Lightly coat a small baking pan (about 8 inches square) with 1 tablespoon of the butter, and then coat with ¼ cup of the bread crumbs, tapping out the excess.

Break the eggs into a bowl and whisk briefly until blended. Whisk in the cream. Add the mozzarella, parsley, prosciutto, pecorino, ¼ cup of the grana, 1½ teaspoons salt, and a couple of pinches of pepper and mix well. Add the mixture to the potatoes and mix thoroughly with a rubber spatula to ensure the ingredients are well combined. Spoon the potato mixture evenly into the prepared pan and level the surface with the spatula. In a small bowl, stir together the remaining ¼ cup each grana and bread crumbs. Sprinkle the bread crumb mixture evenly over the surface. Cut the remaining 4 tablespoons butter into bits and dot the surface.

Place the pan in the oven and bake for 40 minutes, or until the top has lightly browned. Allow the *torta* to cool for a few minutes before cutting into squares. Serve warm or at room temperature.

GIARDINIERA

SERVES 6

This classic pickled vegetable dish is an easygoing, flexible recipe that works well as an antipasto or as an accompaniment to rich pork preparations such as Liver Terrina (page 206) or Coppa di Testa (page 208), or grilled rabbit (page 186). I am partial to the combination of fennel, cauliflower, and carrot, but you could substitute celery, cucumber, or artichoke hearts with good results.

If you cannot locate Calabrian chiles, you can use dried chile flakes in their place, but do not add them to the vinaigrette. Instead, fry ¼ teaspoon chiles flakes in the olive oil just before you add the fennel seeds. This recipe makes more vinaigrette than you will need, but it is a good idea to keep extra on hand to refresh the vegetables before serving them if they have been refrigerated. The vinaigrette also complements salads and tuna *conserva* preparations (page 105).

⅔ cup plus 2 tablespoons extra virgin olive oil

⅓ cup red wine vinegar

3 Calabrian chiles, stemmed and minced (page 76)

Kosher salt

½ head cauliflower, segmented (about 2 cups)

½ teaspoon fennel seeds

1 red onion, sliced ¼ inch thick

1 fennel bulb, cored and sliced lengthwise ¼ inch thick (about 2 cups)

2 carrots, peeled and thinly sliced (about 1 cup)

½ cup water

To make the vinaigrette, whisk together ⅔ cup of the olive oil, the vinegar, and the chiles. Set aside.

Bring a pot of salted water to a boil. Add the cauliflower and blanch for about 4 minutes, or until it begins to soften. Drain and set aside on a plate to cool.

In a 3- to 4-quart pot, heat the remaining 2 tablespoons olive oil over medium heat. Add the fennel seeds, onion, and a pinch of salt and cook for about 3 minutes, or until the onion softens without coloring. Add the fennel and carrots, stir in the water, and continue to cook over medium heat for about 5 minutes, or until the vegetables have softened and most of the water has evaporated. Stir in the cauliflower and cook until the cauliflower is heated through. Taste for seasoning and add salt if needed.

Remove from the heat, add half of the vinaigrette (reserve the remaining vinaigrette for another use), toss well, and let cool to room temperature. Transfer to a bowl and serve, or cover and refrigerate for up to 1 week, then bring to room temperature before serving.

ROASTED CORN WITH BLACK PEPPER

SERVES 6

I prefer corn on the cob, which has far more flavor than corn sawed off a day before and stored in the refrigerator. Our customers must agree because when it is on the menu, we sell more corn than any other side dish. Cutting the ears into 2-inch-long pieces makes them more manageable for eating. It is a little hard to cut through a raw ear of corn, but a sharp serrated knife will get the job done.

While the closest way to replicate the smoky flavor we get in our oven is to grill the corn, you can also prepare the corn in a cast-iron pan. Blanch the shucked ears first in boiling water for a few minutes, and then cut them into 2-inch pieces (this is easier with blanched corn). Season the corn as you would if you were grilling it, and then quickly blacken it on all sides in the pan over high heat.

6 ears very fresh yellow corn
Extra virgin olive oil
Kosher salt
Freshly ground black pepper

Prepare a hot fire in a grill, spreading the coals evenly for direct-heat cooking.

Shuck the corn and wipe off all of the corn silk. With a serrated knife, slice the corn into 2-inch pieces. In a large bowl, toss the ears with olive oil to coat and generous pinches of salt and pepper.

Arrange the corn on the grill rack over the hottest part of the fire and grill, rotating the ears a few times, for about 6 minutes, or until the corn is still slightly crunchy but blistered. If your fire has cooled too much to blister the corn, close the grill to retain some of the heat, which will aid the blistering. Serve immediately.

DESSERT

If you find yourself walking down Naples's congested, cobbled Corso Umberto on your way to the marina, there is a short, delicious detour to take that offers more than respite from urban traffic. Pasticceria Giovanni Scaturchio in the Piazza San Domenico Maggiore serves *sfogliatelle*, thin, toothsome layers of lard-enriched pastry filled with candied orange–studded ricotta. Making them requires time and skill, but the Scaturchio bakers also harbor a secret technique that I have yet to figure out. I have eaten *sfogliatelle* in the United States, and I have made them myself, but nothing comes close to the rich, shell-shaped pastries from Scaturchio.

It is often said that desserts are less important at the Italian table, that fresh fruit or a few cookies is enough to complete a meal. But one short walk through the Spaccanapoli district, Naples's historic center, shows that sweets are everywhere, and it is the rare visitor who is not tempted by the enticing gelati or *semifreddi* served on a hot southern Italian summer day. At home, Campanians do not forsake sweets, either. Instead, they serve simpler renditions of the desserts available at the local *pasticceria*. Cakes filled with nuts and chocolate or lemon zest, baked fruit desserts, and cookies precede espresso or, on special occasions, *passito*, at a meal's end.

Our desserts are inspired by the flavors found in the creations made in both the *pasticcerie* and the homes of southern Italy. We add our own interpretations, too, thanks to Jane Tseng, our pastry chef, whose thoughtful desserts combine a classic Italian sensibility with contemporary technique. With an instinct for balancing sweet flavors with savory, and crunchy textures with smooth, Jane chooses dried or fresh fruits instead of the more traditional candied fruits, tempers sweetness with tart citrus, lightens dense cakes, and uses cookie crumbs as a garnish. The results, shown in the following recipes, are simple and satisfying. We have included a few signature items, such as our ever-popular chocolate *budino* tart seasoned with olive oil and sea salt, and a selection of our cookies, which pair well with Italian dessert wines. Frozen desserts, for which Naples is renowned, are represented in a walnut *semifreddo* and a selection of gelati and sorbetti. We have also added seasonal recipes with unexpected twists. A spin on a savory *panzanella* salad that combines summer blackberries, buckwheat cookies, and *panna cotta* is unlike anything I have eaten in Italy. Yet like all of our desserts, it is Italian in spirit.

SOUTHERN ITALY'S DESSERT WINES

BY SHELLEY LINDGREN

Shades of gold intertwined with the aromas of flowers, fruits, honeys, and nuts, with flavors so concentrated that one sip induces reflection—these are the qualities found in the dessert wines of southern Italy. And they also are what make them delightful finales to a meal.

Italy produces more styles of dessert wine than any other country, and their southern wines are among the most versatile, ranging from light elixirs with hints of orange blossom and honey to denser wines with an almost savory, nutty quality. The sweet wine made from the Zibibbo grape (the local name for Moscato di Alessandria) on the Sicilian island of Pantelleria is distinguished enough to make a case for the entire category of southern Italian dessert wines, and it is just one of Sicily's many singular bottlings. Sicily can also boast Marsala, which is making a comeback after years of being used for little more than cooking; late-harvest Malvasia; and numerous other incarnations of the Moscato grape. There is even evidence that suggests Sicilian technique spread through the Italian mainland, influencing several wines, including Tuscany's classic Vin Santo.

Taught long ago by the Greeks, southern Italian vintners most often make dessert wines by the *appassimento* process, a method of drying grapes to concentrate their sugars that yields a style of sweet wine called *passito*. Because of the risky nature of taking grapes past the point of ripeness and of the low yield relative to labor cost, making *passito* wines requires a special dedication. Though these wines were once prized for their distinctive character and ability to age, today some of them are in danger of extinction, pushed by the global wine market's thirst for dry wines. I can only hope that some of the particularly rare examples, such as Greco di Bianco

from Calabria (of which I am still waiting patiently for my first taste), continue to be produced.

There are many ways to make these *passito* wines, but here are the three main methods.

APPASSIMENTO NATURALE

This is the most natural, and some believe most favorable, way of making *passito* wines in southern Italy. The grapes are allowed to dry naturally on the vine, often aided by vintners who twist grapevines by hand to cut off the vines' supply of sap. After the grapes are harvested, they are dried more thoroughly on racks, trellises, rock walls, trays, or crates. The process requires a temperate climate with low humidity to ensure the grapes dry properly. Taking this into account, it is no wonder that warm, dry southern Italy produces some of the world's best sweet wines from *appassimento naturale*. Wines made from this method worth seeking out include Zibibbo di Pantelleria, made from the local, thick-skinned Moscato di Alessandria grapes grown on the island, and Moscato di Trani from Puglia, particularly the aromatic version produced by Villa Schinosa.

APPASSIMENTO IN PIANTA

Appassimento in pianta occurs when late-harvest grapes attract botrytis, a fungus that preserves their interior while drying it and concentrating its sugars. Botrytis (or *muffa grigia*, as it is also known in Italy) is the "noble rot" that gives French Sauternes, Hungarian Tokaji, and German Trockenbeerenauslese their unique character. In Campania,

Fiano grapes can attract the fungus if the conditions are right. For example, while Feudi di San Gregorio's Privilegio is made through *appassimento forzato*, its Fiano grapes occasionally acquire a touch of botrytis before they are harvested, as was the case in 2004.

APPASSIMENTO FORZATO

Used most often in northern Italy and in southern Italy's cooler mountain regions, *appassimento forzato* calls for "forcing" the grapes to dry in humidity-controlled rooms. Some wineries in warmer climates also choose *appassimento forzato* over *appassimento naturale* for consistency. The Sicilian producer Planeta discovered that drying Moscato grapes naturally in the sun for its Moscato di Noto dessert wine harmed their delicate skin, in effect giving them a sunburn. Now the producer prefers to dry the grapes in a single layer in temperature- and humidity-controlled rooms.

Dessert wines should be sipped and savored, complementing dessert without weighing it down. These wines pair particularly well with desserts made with nuts, honey, and fresh or candied fruits. As the wines' viscous qualities often mimic honey, I will sip a glass of Feudi di San Gregorio Privilegio instead of adding honey to a salty, creamy Gorgonzola or Stravecchio Pecorino. As the flavors of dessert wines are concentrated, I serve the wines in smaller, three-ounce pours, compared to the usual six ounces for dry wines. The wines benefit from a slight chill to mellow their higher alcohol content, but serving them too cold will mute their aromatics.

CHOCOLATE BUDINO TARTLETS WITH SEA SALT AND OLIVE OIL

SERVES 12

When I tasted chocolate custard garnished with sea salt and olive oil on a visit to Italy, I knew I had stumbled on a great idea. So, like most chefs, I tucked the idea away to use myself. Jane added a chocolate tart shell, which provides a nice textural contrast to the smooth filling and also complements the sea salt. Use the leftover egg whites from the recipe to make amaretti (page 263).

It is best to make the tart shells and the filling a day or two before you plan to serve the dessert. The filling needs a minimum of 4 hours to chill and set up. After the initial whisking, avoid stirring the filling as it cools or you will change its texture.

BUDINO FILLING
7 ounces bittersweet chocolate (60 to 70 percent cacao), coarsely chopped
1½ ounces milk chocolate, coarsely chopped
½ cup whole milk
6 egg yolks
⅓ cup sugar
2 cups heavy cream

TART SHELLS
2 egg yolks
1 tablespoon heavy cream
1¾ cups "00" flour (page 79) or all-purpose flour
½ cup unsweetened cocoa powder, preferably natural
7 ounces unsalted butter, at room temperature
⅓ cup sugar
½ teaspoon pure vanilla extract
¼ teaspoon kosher salt

GARNISH
1 teaspoon unrefined sea salt, preferably grey
Extra virgin olive oil

Preheat the oven to 300°F.

To make the *budino* filling, combine the bittersweet and milk chocolates in a heatproof bowl, place over (not touching) barely simmering water in a pot, and leave to melt. Meanwhile, warm the milk in a small pot over medium heat just until it begins to simmer. In a bowl, whisk together the egg yolks and sugar, and then gradually whisk in the warm milk.

When the chocolate has melted, remove from the heat and stir until smooth. Strain the egg yolk mixture through a fine-mesh strainer into the melted chocolate, and stir until combined. In a small pot, heat 1 cup of the cream over medium heat just until it begins to simmer. Remove from the heat and slowly stir the warm cream into the chocolate mixture. Then stir in the remaining 1 cup cream.

Pour the filling into a small baking pan (about 8 inches square) and cover tightly with aluminum foil. Place the pan into a larger baking pan and pour warm tap water into the larger pan to come halfway up the sides of the filling pan. Bake the filling for 50 to 60 minutes, or until the edges appear set but the center is loose and a bit runny.

Remove the pan from the water bath, and briefly whisk the filling in the pan until smooth. Strain through a fine-mesh strainer into another shallow pan and let cool completely, without stirring. Cover and refrigerate for at least 4 hours or up to overnight.

To make the tart shells, in a bowl, whisk together the egg yolks and cream and set aside. In another bowl, sift together the flour and cocoa powder and set aside. In a stand mixer fitted with the paddle, combine the butter, sugar, vanilla, and salt and mix on medium speed for 3 minutes, or until creamy and smooth. Reduce the speed to low, add the flour mixture all at once, and mix for 1 minute, or until barely incorporated. Drizzle in the yolk mixture and mix briefly.

continued

Turn the dough out onto a lightly floured work surface and knead gently for a couple of minutes until it comes together completely. Pat the dough into a round disk, wrap in plastic wrap, and refrigerate for at least 1 hour or up to 4 days.

Lightly butter 12 tartlet pans, each 3½ inches in diameter and ¾ inch deep. On a lightly floured work surface, roll out the dough about ⅛ inch thick. Using a cookie cutter or other template, cut out 4-inch rounds. Gather up the scraps of dough and roll it out again until you have 12 rounds. To line the pans, place a round in each pan and, starting from the center, gently press the dough against the bottom to flatten. Then, using your thumbs, press the dough firmly against the sides. With a paring knife, trim away the excess dough from the rim. Slip the lined pans into the freezer for 20 minutes before baking. Meanwhile, preheat the oven to 350°F.

Transfer the pans from the freezer to a rimmed baking sheet. Bake for 15 to 20 minutes, or until dry and firm to the touch. Transfer the pans to a wire rack and let cool completely. Then gently remove the cooled tart shells from the pans and set aside.

To assemble each tart, spoon about ¼ cup of the chilled filling into the baked shell and gently level off the top with a small offset spatula or butter knife. Place the tarts on individual plates and sprinkle the top of each tart with about ⅛ teaspoon sea salt. Finish each tart with a generous drizzle of olive oil.

MODIFIED BUDINO

If you want to make a simpler variation of this dessert, you can eliminate the tart shell and bake the *budino* filling in ramekins until set. Follow the recipe up until it is time to bake the filling, and instead of using 1 baking pan, pour the filling into 8 (1-cup) ramekins. Cover each ramekin tightly with aluminum foil and place the ramekins in a baking pan at least 2 inches deep. Carefully pour hot tap water into the baking pan to come two-thirds up the sides of the ramekins. Bake until the edges appear to be set but the middle is still loose, about 40 minutes. Carefully remove the ramekins from the pan, let cool, and refrigerate until ready to serve.

WALNUT AND CHOCOLATE SEMIFREDDO WITH CHESTNUT SHORTBREAD AND BITTERSWEET CHOCOLATE SAUCE

SERVES 6 TO 8

I would love to see how Neapolitans prepared a *semifreddo* before the advent of modern refrigeration. Frozen desserts, from *semifreddi* to *sorbetti*, have been specialties of Campania for centuries. Here, walnuts and chocolate give a rustic texture to the frozen cream, which is complemented by buttery, smoky chestnut shortbread.

Allow yourself ample time to prepare and freeze the *semifreddo*, preferably making it the day before you plan to serve it. The instructions call for freezing it in a loaf pan, but you can also freeze it in individual portions. To give the desserts a consistent shape, line jumbo nonstick muffin cups with small circles of waxed paper. Cut the shortbread cookies the same size as the top of a muffin cup. When serving, drizzle a small amount of chocolate sauce in the center of each plate. Place a cookie round on top of the sauce, then invert the *semifreddo* molds on top of each cookie. Save leftover chocolate sauce in a tightly covered container in the refrigerator for up to 2 weeks for serving with gelato.

SEMIFREDDO

⅔ cup walnuts, toasted (page 81) and chopped

2 ounces unsweetened chocolate, grated (about ¼ cup)

2 ounces bittersweet chocolate (70 percent cacao), grated (about ¼ cup)

¼ teaspoon kosher salt

1½ cups heavy cream

1½ teaspoons powdered gelatin

2 tablespoons cold water

4 eggs

¾ cup granulated sugar

CHESTNUT SHORTBREAD

¾ cup (6 ounces) unsalted butter, at room temperature

¼ cup powdered sugar

¼ cup granulated sugar

¾ cup chestnut flour (page 79)

¾ cup "00" flour (page 79) or all-purpose flour

BITTERSWEET CHOCOLATE SAUCE

2 ounces bittersweet chocolate (70 percent cacao), finely chopped

1 ounce unsweetened chocolate, finely chopped

1 cup whole milk

1 tablespoon granulated sugar

To make the *semifreddo*, lightly butter a 4-by-8-inch loaf pan. Then line the buttered pan with waxed paper, leaving at least a 1-inch overhang on all 4 sides.

In a large bowl, mix together the walnuts, unsweetened chocolate, bittersweet chocolate, and ⅛ teaspoon of the salt. Set aside.

continued

In a stand mixer fitted with the whisk attachment, whip the cream on medium-high speed for about 3 minutes, or until it forms medium peaks. Transfer to a bowl, cover, and refrigerate. Wash the mixer bowl and whisk to use for the egg yolks.

In a small bowl, sprinkle the gelatin over the cold water and set aside for at least 3 minutes to soften.

Combine the eggs, sugar, and remaining ⅛ teaspoon of salt in the top pan of a double boiler (or in a heatproof bowl) and place over (not touching) gently simmering water in the lower pan. Whisk together for 3 minutes, or until the mixture is hot and frothy and registers about 160ºF on an instant-read thermometer. Transfer the egg mixture to the cleaned mixer bowl, fit the mixer with the whisk attachment, and whip on medium speed for 3 minutes, or until the mixture has cooled slightly. Pour in the gelatin mixture and continue to whip for about 5 minutes longer, or until lukewarm.

Using a rubber spatula, gently fold the egg mixture into the chocolate-walnut mixture just until combined. Add a few spoonfuls of this combined mixture to the whipped cream and stir gently to mix. Then add the cream all at once to the egg-chocolate mixture and gently incorporate it until the batter is smooth.

Pour the batter into the prepared loaf pan, fold the overhanging waxed paper over the top, and cover with plastic wrap. Place in the freezer for at least 3 hours but preferably overnight, or until firmly set.

To make the chestnut shortbread, in the stand mixer fitted with the paddle attachment, combine the butter, powdered sugar, and granulated sugar and beat on medium-high speed for about 2 minutes, or until creamy and smooth. Reduce the speed to low, add the chestnut flour and "00" flour, and mix for about 1 minute, or until partially incorporated. Increase the speed to medium and mix for about 2 minutes, or until the flours are completely incorporated and the dough is smooth.

Line 2 baking sheets with parchment paper. On a lightly floured work surface, roll out the dough into a rectangle (that will fit on a baking sheet) about ½ inch thick. Transfer the dough to 1 of the prepared baking sheets and refrigerate until firm, about 30 minutes. Meanwhile, position the oven racks so that one is in the center of the oven and the other is in the upper third, then preheat the oven to 325°F.

Remove the dough from the refrigerator. Using a sharp knife, cut the dough into 3-by-3½-inch rectangles (they will be about the same size as the slices of *semifreddo*) and place on the prepared baking sheets, spacing them about 1 inch apart.

Bake the cookies for about 15 minutes, rotating the sheets once from front to back, or until the edges are browned and the tops feel firm to the touch. Transfer the sheets to wire racks and let the cookies cool completely.

To make the chocolate sauce, combine the bittersweet chocolate and unsweetened chocolate in a medium heatproof bowl. In a small pot, heat the milk over medium heat until warm. Stir in the sugar and bring to a simmer. Remove from the heat, pour one-third of the hot sweetened milk over the chocolate, and let stand, undisturbed, for about 5 minutes. Then whisk the mixture together until smooth and shiny. Gradually add the remaining sweetened milk while whisking constantly. Keep warm until needed. If making in advance, let cool completely, store tightly covered in the refrigerator, and reheat gently in a water bath.

To serve, drizzle a small amount of chocolate sauce in the center of each plate and top with a cookie. Remove the *semifreddo* from the freezer, invert it onto a clean surface, lift off the pan, and peel off the waxed paper. Heat a sharp knife under hot water, dry the knife with a towel, and cut the *semifreddo* into slices about 1¼ inches thick. Place each slice on top of a shortbread cookie, and then garnish with a generous drizzle of chocolate sauce.

HONEY PANNA COTTA WITH PANZANELLA OF BLACKBERRIES AND BUCKWHEAT COOKIES

SERVES 6

Sweet and earthy, spicy and herbal, this is one of Jane's favorite desserts. The *panna cotta* is a cool, creamy complement to the basil, buckwheat cookies, blackberries, and pepper. It is easy to make but requires time to set. Start the day before or the morning of the day you plan to serve it.

HONEY PANNA COTTA
2 teaspoons powdered gelatin
2 tablespoons cold water
2 cups heavy cream
¼ cup plus 1 tablespoon honey
⅛ teaspoon kosher salt

BUCKWHEAT COOKIES
½ cup buckwheat flour
½ cup "00" flour (page 79) or all-purpose flour
⅓ cup sugar
½ teaspoon kosher salt
¼ teaspoon baking powder
½ cup (4 ounces) cold unsalted butter, cut into cubes
1 egg yolk
1 tablespoon heavy cream

PANZANELLA
1 pint blackberries, picked over
2 to 3 teaspoons sugar
1 teaspoon freshly squeezed lime juice
6 large fresh basil leaves
Freshly ground black pepper

To make the *panna cotta*, in a small bowl, sprinkle the gelatin over the water and let soften for at least 3 minutes. In a small pot, heat 1 cup of the cream over medium heat until warm. Stir in the honey and salt and continue to heat the mixture until it begins to simmer. Remove from the heat, add the gelatin, and slowly stir in the remaining 1 cup cream.

Divide the mixture among 6 nonstick standard muffin cups or 6 (3-ounce) paper cups. Cover with plastic wrap and refrigerate until set, at least 4 hours.

To make the cookies, in a food processor, combine the buckwheat flour, all-purpose flour, sugar, salt, and baking powder and pulse to blend. Scatter the butter over the flour mixture and pulse until the mixture appears coarse and crumbly. Add the egg yolk and cream and pulse a few more times. The dough will appear as if it is starting to come together, though it will still be somewhat dry and crumbly.

Transfer the dough to a lightly floured surface and knead gently for about 2 minutes, until it comes together. Divide the dough into 3 equal portions. Using your fingers, and widening the distance between them as the dough extends, roll each portion back and forth into a long rope ¼ to ½ inch in diameter. Transfer the ropes to a baking sheet and freeze for 30 minutes.

Meanwhile, position the oven racks so that one is in the center of the oven and the other is in the upper third, then preheat the oven to 325°F. Line 2 baking sheets with parchment paper or lightly butter them.

Remove the dough from the freezer. Using a sharp knife, cut each log into ¼-inch-thick slices, and place the slices on the prepared baking sheets, spacing them 1 inch apart.

Bake the cookies, rotating the sheets once, for 15 minutes, or until they are medium gold and slightly puffed. Transfer the sheets to wire racks and let the cookies cool.

To make the *panzanella*, in a bowl, toss the blackberries with the sugar to taste and the lime juice and let stand at room temperature for 1 hour. Right before serving, tear the basil into small pieces, scatter over the berries, and toss to mix. Toss in the cookies and mix until they are moistened.

To serve, unmold each *panna cotta* by running a paring knife around its edge and inverting it onto a plate, placing it off-center. Divide the *panzanella* evenly among the plates, and finish each plate with a grind of black pepper.

BAKED PEACHES WITH AMARETTI AND VANILLA ZABAGLIONE

SERVES 6

It is hard to make great peaches any better. But this simple baked preparation, in which the pit is removed and replaced with a filling of crushed amaretti, heightens the flavor of the peaches without overpowering their inherent goodness. The zabaglione we pair with the peaches offers a sophisticated alternative to whipped cream.

Store-bought amaretti work well if you don't want to make the cookies from scratch. If you are baking the amaretti specifically for this recipe, be sure to leave out the aniseeds.

VANILLA ZABAGLIONE
1 cup heavy cream
1 vanilla bean
1 teaspoon powdered gelatin
2 tablespoons water
1 egg
5 egg yolks
½ cup sugar
Pinch of kosher salt

BAKED PEACHES
1 egg yolk
1 tablespoon sugar
⅛ teaspoon kosher salt
½ cup finely crushed Anise Amaretti made
    without aniseeds (page 263), or as needed,
    plus ¼ cup for garnish
3 tablespoons unsalted butter, melted and
    cooled slightly
2 teaspoons honey
6 peaches
½ lemon

To make the vanilla zabaglione, place the cream in the bowl of a stand mixer fitted with the whisk attachment. Using a sharp paring knife, split the vanilla bean in half lengthwise. With the back of the knife or with a spoon, scrape out the seeds into the cream. Reserve the pods. With the mixer on medium-high speed, whip the cream for about 3 minutes, or until it forms medium peaks. Transfer the whipped cream to a new bowl, cover, and refrigerate. Wash the mixer bowl and whisk and set aside for using later.

In a small bowl, sprinkle the gelatin over the water and set aside to soften for at least 3 minutes.

Combine the egg, egg yolks, sugar, and salt in the top pan of a double boiler (or in a heatproof bowl) and place over (not touching) gently simmering water in the lower pan. Whisk together for about 4 minutes, or until the mixture is hot and frothy and registers about 160° F on an instant-read thermometer. Transfer the egg mixture to the cleaned mixer bowl, fit the mixer with the whisk attachment, and whip on medium speed for about 3 minutes, until the mixture has cooled slightly. Pour in the gelatin mixture and whip for about 3 minutes longer, or until lukewarm.

Using a rubber spatula, gently fold half of the whipped cream into the egg mixture. Then fold in the remaining cream just until evenly incorporated. Add the reserved vanilla pods to the mixture; they will continue to flavor the zabaglione as it sets. Cover and refrigerate for at least 1 hour or overnight.

To make the filling for the peaches, in a bowl, whisk together the egg yolk, sugar, and salt until frothy. Using the rubber spatula, fold in the crushed amaretti, followed by 1 tablespoon of the butter. The filling should be soft but not runny. If the filling seems too runny, add additional crushed amaretti. Transfer the filling to a storage container, cover, and refrigerate for about 30 minutes, or until firm enough to scoop into balls.

Preheat the oven to 425°F. Lightly butter a baking pan large enough to accommodate the peaches in a single layer once they are halved.

To bake the peaches, in a small bowl, combine the remaining 2 tablespoons butter with the honey and set aside. Halve the peaches, remove the pits, and rub the cut sides with lemon. Using a pastry brush or your fingers, coat the cut sides generously with the butter mixture, avoiding the pit indentation.

Place the peaches, cut side down, in the pan and bake for about 10 minutes, or until the skin has slightly darkened. Remove from the oven, and leave the oven on.

Turn the peaches cut side up. Remove the amaretti mixure from the refrigerator. For each peach half, scoop up about 1 tablespoon of the amaretti mixture and roll it between your palms into a ball. The ball should fit comfortably in the hollow left by the pit, so if you are using smaller peaches, you may need to form smaller balls. Place a ball in each hollow.

Return the peaches to the oven and bake for 10 to 15 minutes, or until the filling puffs and browns. Remove the pan from the oven and let the peaches cool slightly before serving. The skins will have loosened from the peaches in the heat of the oven. If you want to remove them, do so once the peaches are cool enough to handle.

To serve, remove the vanilla pods from the zabaglione and discard. Spoon the zabaglione onto individual plates, dividing it evenly. Place 2 peach halves, one cut side up and one cut side down, on each bed of zabaglione. Garnish each serving with a sprinkle of crushed amaretti and serve immediately. The peaches are best when served warm.

PISTACHIO AND ALMOND CAKE WITH ORANGE SALAD

SERVES 6 TO 8

This homespun loaf cake evokes the nut tree–covered hills of Avellino and the lemon-scented Amalfi coast. The cake batter is primarily ground raw nuts, generously flavored with lemon zest. The latter gives the finished cake a pronounced citrus flavor that pairs well with the orange salad.

PISTACHIO AND ALMOND CAKE
1⅓ cups unsalted shelled pistachio nuts
1⅓ cups blanched whole almonds
½ cup plus 2 tablespoons (5 ounces) unsalted butter, at room temperature
¾ cup plus 3 tablespoons sugar
3 lemons
½ teaspoon pure vanilla extract
3 eggs
½ cup plus 1 tablespoon "00" flour (page 79) or all-purpose flour
¼ teaspoon kosher salt

ORANGE SALAD
3 blood oranges
2 Valencia, navel, or blood oranges
¼ cup orange marmalade
1 teaspoon freshly squeezed lemon juice

½ cup plain whole-milk yogurt
Unsalted shelled pistachio nuts

To make the cake, preheat the oven to 300°F. Butter a 4-by-8-inch loaf pan. Then, using a sifter or a fine-mesh strainer, dust it with flour, tapping out the excess.

In a food processor, combine the pistachios and almonds and pulse until finely ground. Set aside.

Combine the butter and sugar in the bowl of a stand mixer. Grate the zest from the lemons directly into the bowl. Fit the mixer with the paddle attachment and beat on medium speed for about 2 minutes, or until smooth and creamy. Mix in the vanilla just until incorporated. On low speed, gradually add the nuts and mix just until incorporated. Then add the eggs, one at a time, mixing after each addition just until incorporated. Stir in the flour and salt and mix just until incorporated.

Spoon the batter into the prepared loaf pan. Bake until a skewer inserted into the middle of the cake comes out clean, about 45 minutes. Let cool in the pan on a wire rack for 10 minutes. Then, run a paring knife around the inside of the pan to loosen the cake sides, invert the cake onto a plate, and lift off the pan. At this point, the cake can be served warm or allowed to cool completely before being sliced and reheated.

To make the orange salad, cut a slice off the top and bottom of 1 orange, stand the orange upright, and cut downward to remove the rind and pith in thick strips. Cut the orange crosswise into ¼-inch-thick slices, capturing any juice. Repeat with all of the remaining oranges. Set the oranges slices aside until needed.

Gently heat the marmalade in a pot over low heat for about 3 minutes, or until syrupy. Add any captured orange juice along with the lemon juice to the marmalade. Remove the pot from the heat and add 1 to 2 tablespoons water to thin the marmalade to the consistency of a vinaigrette. Let cool.

To serve, preheat the oven to 400°F. Cut the cake into generous slices and place on a baking sheet. Bake the slices, turning them over once, for about 5 minutes, or until warm and slightly toasted on both sides.

Place 4 or 5 orange slices on each plate and drizzle generously with the marmalade syrup. Place the warm pieces of cake next to the orange slices and top with a dollop of yogurt and a few pistachios. Serve immediately.

COOKIES

Sometimes all diners want to do after a meal is nibble on small treats. That's when a plateful of sophisticated cookies makes a perfect ending, especially when paired with a honey-hued *passito*. Our cookies are sweet but frequently include a savory undertone, such as sea salt. They also give us an often-discarded asset: cookie crumbs. Just as bread crumbs add texture to savory dishes, cookie crumbs are an effective, easy way to garnish desserts. Our pastry chef, Jane Tseng, garnishes creamy desserts and cakes with a pinch of crumbs, incorporates *croccante* crumbs into parfaits, and uses amaretti crumbs in a filling for baked peaches (page 254). Topping frozen desserts like *semifreddo* and gelato with a pinch of cookie crumbs gives them crunch and style.

CHOCOLATE AND SEA SALT SHORTBREAD COOKIES

MAKES ABOUT 50 COOKIES

Sea salt accentuates the deep chocolate flavor of these crumbly shortbread cookies, making them unexpectedly complex additions to any cookie plate.

1¾ cups plus 1 tablespoon "00" flour (page 79)
    or all-purpose flour
½ cup plus 1 tablespoon unsweetened cocoa powder,
    preferably natural
¾ teaspoon baking powder
1 cup (8 ounces) unsalted butter, at room temperature
¾ cup sugar
8 ounces bittersweet chocolate (70 percent cacao),
    coarsely chopped
1 teaspoon pure vanilla extract
¾ teaspoon sea salt

In a large bowl, sift together the flour, cocoa, and baking powder. Set aside.

In a stand mixer fitted with the paddle attachment, combine the butter and sugar and beat on medium speed for about 2 minutes, or until pale and smooth. Switch to low speed and add the flour mixture in 3 additions, beating after each addition just until incorporated. Add the chocolate, vanilla, and salt and mix briefly just until incorporated.

Divide the dough in half. Place half of the dough on a lightly floured work surface. Using your fingers, and widening the distance between them as the dough extends, roll the dough back and forth into a log about 1 inch diameter. Repeat with the second half. Wrap the logs separately in plastic wrap and refrigerate for about 1 hour, or until firm.

Position the oven racks so that one is in the center of the oven and the other is in the upper third, then preheat the oven to 300°F. Line 2 baking sheets with parchment paper or lightly butter them.

Using a sharp knife, cut the logs into ¼-inch-thick rounds, and arrange the rounds on the prepared baking sheets, spacing them about 1½ inches apart. Bake, rotating the sheets once from front to back, for 15 to 20 minutes, or until baked through but still soft. Transfer the sheets to wire racks. The cookies will firm up as they cool.

Store in an airtight container at room temperature for up to 1 week.

CROCCANTE

MAKES ABOUT 30 COOKIES

Named after a classic Italian almond brittle for their sweet nuttiness, these simple, satisfying cookies are ideal accompaniments to such creamy desserts as gelato, *semifreddo*, and *panna cotta*.

1 cup (8 ounces) unsalted butter at room temperature
1 cup plus 2 tablespoons sugar
1 egg
1 teaspoon pure vanilla extract
1¾ cups "00" flour (page 79) or all-purpose flour
¼ teaspoon kosher salt
1½ cups sliced natural almonds

In a stand mixer fitted with the paddle attachment, combine the butter and sugar and beat on medium speed for about 2 minutes, or until smooth and creamy. Add the egg and vanilla and beat briefly to incorporate. Switching to low speed, mix in the flour and salt, and then add the almonds and mix just until incorporated.

Lay a large piece of plastic wrap on a work surface. Scrape the dough onto the plastic wrap and pat it into a 6-inch square. Cover completely with the plastic wrap and refrigerate for about 1 hour, or until firm.

Position the oven racks so that one is in the center of the oven and the other is in the upper third, then preheat the oven to 350°F. Line 2 baking sheets with parchment paper or lightly butter them.

On a lightly floured work surface, roll out the dough in a rectangle or square ¼ inch thick. With a sharp knife, cut into 1-by-2-inch rectangles, and arrange them on the prepared baking sheets, spacing them 1 inch apart.

Bake the cookies, rotating the sheets once from front to back, for about 12 minutes, or until the tops are a deep gold. Transfer the sheets to wire racks and let cool completely.

Store in an airtight container at room temperature for up to 1 week.

Clockwise from top left:
Ricciarelli, Anise Amaretti,
Chocolate and Sea Salt
Shortbread Cookies, and
Croccante

RICCIARELLI

MAKES ABOUT 8 DOZEN COOKIES

These cookies are sweetened with almond paste instead of sugar. Similar to marzipan but slightly coarser and less sweet, almond paste can be found in the baking section of specialty foods stores and well-stocked markets or through mail order.

This recipe yields a large number of cookies and cannot be successfully halved. If you want a smaller batch, bake only what you need and freeze the remaining dough logs for up to 1 month.

1²/₃ cups blanched whole almonds
12 ounces almond paste
1 egg white
½ tablespoon pure vanilla extract
½ teaspoon baking powder
¼ teaspoon kosher salt

In a food processor, pulse the almonds until finely ground.

In a stand mixer fitted with the paddle attachment, briefly mix the almond paste on medium-low speed to break it up. Add the ground almonds and mix on medium-low speed for about 3 minutes, or until smooth. Add the egg white and mix on medium speed for about 2 minutes, or until a stiff dough forms. Add the vanilla, baking powder, and salt and mix just until incorporated.

Divide the dough into 4 equal portions. Place 1 portion on a lightly floured work surface. Using your fingers, and widening the distance between them as the dough extends, roll the dough back and forth into a log about 1 inch in diameter and 12 inches long. Repeat with the remaining portions. Wrap the logs separately in plastic wrap and refrigerate for about 1 hour, or until firm.

Position the oven racks so that one is in the center of the oven and the other is in the upper third, then preheat the oven to 300°F. Line 2 baking sheets with parchment paper or lightly butter them.

Slice the dough from 2 of the logs into ½-inch-thick rounds, and arrange the rounds on the prepared baking sheets, spacing them about 1½ inches apart. Bake the cookies, rotating the pans once from front to back, for about 12 minutes, or until golden but still soft. They will harden as they cool. Transfer the sheets to wire racks and let cool completely. Once the sheets have cooled, slice and bake the remainder of the cookie dough, if needed.

Store in an airtight container at room temperature for up to 1 week.

ANISE AMARETTI

MAKES ABOUT 34 COOKIES

Amaretti are traditionally made with only almond extract, but we use both extract and aniseeds. The latter add a note of complexity to this crunchy, airy cookie, particularly when served with a dessert wine. If you are making these cookies specifically for the baked peaches on page 254, omit the aniseeds.

1¾ cups whole natural almonds
¾ cup plus 2 tablespoons powdered sugar
1 teaspoon cornstarch
½ teaspoon kosher salt
⅓ cup granulated sugar
2 egg whites
Pinch of cream of tartar
1 teaspoon pure almond extract
1 tablespoon aniseeds

Position the oven racks so that one is in the center of the oven and the other is in the upper third, then preheat the oven to 300°F. Line 2 baking sheets with parchment or lightly butter them.

In a food processor, pulse the almonds until finely ground. Transfer to a medium bowl. Sift together the powdered sugar and cornstarch over the almonds, and then whisk in the salt. Set aside.

In a very clean bowl, using a whisk or a handheld mixer on medium-high speed, whip together the granulated sugar, egg whites, and cream of tartar for about 5 minutes, or until the whites are bright white and thick enough so that when a small amount is lifted on the whisk or beater, it falls back onto the surface in a slowly dissolving ribbon. (The quantity is too small to be beaten in a stand mixer.) Using a rubber spatula, fold in the almond extract, followed by the sugar-almond mixture, mixing gently until the batter is well combined.

Fit a pastry bag with a ½-inch plain or star tip. Twist the pastry bag just above the tip (to keep the batter from leaking out). Place the bag, tip down, in a large drinking glass or liquid measuring pitcher and fold the top of the bag over the rim of the glass, forming a cuff. Spoon the batter into the pastry bag, filling it no more than two-thirds full. (If you do not have a pastry bag, you can use a plastic freezer storage bag. Spoon the batter into the bag and snip off about ½ inch from a bottom corner when you are ready to begin piping.)

Lift the bag out of the glass, unfolding the top, and then twist the top tightly, forcing out any air. Untwist the bag just above the tip. With one hand firmly holding the top of the bag and the other hand guiding the tip, pipe the batter in 1-inch mounds onto the prepared baking sheets, spacing the mounds about 1½ inches apart. For control (and to avoid a mess), always squeeze the batter only from the top hand, not the guiding hand. Sprinkle the cookies with the aniseeds, dividing them evenly.

Bake the cookies, rotating the pans once from front to back, for about 35 minutes, or until lightly golden and cooked through. Transfer the sheets to wire racks and let cool completely.

These cookies are highly susceptible to humidity, so once they have cooled, transfer them to an airtight container. They will keep at room temperature for up to 2 weeks.

GELATI AND SORBETTI

When Jane started at A16, she insisted that we purchase a commercial ice cream maker. Now I don't know what we would do without it. Some of the tastiest items on our menu are found on our ever-changing selection of gelati, and I regularly sneak a spoonful for an instant afternoon pick-me-up.

Not only are these recipes delicious, they are also simple to make at home. Most ice cream recipes call for making a custard base, in which egg yolks are gradually combined with hot cream, but our gelato base is made with milk and without eggs. That means our recipes are probably different from other ice cream recipes you have made before, so here are a few tips to keep in mind.

For the best results, make the gelato base a day or two before you plan to serve the gelato, so it is well chilled before it goes into the ice cream maker, and then churn it early on the day you serve it. Before you churn it, freeze the storage container you will be using, so that as soon as the gelato comes out of the machine, it will go directly into an ice-cold environment, eliminating any possibility that it will begin to melt. A metal container is best, but plastic tubs work fine, too. Slip the container into the freezer immediately and serve the gelato the same day. Gelato made with milk freezes harder than ice cream made with cream and eggs, so if it is stored any longer, it will get icy.

Churn the gelato according to the manufacturer's instructions that came with your machine. Our bases freeze fast, so we recommend putting the paddle in the ice cream maker prior to pouring in the gelato base. This ensures you won't run into trouble trying to fit it into the base while the gelato begins to freeze to the walls of the machine. Some recipes warn against overchurning ice cream, but since these recipes do not contain cream or eggs, it is unlikely that will happen. Yet as soon as you see the base has achieved a creamy, frozen consistency reminiscent of soft-serve ice cream, transfer it to the well-chilled storage container and put it in the freezer.

CHOCOLATE GELATO

MAKES 2 QUARTS

The first time Jane made this chocolate gelato at A16, she was fighting a cold. Unimpressed by her first taste, she put it in the freezer and forgot about it. The next day, she found a note on the freezer from the kitchen staff demanding that she never stop making it. The gelato has been a fixture on the menu (and a staff favorite) ever since. The two keys to its addictive nature are good-quality bittersweet chocolate and the addition of vanilla, which accentuates the chocolate flavor.

1 quart whole milk
1 tablespoon plus 1½ teaspoons cornstarch
1 vanilla bean
½ cup light corn syrup
⅓ cup sugar
½ teaspoon kosher salt
8 ounces bittersweet chocolate (about 70 percent cacao), coarsely chopped
1 teaspoon pure vanilla extract

Place 2 tablespoons of the milk in a small bowl. Whisk in the cornstarch to make a slurry and set aside.

In a pot, add the remaining milk and the vanilla bean and bring to a boil over medium heat. Whisk in the slurry, corn syrup, sugar, and salt. Remove the vanilla bean, rinse off, and freeze for future use. Return the mixture to a boil and whisk in the chocolate until completely smooth. Strain the base through a fine-mesh strainer into a bowl and let cool to room temperature. Once cool, stir in the vanilla extract. Cover and refrigerate for at least 3 hours or preferably overnight.

Whisk the base, then pour it into an ice cream maker and churn according to the manufacturer's instructions. The gelato should be the consistency of soft-serve ice cream. Store in a chilled container in the freezer.

Clockwise from top:
Chocolate Gelato, Grapefruit
Sorbetto, Bitter Caramel
Gelato, and Honey Gelato

HONEY GELATO

Just as vanilla is a staple American ice cream flavor and a suitable match for nearly every pie or cake, honey gelato has a natural affinity for fruit- and nut-filled Italian desserts. We like to use a rich local honey made by bees that have had a chance to mingle with some wildflowers. If the honey you have on hand is light in color and mild in flavor, you can concentrate it by placing it in a small sauté pan and caramelizing it over medium-low heat for about 1 minute, or until it darkens slightly.

3¾ cups whole milk
¼ cup heavy cream
1 tablespoon plus 1½ teaspoons cornstarch
½ cup light corn syrup
¼ cup sugar
½ teaspoon kosher salt
½ cup honey

In a pot, combine the milk and cream. Transfer 2 tablespoons of the milk mixture to a small bowl. Whisk in the cornstarch to make a slurry and set aside.

Place the pot over medium heat and bring to a boil. Whisk in the slurry, corn syrup, sugar, and salt. Return the mixture to a boil, whisking to ensure all of the ingredients are thoroughly incorporated, then strain through a fine-mesh strainer into a bowl. Whisk the honey into the hot liquid, and then let cool to room temperature. Cover and refrigerate for at least 3 hours or preferably overnight.

Whisk the base, then pour it into an ice cream maker and churn according to the manufacturer's instructions. The gelato should be the consistency of soft-serve ice cream. Store in a chilled container in the freezer.

BITTER CARAMEL GELATO

The bitter nature of the caramel, which is taken nearly to the point of burning, and the flavor of the salt give an edge to this gelato that keeps it from being too sweet.

1½ cups sugar
⅓ cup heavy cream
2 teaspoons kosher salt
1 quart whole milk
2 tablespoons cornstarch
1 vanilla bean

In a 3- to 4-quart heavy-bottomed pot, combine the sugar and a few drops of water. Place over medium heat and cook, without stirring, for about 3 minutes, or until the sugar begins to liquefy and turns golden. At this point, watching carefully, continue to cook the sugar, swirling the pan but not stirring, for about 2 minutes more, or until it changes to a deep amber color. Remove the pan from the heat and continue to swirl it for another 30 seconds, or until the caramel starts to smoke. Standing back from the pan to prevent spatters that can cause burns, add the cream all at once. The cream will cause the caramel to seize up. Stir the mixture off the heat for about 1 minute, or until smooth. Stir in the salt and set aside.

Place 2 tablespoons of the milk in a small bowl. Whisk in the cornstarch to make a slurry and set aside.

In a 3- to 4-quart pot, heat the remaining milk with the vanilla bean over medium-high heat until it starts to simmer. Whisk in the caramel mixture, and then whisk in the slurry until all of the ingredients are thoroughly incorporated. Remove from the heat and let cool completely. Cover and refrigerate for at least 3 hours or preferably overnight.

Remove the vanilla bean, rinse off, and freeze for future use. Whisk the base, then pour it into an ice cream maker and churn according to the manufacturer's instructions. The gelato should be the consistency of soft-serve ice cream. Store in a chilled container in the freezer.

GRAPEFRUIT SORBETTO

MAKES ABOUT 1 QUART

Citrus groves perfume the southern coast of Italy, the fruits ranging from pointy Amalfi lemons to the famed bergamots of Calabria. This refreshing *sorbetto* features grapefruit, which is much easier to find in the United States than in Italy, and recasts the tart citrus variety as a palate-cleansing intermezzo or a light dessert.

¼ cup sugar
1 teaspoon powdered pectin
1 quart freshly squeezed grapefruit juice
¼ cup light corn syrup
1 tablespoon freshly squeezed lemon juice

In a small bowl, mix together the sugar and pectin. Combine 1 cup of the grapefruit juice with the corn syrup in a small pot. Bring to a simmer over medium heat, whisk in the sugar mixture, and then continue whisking for about 1 minute, or until the sugar and pectin are completely dissolved.

Pour the remaining 3 cups grapefruit juice and the lemon juice into a medium bowl. Add the sugar mixture into the juice gradually, whisking in about 1 tablespoon at a time until the sugar mixture is completely incorporated and the base is smooth. At this point, the base can be covered and stored in the refrigerator for up to 2 days before churning, or it can be cooled down in an ice bath until well chilled and then churned immediately.

Whisk the base, then pour it into an ice cream maker and churn according to the manufacturer's instructions. The *sorbetto* should be smooth and semisolid. Store in a chilled container in the freezer. The *sorbetto* is best if served the day it was churned.

YOGURT SORBETTO

MAKES ABOUT 1½ QUARTS

While frozen yogurt falls in and out of fashion, yogurt *sorbetto* remains a classic. Refreshingly tart, it complements baked fruits and nut-filled cakes. For best results, drain your yogurt overnight before making the base.

2 quarts whole-milk plain yogurt
¾ cup sugar
⅓ cup light corn syrup
⅓ cup water
1 teaspoon freshly squeezed lemon juice

Line a strainer with 3 layers of cheesecloth and place it over a large bowl. Spoon the yogurt into the strainer and let it drain overnight in the refrigerator.

To make a sugar syrup, in a pot, whisk together the sugar, corn syrup, and water, and then bring to a boil over medium-high heat. Remove from the heat and let cool completely.

In a large bowl, whisk together the yogurt, sugar syrup, and lemon juice. At this point, the base can be covered and stored in the refrigerator for up to 2 days before churning, or it can be cooled down in an ice bath until well chilled and then churned immediately.

Whisk the base, then pour it into an ice cream maker and churn according to the manufacturer's instructions. The *sorbetto* should be smooth and semisolid. Store in a chilled container in the freezer. The *sorbetto* is best if served the day it is churned.

RESOURCES

Part of the fun of delving into new recipes is discovering a great source for a hard-to-find ingredient. This guide is structured as a starting point from which you will find your own favorite sources, depending on where you live and what you cook. A number of specialty stores and butcher shops ship their goods; we have made a note when mail order is available.

ANCHOVIES, SALT-PACKED

A.G. Ferrari (multiple locations)
14234 Catalina Street
San Leandro, CA 94577-5512
877.878.2783
www.agferrari.com
Mail order.

Formaggio Kitchen (multiple locations)
244 Huron Avenue
Cambridge, MA 02138
888.212.3224
www.formaggiokitchen.com
Mail order.

Gustiamo Inc.
1715 W. Farms Road
Bronx, NY 10460
877.907.2525
www.gustiamo.com
Mail order.

BUCKWHEAT FLOUR

Boulette's Larder
1 Ferry Building #48
San Francisco, CA 94111
415.399.1155
www.bouletteslarder.com

BOTTARGA

Boulette's Larder
1 Ferry Building #48
San Francisco, CA 94111
415.399.1155
www.bouletteslarder.com

Fresca Italia
200 Valley Drive #14
Brisbane, CA 94005
415.468.9800
www.frescaitalia.com
Contact for local retailers that carry their products.

Gustiamo Inc.
1715 W. Farms Road
Bronx, NY 10460
877.907.2525
www.gustiamo.com
Mail order.

CALABRIAN CHILES

Italian Food Imports
324 Main Street
Medford, MA 02155
781.395.0400
www.italianfoodimports.com
Mail order.

Lucca Delicatessen
2120 Chestnut Street
San Francisco, CA 94123
415.921.7873
www.luccadeli.com

CAPERS, SALT-PACKED

A.G. Ferrari (multiple locations)
14234 Catalina Street
San Leandro, CA 94577-5512
877.878.2783
www.agferrari.com
Mail order.

Taylor's Market
2900 Freeport Boulevard
Sacramento, CA 95818
877.770.6077
www.taylorsmarket.com
Mail order through Amazon.com.

CHEESES

The Cheese Works
22 North Loop Road
Alameda, CA 94502 (West Coast location)
800.477.5262
www.thecheeseworks.com
Contact for local retailers that carry their products.

Cowgirl Creamery (multiple locations)
1 Ferry Building #17
San Francisco, CA 94111
415.362.9354
www.cowgirlcreamery.com
Carries Gioia Burrata.

Formaggio Kitchen (multiple locations)
244 Huron Avenue
Cambridge, MA 02138
888.212.3224
www.formaggiokitchen.com
Mail order.

Fresca Italia
200 Valley Drive #14
Brisbane, CA 94005
415.468.9800
www.frescaitalia.com
Contact for local retailers that carry their products.

Gioia Cheese Co.
1605 Potrero Avenue
South El Monte, CA 91733
626.44.6015
For Burrata, mozzarella, and ricotta. Contact for local retailers that carry their products.

CHESTNUTS AND CHESTNUT FLOUR

Allen Creek Farm
29112 NW 41st Avenue
Ridgefield, WA 98642
360.887.3669
www.chestnutsonline.com
Mail order.

FLOUR, CAPUTO "00"

Forno Bravo
399 Business Park Court #104
Windsor, CA 95492
800.407.5119
www.fornobravo.com
Mail order.

Lucca Delicatessen
2120 Chestnut Street
San Francisco, CA 94123
415.921.7873
www.luccadeli.com

Pennsylvania Macaroni Company
2010-2012 Penn Avenue
Pittsburgh, PA 15222
412.471.8330
www.pennmac.com
Mail order.

HONEY

Marshall's Farm Natural Honey
159 Lombard Road
American Canyon, CA 94503
800.642.4637
www.marshallshoney.com
Mail order.

MEAT (BEEF, GOAT, LAMB, PORK, AND POULTRY)

INFORMATION AND NATIONAL CONTACTS

Heritage Foods USA
P.O. Box 827
New York, NY 10150
212.980.6603
www.heritagefoodsusa.com

CALIFORNIA

Baron's Meats (multiple locations)
1650 Park Street
Alameda, CA 94501
510.864.1915
www.baronsmeats.com
Carries natural beef, lamb, pork, poultry, and rabbit from local producers. Can accommodate most special orders with advance notice.

Bi-Rite Market
3639 18th Street
San Francisco, CA 94110
415.241.9760
www.biritemarket.com
Carries natural beef, lamb, and poultry and supplies pork raised by farmers affiliated with Heritage Foods USA.

Bryan's Quality Meats
3473 California Street
San Francisco, CA 94118
415.752.3430
Carries natural beef, lamb, pork, and poultry.

Café Rouge
1782 4th Street
Berkeley, CA 94710
510.525.2707 (butcher's phone number for special orders)
www.caferouge.net
Carries natural beef, lamb, pork, and poultry and can accommodate special orders with advance notice.

Drewes Bros. Meats
1706 Church Street
San Francisco, CA 94131
415.821.0515
www.drewesbros.com
Carries natural beef, lamb, pork, and poultry, including beef rib roasts, beef short ribs, and game hens.

Enzo's Meat & Poultry
5655 College Avenue
Oakland, CA 94618
510.547.5839
www.rockridgemarkethall.com
Carries natural beef, pork, and poultry.
Mail order.

Golden Gate Meat Company
1 Ferry Plaza, #13
San Francisco, CA 94111
415.861.3800
www.goldengatemeatcompany.com
Carries beef, lamb, pork, poultry, fresh rabbit, offal, and specialty cuts.

Marin Sun Farms
P.O. Box 1136
Point Reyes Station, CA 94956
415.663.8997
www.marinsunfarms.com
Pasture-raised beef, goat, lamb, and pork sold at farmers' markets and San Francisco Bay Area butcher shops.

Niman Ranch
1600 Harbor Bay Parkway, Suite 250
Alameda, CA 94502
866.808.0340
www.nimanranch.com
Natural beef, lamb, and pork, including pork belly and spareribs. *Mail order.*

Prather Ranch Meat Co.
1 Ferry Plaza, #32
San Francisco, CA 94111
415.391.0420
www.pratherranch.com
Carries pasture-raised beef, Berkshire pork, and rendered lard. Will take orders for custom cuts, such as skin-on pork shoulder.

COLORADO

Napa Valley Lamb Company
Don and Carolyn Watson
4925 Swainsona Drive
Loveland, CO 80537
970. 663.1396
www.woolyweeders.com
Whole lamb.

ILLINOIS

Gepperth's Market
1964 N. Halsted Street
Chicago, IL 60614
773.549.3883
www.gepperthsmarket.com
Carries lamb, prime rib, specialty cuts of pork, and occasionally rendered lard.
Mail order.

Marketplace on Oakton
4817 W. Oakton Street
Skokie, IL 60077
877.677.9330
www.marketplaceonoakton.com
Carries beef and pork, including pork belly, pork fat, pigs' heads, pig livers, and trotters.

Paulina Meat Market
3501 N. Lincoln Avenue
Chicago, IL 60657
773.248.6272
www.paulinameatmarket.com
Carries beef, pork shanks, pork belly, pork fat, and short ribs. *Mail order.*

MASSACHUSETTS

The Butcher Shop
552 Tremont Street
Boston, MA 02118
617.423.4800
www.thebutchershopboston.com
Can accommodate special orders for beef, goat, lamb, pork (including head, belly, fat, and trotters), and poultry with advance notice.

Savenor's Market (multiple locations)
160 Charles Street
Boston, MA 02114
617.723.6328
www.savenorsmarket.com
Carries prime rib, lamb, natural pork, and poultry and can accommodate special orders with advance notice.

NEW YORK

Florence Prime Meat Market
5 Jones Street
New York, NY 10014-5638
212.242.6531
Prime rib roasts.

Flying Pigs Farm
246 Sutherland Road
Shushan, NY 12873-1805
518.854.3844
www.flyingpigsfarm.com
Sells shanks, fresh belly, heads, skin, and,
on occasion, liver and trotters. Mail order
or call in advance for a pickup at New York
City's Union Square Greenmarket.

O. Ottomanelli's & Sons Meat Market
285 Bleeker Street
New York, NY 10014-4108
212.675.4217
Carries beef, lamb, pork belly, quail, and
specialty cuts.

Violet Hill Farm
P.O. Box 959
Livingston Manor, NY 12758
845.439.8040
http://vilothillarabians.tripod.com/
violethillfarm/
Goat and other pastured-raised meats.
Available at New York City's Union Square
Greenmarket. *Mail order.*

OREGON

Nicky USA
223 SE 3rd Avenue
Portland, OR 97214
800.469.4162
www.nickyusa.com
Natural beef, goat (whole), lamb (whole
or butchered), poussin, rabbit, and quail.
Mail order.

PENNSYLVANIA

D'Angelo Bros. Meat Market
909 South 9th Street
Philadelphia, PA 19147
215.923.5637
www.dangelobros.com
Specializes in game meats, poussin, and
quail. *Mail order.*

WASHINGTON

Don and Joe's Meats
85 Pike Street
Seattle, WA 98101
206.682.7670
www.donandjoesmeats.com
Carries natural beef, lamb, tripe, pork, and
pork liver and can special order whole pigs.

Wooly Pigs (Heath Putnam)
505 W. Riverside Avenue, Suite 500
Spokane, WA 9901
509.536.4083
www.woolypigs.com
Raises Mangalitza and other heritage pig
breeds. Can ship whole or half pigs, also
occasionally has a frozen inventory of
smaller cuts. *Mail order.*

MOSTO/SABA/VINCOTTO

Italian Food Imports
324 Main Street
Medford, MA 02155
781.395.0400
www.italianfoodimports.com
Mail order.

Zingerman's
620 Phoenix Drive
Ann Arbor, MI 48108
888.636.8162
www.zingermans.com
Mail order.

MUSHROOMS, WILD

Panexotic
112 Squaw Valley Road
McCloud, CA 96057
415.713.4569
www.panexotic.biz
Contact for local retailers that carry their
products. *Mail order.*

OLIVE OIL

Casa de Case (Howard Case)
224 Carl Street
San Francisco, CA 94117
415.759.6360
www.casesf.com
Mail order.

PASTAS, DRIED

A.G. Ferrari (multiple locations)
14234 Catalina Street
San Leandro, CA 94577-5512
877.878.2783
www.agferrari.com
Mail order.

Gustiamo Inc.
1715 W. Farms Road
Bronx, NY 10460
877.907.2525
www.gustiamo.com
Mail order.

Surfas Restaurant and Supply
3975 Landmark Street
Culver City, CA 90232
866.799.4770
www.surfasonline.com
Mail order.

PASTA AND PIZZA EQUIPMENT

Forno Bravo
399 Business Park Court #104
Windsor, CA 95492
800 407.5119
www.fornobravo.com
Pizza-making equipment.

Pasta Biz (Emilio Mitidieri)
2129 Harrison Street (showroom, by
appointment only)
San Francisco CA 94110
415.621.1909
www.pastabiz.com
Pasta machines for home cooks and
for restaurants.

Surfas Restaurant and Supply
3975 Landmark Street
Culver City, CA 90232
866.799.4770
www.surfasonline.com
Pasta machines and pizza-making equipment.
Mail order.

POLENTA

Anson Mills
1922-C Gervais Street
Columbus, S.C. 29201
803.467.4122
www.ansonmills.com

PORK, CURED (GUANCIALE, PANCETTA, PROSCIUTTO, PROSCIUTTO COTTO)

Fox & Obel
401 East Illinois Street
Chicago, IL 60611
312.410.7301
www.fox-obel.com
Carries guanciale, pancetta, prosciutto,
cut to order. *Mail order.*

Fresca Italia
200 Valley Drive #14
Brisbane, CA 94005
415.468.9800
www.frescaitalia.com
Contact for local retailers that carry
their products.

La Quercia
400 Hakes Drive
Norwalk, Iowa 50211
515.981.1625
www.laquercia.us
Produces guanciale, pancetta, and
prosciutto. Mail order and sold at most
Whole Foods.

Lucca Delicatessen
2120 Chestnut Street
San Francisco, CA 94123
415.921.7873
www.luccadeli.com
Pancetta, prosciutto, prosciutto cotto.

Pennsylvania Macaroni Company
2010-2012 Penn Avenue
Pittsburgh, PA 15222
412.471.8330
www.pennmac.com
Supplies prosciutto and prosciutto cotto.
Mail order.

PRODUCE

Mariquita Farm
P.O. Box 2065
Watsonville, CA 95077
831.761.8380
www.mariquita.com
Distributes produce through community-
supported agriculture (CSA) members in
some northern California counties and sells
produce through San Francisco restaurants
during weekly produce drop-offs.

SAN MARZANO TOMATOES

A.G. Ferrari (multiple locations)
14234 Catalina Street
San Leandro, CA 94577-5512
877.878.2783
www.agferrari.com
Mail order.

Gustiamo Inc.
1715 W. Farms Road
Bronx, NY 10460
877.907.2525
www.gustiamo.com
Mail order.

Taylor's Market
2900 Freeport Boulevard
Sacramento, CA 95818
877.770.6077
www.taylorsmarket.com
Mail order through Amazon.com.

SAUSAGE MAKING

The Sausage Maker
1500 Clinton Street, Building 123
Buffalo, NY 14206-3099
888.490.8525
www.sausagemaker.com
Supplies grinders, hog casings, and
sausage-making equipment. *Mail order.*

SEAFOOD

Citarella (multiple locations)
2135 Broadway
New York, NY 10023
212.874.0383
www.citarella.com
Carries halibut, fresh sardines, octopus,
and squid. *Mail order.*

Dirk's Fish and Gourmet Shop
2070 N. Clybourn Avenue
Chicago, IL 60614
773.404.3475
www.dirksfish.com
Carries halibut, cod, and frozen squid ink.
Mail order.

Monterey Fish Market
1582 Hopkins Street
Berkeley, CA 94707
510.525.5600
www.montereyfish.com
Carries Dungeness crab, California salmon,
halibut, and fresh sardines.

San Francisco Fish Company
1 Ferry Building #31
San Francisco, CA 94111
415.399.1111
www.sanfranfishco.com
Carries Dungeness crab, fresh octopus,
local prawns, salmon, and fresh sardines.

SEAFOOD SUSTAINABILITY

Monterey Bay Aquarium Seafood Watch
www.mbayaq.or/cr/seafoodwatch.asp

SLOW FOOD USA

www.slowfoodusa.org

SPICES

Le Sanctuaire
315 Sutter Street, 5th floor
San Francisco, CA 94108
415.986.4216
www.le-sanctuaire.com
Carries aniseeds, bay leaves, dried chile
flakes, dried oregano, fennel seeds, and
peppercorns.

WINE

CALIFORNIA

Biondivino
1415 Green Street
San Francisco, CA 94109
415.673.2320
www.biondivino.com

Ferry Plaza Wine Merchant & Wine Bar
1 Ferry Building #23
San Francisco, CA 94111
415.391.9400
www.fpwm.com
Mail order.

K&L Wine Merchants (multiple locations)
638 4th Street
San Francisco, CA 94107
www.klwines.com
Mail order.

Swirl on Castro
572 Castro Street
San Francisco, CA 94114
415.864.2262
www.swirloncastro.com

The Wine House
2311 Cotner Avenue
Los Angeles, CA 90064
800.626.9463
www.winehouse.com
Mail order.

ILLINOIS

Sam's Wines and Spirits (multiple locations)
1720 N. Marcey Street
Chicago, IL 60614
312.664.4394
www.samswine.com

NORTHEAST

Brix Wine Shop
1284 Washington Street
Boston, MA 02118
617.542.2749
www.brixwineshop.com
Special orders on request.

Italian Wine Merchants
108 East 16th Street
New York, NY 10003
212.473.2323
www.italianwinemerchant.com

Vestry Wines
65 Vestry Street
New York, NY 10013
212.810.2899
www.vestrywines.com

INTERNET

Garagiste
www.garagistewine.com
888.264.0053

WINE LITERATURE

Attilio, Scienza. **Atlante dei Vini Passiti Italiani.** Rome: Gribaudo, 2006.
  Written in Italian, this resource explains and celebrates Italy's dessert-wine heritage.

Bastianich, Joseph, and David Lynch. **Vino Italiano: The Regional Wines of Italy.** New York: Clarkson Potter, 2002.
  This comprehensive, region-by-region work is filled with fascinating stories about the wines and winemakers of Italy, as well as technical information on import laws, the DOC system, and the many grapes of Italy. It is required reading for anyone seeking to deepen their knowledge of the modern Italian wine world.

Belfrage, Nicolas. **Brunello to Zibibbo: The Wines of Tuscany, Central and Southern Italy.** London: Mitchell Beazley, 2003.
  By providing a tour through central and southern Italy through its grapes, Nicolas Belfrage celebrates Italy's viticultural biodiversity and describes its best wines.

Duemilavini 2007. Rome: Bibenda Editore, 2007.
  The annual guide put forth by the Italian Sommeliers Association (and written in Italian), Duemilavini covers more than fifteen hundred Italian wines and lists wine-friendly restaurants throughout Italy.

Gambero Rosso Italian Wines 2007. New York: Gambero Rosso Editore, 2007.
  The annual, definitive Italian wine guide, whose Tre Bicchiere (Three Glasses) award has become a standard of excellence for the Italian wine industry.

Kramer, Matt. **Matt Kramer's Making Sense of Italian Wine: Discovering Italy's Greatest Wines and Best Values.** Philadelphia: Running Press, 2006.
  In this lively, incisive, and opinionated exploration of Italian wine, Matt Kramer renders an often-challenging subject accessible.

Robinson, Jancis. **Vines, Grapes, and Wines: The Wine Drinker's Guide to Grape Varieties.** London: Mitchell Beazley, 1992.
  This comprehensive survey of grape varieties explains both the familiar and the obscure.

ONLINE RESOURCES

www.inumeridelvino.it
An Italian website (with handy side-by-side English translations) analyzing Italian wine industry statistics and trends.

www.italianmade.com
The official site of the Italian Trade Commission, which includes extensive information on regional foods and wines from Italian wine authority Burton Anderson.

www.lavinium.com
Written in Italian by wine professionals and aficionados, this online wine magazine shares news and information on Italian wine, grapes, growing regions, and culture.

www.vinowire.simplicissimus.it
An English news source, launched in 2008, that provides weekly news updates and analysis of the Italian wine industry.

INDEX